About the

THOMAS C. FOSTER is a professor of English at the University of
Michigan–Flint, where he teaches classic and contemporary fiction,
drama, and poetry, as well as creative writing and composition. In
addition to *How to Read Novels Like a Professor*, he is the author
of *How to Read Literature Like a Professor* and several books on
twentieth-century British and Irish fiction and poetry. He lives in
East Lansing, Michigan.

How to Read
Novels
Like a
Professor

Also by Thomas C. Foster

How to Read Literature Like a Professor

How to Read
Novels
Like a
Professor

Thomas C. Foster

HARPER

NEW YORK • LONDON • TORONTO • SYDNEY

HARPER

HOW TO READ NOVELS LIKE A PROFESSOR. Copyright © 2008 by Thomas C. Foster. All rights reserved. Printed in the United States of America. No part of this book may be used or reproduced in any manner whatsoever without written permission except in the case of brief quotations embodied in critical articles and reviews. For information address HarperCollins Publishers, 10 East 53rd Street, New York, NY 10022.

HarperCollins books may be purchased for educational, business, or sales promotional use. For information please write: Special Markets Department, HarperCollins Publishers, 10 East 53rd Street, New York, NY 10022.

FIRST EDITION

Designed by Jamie Kerner-Scott

Library of Congress Cataloging-in-Publication Data is available upon request.

ISBN 978-0-06-134040-6

10 11 12   ID/RRD   10 9 8 7 6

For Linda Wagner-Martin,
without whom the profession would be immensely poorer

Acknowledgments

IN WRITING THIS BOOK and indeed for years before, I have had the privilege of being surrounded by great people and have shown my gratitude by exploiting them shamelessly. I am deeply indebted to colleagues at the University of Michigan–Flint and Michigan State University for many conversations, much advice, and editorial assistance. Professors Fred Svoboda, Alicia Kent, Steve Bernstein, Anjili Babbar, Jan Bernsten, and Leonora Smith have been unstinting in their contributions and their patience, which I have tried on many occasions. Their responses and suggestions inform this book in too many places to count. My profound thanks to Professor Jan Furman for her critical acumen, her generous support, and her willingness to express doubt regarding my flakier efforts. She is the best—and toughest—editor I could ever hope for. My thanks, too, to Diane Saylor and Nicole Bryant for observations, questions, and coffee.

It is no exaggeration to say that this book would not exist without my students. They never fail to teach me, and I am as obliged to them for their doubts as for their belief. They would probably be justified in charging me tuition. The same is true of readers of this book's predecessor, *How to Read Literature Like a Professor*, especially those many who have taken the time to correspond. Their many comments, questions, and ideas have shaped the present text.

More than one, in fact, requested early on that I write this very book; I should have heeded them sooner.

My thanks also to my editor, Rakesh Satyal, and the staff at HarperCollins, as well as to my agent, Faith Hamlin, and her assistant, Courtney Miller-Callihan. The process by which an idea becomes a manuscript and eventually a book is the furthest thing from mechanical, and at every stage, this one has fallen into the best of hands.

And finally, to my family I offer my most profound gratitude and love. My sons, Rob and Nate, have listened patiently and offered ideas and support when we were supposed to be fishing or hunting or building something, and I appreciate their efforts, and them, mightily. I have no idea how I could possibly have done any of this work over all these years without my wife, Brenda, offering her love and support. Her acceptance of my manifold shortcomings and idiosyncrasies is heroic, her tolerance for the slide-zone that is my workspace nothing short of saintly.

It remains only to be said that none of these excellent persons is in any way accountable for the shortcomings in these pages. The errors, as always, are purely mine.

Contents

Preface: Novel Possibilities, or All Animals Aren't Pigs?   xiii

Introduction: Once Upon a Time: A Short, Chaotic, and Entirely
       Idiosyncratic History of the Novel   1

1   Pickup Lines and Open(ing) Seductions,
     or Why Novels Have First Pages   21

2   You Can't Breathe Where the Air Is Clear   37

3   Who's in Charge Here?   45

4   Never Trust a Narrator with a Speaking Part   56

5   A Still, Small Voice (or a Great, Galumphing One)   67

6   Men (and Women) Made out of Words,
     or My Pip Ain't Like Your Pip   80

7   When Very Bad People Happen to Good Novels   89

8   Wrinkles in Time, or Chapters Just Might Matter   99

9   Everywhere Is Just One Place   109

10   Clarissa's Flowers   117

11   Met-him-pike-hoses   131

12   Life Sentences   145

13   Drowning in the Stream of Consciousness   160

14   The Light on Daisy's Dock   172

15   Fiction About Fiction   182

16   Source Codes and Recycle Bins   197

Interlude: Read with Your Ears   213

17   Improbabilities: Foundlings and Magi, Colonels
         and Boy Wizards   227
18   What's the Big Idea—or Even the Small One?   239
19   Who Broke My Novel?   250
20   Untidy Endings   264
21   History in the Novel/The Novel in History   279
22   Conspiracy Theory   291

Conclusion: The Never-Ending Journey   303
Reading List: Criticism of the Novel   309

Preface

Novel Possibilities, or All Animals Aren't Pigs?

WHEN HUCK AND JIM are floating south on their raft, where are we? How is it that we can identify with a being as monstrous, literally, as John Gardner's Grendel? Have you ever been Lucy Honeychurch? Leopold Bloom? Humbert Humbert? Tom Jones? Bridget Jones? The novels we read allow us to encounter possible persons, versions of ourselves that we would never see, never permit ourselves to become, in places we can never go and might not care to, while assuring that we get to return home again. At the same time, the novel holds out its own possibilities, narrative miracles, and tricks that are rewards in themselves, seductions for unsuspecting and even canny readers.

Much of the continuing appeal of the novel lies in its collaborative nature; readers invest themselves in the characters' stories, becoming actively involved in the creation of meaning. At the same time, they are rewarded by pleasures that are more intimate than the essentially vicarious genres of drama and film. That give-and-take between creator and audience starts in the first line, runs through the last word, and causes the novel to stay in our minds long after we close the cover.

And it is a real give-and-take. The novel begs to be read from its opening words, tells us how it would like to be read, suggests things we might look for. We readers decide whether we'll go with the program, even whether we'll read the book or not. We decide whether we agree with the author about what's important, we bring our understanding and imagination to bear on characters and events, we involve ourselves not merely in the story but in all aspects of the novel, we collude in the creation of meaning. And we carry the book with us and keep it alive, sometimes centuries after the author himself is dead. Active and engaged reading is critical to the life of the novel and rewarding and fulfilling in the life of the reader.

In 1967, the novel was in a bad way, or so it seemed. Two seminal essays by writers with distressingly similar names appeared in American publications, fortelling doom and gloom. The French critic and philosopher Roland Barthes published an essay called "The Death of the Author" in the journal *Aspen*. In that essay, Barthes places the whole responsibility for the construction of meaning and significance, that is to say the interpretive enterprise, on the reader, the writer (whom he prefers to call a "scriptor") being little more than a conduit through which the accumulated culture pours its *texts*. Barthes is being more than a little impish in denying the author the quasi-divine *author*ity he was accorded in earlier understandings of literary creation. But what he is chiefly supporting is the role of active and creative reading, something about which we will have occasion to discuss throughout the book. Perhaps more alarmingly, the American novelist John Barth published "The Literature of Exhaustion" in *The Atlantic Monthly*, in which he seemed to many readers to suggest that the novel was on its deathbed. What he in fact argued was that the novel as we had known it was pretty largely played out, the "exhaustion" of the essay's title referring to exhausted possibilities. Fiction, he suggested, was going to have to find something new to do in order to reinvigorate itself. There was a lot of talk of the "death" of old ways in 1967, a lot of emphasis on newness, its signature event being the accumulation of outrageous humanity around the intersection of Haight and Ashbury streets in San Francisco.

What Barth seemed not to know (although with him, a lot of seeming is disingenuous) was that help was on the way. That same year, a novel was being published by a writer in Colombia and another was being composed by a writer in England, and they would offer ways forward from the apparent impasse. The English novelist John Fowles was composing *The French Lieutenant's Woman*, possibly the first major commercial novel to seriously address changes in the landscape of fictional theory. At the beginning of Chapter 13, he says of his faux-historical novel that it cannot be a conventional Victorian novel despite its outward appearance as such because "I live in the age of Alain Robbe-Grillet and Roland Barthes." Instead, the novel teases readers with Victorian characters and settings even as it reminds them that it is a fictional, twentieth-century work that is merely employing Victorian conventions for its own ends. The literary gamesmanship did not harm sales; *The French Lieutenant's Woman* was the best-selling novel in America in 1969. The Colombian novel was, of course, Gabriel García Márquez's *One Hundred Years of Solitude*, which would appear in English three years later. The solution it offered was not one of metafictional play but of the wild eruption of the fabulous amidst the commonplace, what would become known as "magic realism." These works and writers changed everything, so much so that Barth returned to *The Atlantic* in 1979 with an essay called "The Literature of Replenishment," in which he admitted things had changed more in a dozen years than he could have foreseèn and that maybe, just maybe, this novel thing did have a future. He cites García Márquez and Italo Calvino in particular as reinvigorating the form. So what does it mean to say that they "changed everything"? Did everyone begin copying what they did? No, even they didn't copy what they did. There is only one *One Hundred Years of Solitude*, and even García Márquez can't write a second one. But those novels showed possibilities in the form that had not been tried in quite the same way before, things a writer might do with fiction that would be sufficiently new and interesting to keep readers hanging around.

I believe, moreover, that the essays and the novels in question show something else: the history of the genre. The novel is always dying, always running out of steam, and always being renewed, reinvented. We might say, following the philosopher Heraclitus, one cannot step in the same novel twice. To stay put is to stagnate. Even those novelists we value for their sameness—Charles Dickens, George Eliot, Ernest Hemingway—are constantly changing and growing. They move, if only slightly, from one novel to the next; they set themselves new challenges. Those who stand pat soon seem stale, flat, and unprofitable. As it is with individual writers, so it is with the form itself. The movement is neither inevitably forward nor backward; "progress" in matters literary is chiefly an illusion. But movement there is and movement there must be. In a genre called "novel," readers have some right to expect novelty. That's only fair, isn't it?

A FRIEND OF MINE, a colleague in another discipline, noted the very slight change between the previous book's title and this one and asked, "So how are novels different from literature?" It's an excellent question, one that the literature priesthood would never think to ask but that lay people will come up with right off. I was reminded of the old syllogism, "All pigs are animals, but not all animals are pigs." We can say roughly the same thing in literary terms by substituting "novels" for "pigs" and "literature" for "animals." Are all novels literature? We could get some disagreement here from inside and outside the academy. A sizable percentage of literary people want to maintain walls around their little corner of heaven, although rarely do they concur on whom to wall in or wall out. Would Jonathan Franzen, for instance, object to being lumped in with Jackie Collins? Nor am I suggesting that the quality of all writing is the same. There are significant differences in quality between novels, as between poems, stories, plays, movies, songs, and dirty limericks. I would, however, suggest that they all belong to the same field of human endeavor, and we can call that field "literature." Drawing distinctions comes later. For me, there is writing (in which I would include oral forms of entertainment and instruction, since when they reach me, they're generally written down), and writing comes in two forms, good and bad. Okay, sometimes execrable, which could be a third category but which I think we can fold into "bad" writing more generally. All right then, so all novels are literature. All literature, on the other hand, is not novels. We have lyric poetry, epic poetry, verse drama, verse romance, short story, drama, and whatever those things are that Woody Allen and David Sedaris are wont to publish in *The New Yorker*. Among others. That only leaves one question.

Are novels pigs?

There are many elements common to all forms of literature, many sorts of signification we can see whether the writing in question is a poem, play, or novel—pattern making, imagery, figurative language, use of detail, invention, it's a long list. There are also, however, elements that are specific to each genre. Our discussion in this book is concerned with the specific formal elements of one genre, the novel. I know, I know, those structural components, things like chapters—point of view, style, voice, beginnings and endings, and characterization—seem dull as ditchwater. They're the groaners in English class, right? *Oh, no, not flat and round characters again.* But they don't have to be that. Because they're also the portals to meaning, the doors and windows where possibilities establish themselves. In choosing this opening and not another, the writer has closed off some options but opened up several others. A method of revealing characters both limits and determines what sorts of characters can be revealed. The way the story is told, in other words, is as important as the story being told.

And how readers will respond. I can't go as far as Barthes in killing off the author, but I'm with him on the importance of the reader. We are the ones, after all, who exist long after the author (the real, physical being) is in the grave, choosing to read the book, deciding if it still has meaning, deciding what it means for us, feeling sympathy or contempt or amusement for its people and their problems. Take just the opening paragraph. If, having read that, we decide the book isn't worth our time, then the book ceases to exist in any meaningful fashion. Someone else may cause it to live again another day in another reading, but for now, it's as dead as Jacob Marley. Who's as dead as a doornail. Did you have any idea you held so much power? But with great power comes great responsibility. If we readers are going to hold the life and death of novels in our hands, we should probably find out more about them.

How to Read
Novels
Like a
Professor

Introduction

Once Upon a Time:
A Short, Chaotic, and Entirely Idiosyncratic
History of the Novel

IRIS MURDOCH ONLY WROTE one novel in her lifetime. But she wrote it twenty-six times. Anthony Burgess never wrote the same book twice. And he wrote about a thousand. Are those characterizations accurate? Fair? Of course not. You will hear from time to time that criticism of Murdoch, and in fairness, they are pretty similar. *The Green Knight* (1993), her last novel before the Alzheimer's-damaged *Jackson's Dilemma*, isn't all that far from *Under the Net* (1954). Same class, same sorts of problems, same ethical preoccupations. Strong characterization and strong plotting. All this was deemed a positive virtue during her lifetime: her fans could count on a new-yet-familiar novel every two to three years. Those novels would always be solid and, once in a while, as with the Booker Prize–winning *The Sea, the Sea* (1978), they would knock your socks off.

And Burgess? He has his consistencies, as well. But nothing in the early novels can prepare the reader for *A Clockwork Orange*

(1962), which is wildly unlike the Enderby novels of the 1970s, which are formally quite distant from the experimentalism of *Napoleon Symphony* (1974) or the historical artfulness and Elizabethan language of his novels on Shakespeare, *Nothing Like the Sun* (1964), and Christopher Marlowe, *A Dead Man in Deptford* (1993), or the Maugham-like performance of what many call his masterpiece, *Earthly Powers* (1980), to say nothing of his novels in verse. Where readers of Murdoch can begin a new novel with a quiet confidence, opening a Burgess book is an exercise in anxiety: what the devil is he up to *this* time?

Does it matter, this difference in uniformity? Not really. After all, each novel would have both its return audience and its newcomers, so each book had to teach its readers how to deal with it, as if for the first time, which for some it was.

It always is. Every novel is brand-new. It's never been written before in the history of the world. At the same time, it's merely the latest in a long line of narratives—not just novels, but narratives generally—since humans began telling stories to themselves and each other. This is the basic dialectic of literary history. The impulse to originality clashes with the received tradition of things already written. Miraculously, neither ever seems to overwhelm the other, and novels keep appearing, as do audiences to read them. Even so, some novels are more traditional, some more experimental, some impossible to classify.

Let's go back to a time when the novel really was new. Once upon a time, there weren't any novels. There were other things that were narrative and lengthy—epics, religious or historical narratives of the tribe, prose or verse romances, nonfictional narratives like travelogues. You know, *The Iliad* and *The Odyssey*, *The Epic of Gilgamesh*, the *Táin Bó Cuailgne* in Ireland, the romances of Chrétien de Troye and Marie de France. Plenty of candidates out there. Just not novels. Then some things began emerging, sporadically. It may be that the Catalan writer Joanot Martorell's *Tirant lo Blanc*, first published in Valencia in 1490, is the first European novel we can recognize as such. Note the date. Columbus hadn't sailed the sea to discover modernity yet, but he was about to. The rise of the novel coincides with the rise of the modern world—exploration, discovery, invention, development, oppression, industrialization, exploitation, conquest, and violence—and that's no coincidence. It took more than movable type to make the novel possible; it took a new age. But I digress.

Rightly or wrongly, there are two novels we generally think of as the "first"—and they're seventy years apart. In 1678 someone, perhaps Madame de La Fayette, published a little novel of profound significance. Its popularity was such that people lined up at the publishers waiting, sometimes for months, for their copies. Take that, Harry Potter. The book is called *La Princesse de Clèves*, and its chief claim to fame is not as a first novel but as the first *roman d'analyse*, a novel of analysis, a book that investigates emotions and mental states, pushing well beyond the mere conveying of plot. Some readers three hundred and some years later may find the tale a little clunky for their tastes, although the clunkiness largely resides in the surface details, in how persons in the novel speak and address one another and how the writer handles character presentation. The mores of the novel are not ours, but they are genuine in themselves, as are the consequences that grow out of the dictates of conscience. For its time (published within a decade of the Sturm und Drang that is *Paradise Lost*), the narrative is an extremely subtle performance, and writers as various as Jane Austen, Henry James, Gustave Flaubert, and Anita Brookner couldn't do what they do without it. Madame de La Fayette is one of the giants of the novel, but she's just a kid.

At the yonder end of the century, 1605 to be exact, a book came out that really set the world on its ear. Here's what I heard the amazing Mexican novelist Carlos Fuentes say at a conference once: "All of Latin American literature grows out of *Don Quixote*." Not fiction or novels. Literature. All of it. The Hispanic world gets to claim Miguel de Cervantes and his masterpiece, of course, but it has to share with the rest of us. The book is simply too big for any one group to own. It's goofy and serious, hilarious and sad, satiric and original. And it's first. Okay, okay, there are lots of "first" novels. But this is a big first. Cervantes shows everyone else what might be done. He parodies earlier narrative forms as his Quixote descends into confusion between the world of the too-many romances he has read and the dull world life has saddled him with. Cervantes uses an out-of-touch figure locked in some never-never past to make commentary on the author's here-and-now. His hero is comic, certainly, but there's a forlorn quality there, too, as we watch someone too far gone in fantasy to notice, whose gestures, as in his championing of Dulcinea and his tilting at windmills, are both noble and pathetic, uplifting and pointless. When a character gives his name to an entire class of enterprise, he's really captured our imagination. Don Quixote and Sancho Panza are seared into the Western imagination; they form an archetypal pairing, so much so that, three and a half centuries later, William Hanna and Joseph Barbera could build a cartoon empire on the formula. Yogi and Boo Boo, Quick-Draw McGraw and Baba Louis, Fred Flintstone and Barney Rubble are all variations on the clueless nobleman and his long-suffering, devoted servant. Now *that's* a legacy. Cervantes takes the old and makes something completely new. More—he says to other writers, you can do this too, ignore convention, invent, make it up as you go. And make it up he does. No one had ever seen anything quite like it before. And no one has since. Everyone tries to measure up to Cervantes, of course, but the attempt is, well, quixotic.

At that time, of course, and for a number of years afterward, every novel was experimental. If a genre hasn't been around long enough to establish conventions, then there can be no such thing as a "conventional" specimen. In the late seventeenth and early eighteenth centuries, writers of this new form understood that it was new, that it was . . . novel.

A word or two on literary terms: despair of definitions. What we call a novel would nearly everywhere in non-Anglophone Europe be a *roman*. That term derives from *romanz*, the universal term for lengthy narratives in verse prior to the age of print. The word "novel," by contrast, comes from the Italian term *novella*, meaning new and small. English removed the diminutive, stuck with the "new" part, and a term was born. Fictional narratives of book length would come to be known as novels. The term "romance" has been kept for a certain sort of fictional narrative, one that was more stylized, more action-driven, more reliant on character types than psychologically realistic characters, often with improbable actions. Gothic tales, adventure stories, the books of Nathaniel Hawthorne and Bram Stoker, westerns and thrillers, and, yes, bodice rippers would all come under the heading of the romance. The distinction remained in greater or lesser use for a couple of centuries, yet it was always an imprecise science. *The Scarlet Letter* is pretty clearly a romance, *The Portrait of a Lady* a novel. But what about *Moby Dick*? *The Adventures of Huckleberry Finn*? *Bleak House*? You see the problem. Terms are often butter knives employed where surgical precision is demanded. These days, hardly anyone differentiates between the two. When was the last time you heard someone speak of a Stephen King romance? The problem is compounded when "romance" is instantly connected with "Harlequin." So we'll stick with "novel" here as our choice for book-length fictions, knowing that it doesn't mean anything very exact. But it does mean something, and we can mostly agree on its broad definition.

But back to the early days. These new novelists did not make up their new form out of thin air. There were established forms, most of them nonfictional, for prose narrative: prose romances, letters, sermons, confessions, travel narratives, captivity narratives, histories, memoirs. And the big one, of course, the biography or "life." Samuel Richardson's novels are epistolary; that is, they are composed as a series of letters. His most famous novel is *Clarissa* (1748), which at something over a million words is a whole bunch of letters. Daniel Defoe's *Robinson Crusoe* (1719) follows the form of a travel narrative of a castaway—the actual model was Alexander Selkirk—while *Moll Flanders* (1722) uses the form of the confession and the story, very loosely, of Mary Carleton. One of the conventions of the confession is that the sinner basks in the glory of her redemption, but Moll's narrative is much more energetic, and convincing, about her sins than about her salvation.

The bottom line, for me, is that in the early days of the novel, it was all exciting. Readers couldn't say, "Oh, we've seen that before; that's so old hat." Every novel was experimental, every foray opened new ground. That may not have been the case, of course, but it's certainly how it looks from the twenty-first century. Now, the thing about experimentalism is that not all experiments turn out equally well. One thing that would inevitably occur is that novelists would discover, over the course of a century or so, that some narrative structures worked better than others, that it was hard to construct compelling, organized, and direct narratives out of letters, for instance. Richardson's epistolary adventures did not set off a tidal wave of like works. Lucky for us.

So what works best? Linear narrative, plots centering around individuals either growing up or coming apart, characters in whom readers can invest large emotional capital, and clear resolutions that give emotional pleasure. In other words, the formula of the Victorian novel.

All you need is time.

How much time? How about as much as two years? These novels (and they include most of the British novels of the era) were published monthly, either in magazines or in freestanding installments (you simply walked into your neighborhood bookstand and purchased this month's installment, boxed, of the new William Makepeace Thackeray novel), or weekly, in such newspapers as Dickens's *Household Hints* or *The Graphic*. This latter paper was a combination of our *USA Today*, *The New Yorker*, and *People*. When Thomas Hardy published his penultimate novel, *Tess of the D'Urbervilles*, in the early 1890s, installments appeared each week except two: the week of the Henley-on-Thames rowing regatta and the week of the marriage of Prince Aribert of Anhalt to Princess Marie Louise of Schleswig-Holstein (you can't make this stuff up). Those two editions were wholly taken up with which famous people were there to be seen and detailed descriptions of ladies' gowns, bridesmaids' dresses, and the doings of the beautiful people. Some things never change.

Here's how it worked: each installment would contain a pre-specified number of words, usually two chapters of, say, four thousand words each. This would go on month after month (or week after week), sometimes for as much as two years, until the final episode was reached. That last episode would contain twice the usual number of chapters, in part because the final chapters were often a matter of wrapping up many, many loose ends and were therefore not inevitably riveting and in part to give readers a reward for patient loyalty.

So what did the serial novel look like? Chiefly, like soap operas (with less explicit sex). And for the same reasons that soap operas look the way they do, only slower. Here are the problems of telling a story over time:

- Maintaining continuity
- Making information manageable
- Keeping audience loyalty

Continuity is a huge issue in any sort of serial narrative. You have to have consistency, so that characters act the same way last week and this. You have to periodically renew readers' acquaintance with characters they haven't seen for a while or with the events to date. Often, installments start with a recap of previous happenings—kind of like elementary school, where the first month or two of every fall is spent on last year's math.

Information management? Dickens often had scores if not hundreds of characters—with names—in his triple-decker novels. And months might pass between one appearance and the next for minor characters. How to keep them memorable: that's the problem. Well, you would (if you were Dickens) give them odd names, weird quirks, grotesque appearances, goofy catchphrases. Magwitch, Jaggers, Wemmick, Miss Havisham, Joe Gargery and Mrs. Joe. And that's just *Great Expectations*. Wemmick worries constantly about his old father, whom he calls the "Aged P." Miss Havisham wears her fifty-year-old wedding dress and sits among the ruins of the never-consumed wedding feast. Think you're likely to forget them? In *David Copperfield*, Mrs. Micawber says, virtually every time she appears, "I shall never leave Mr. Micawber." No one ever, ever asked her to. So why does she say it? For our benefit. We haven't seen her since March, it's June, and we might forget her among the Barkuses and Peggottys. As if.

Audience loyalty? Give 'em a reason to come back tomorrow, next week, next month. To accomplish this, the narrative must be plot-heavy; that is, story must be the driving force, rather than theme or form or originality or anything else. And the most important element of plot is the uptick in intensity at the end of the episode. In other words, you leave something big about to happen at the end of the episode: the cliff-hanger. The most famous example we have is the season-ending question: who shot J.R. on *Dallas*? Well, the Victorians had their who-shot-J.R. questions, too. The most famous involves Charles Dickens's *The Old Curiosity Shop*, where one episode left its young heroine, Little Nell, desperately ill.

We have a desire to divorce art from commerce, to decry the influence of money on movies or corporate underwriters on museums, but the fact of the matter is that most art is influenced to some degree by business issues. If it isn't, like lyric poetry, it's because there's no money to be made. Maybe that's another point in favor of the lyric.

In any case, the real money for novelists during Victorian days was in serial publication. First, many writers made a lot of money from the contract with the journals, and second, the exposure and interest led to greater sales when the novel appeared in book form. Now, length and number of installments were a matter of serious business. Writers could expect to make anywhere from £50 (that's pounds sterling for us Yanks) for a novel by a comparative unknown to £10,000 for a work by a major author.

And negotiations could be a tricky affair. George Eliot (real name, Mary Anne Evans), the most famous author of her day, whose husband (George Henry Lewes) acted as her agent, was offered £10,000 for her novel *Romola*, to be released in sixteen installments. George Lewes countered with a cut to £7,000 for twelve installments. When the final version ran to fourteen installments, Eliot received no pay for the extra two. The art of the deal, indeed.

Then, assuming the novel was any kind of success, it would get published twice more, first as a three-volume novel in cheap bindings and then, if it was deemed worthy, in an expensive, leather-bound single volume. Those three-volume cheapies came to be known as triple-deckers.

Did it work, this Victorian formula?

Did it ever. The "serious" or "literary" novel has never enjoyed the mass appeal, not before and certainly not since, that it did in the Victorian era. Readers were hooked. Subscriptions could jump by tens of thousands during the run of a particularly exciting new novel. Bookstalls could be picked clean in an hour. Thackeray and Dickens and Eliot and Hardy and George Meredith became very rich indeed off the serialized novel. Even in the United States, where serialization did not catch on the same way, the conventional novel proved hugely successful for Nathaniel Hawthorne and Mark Twain and William Dean Howells and even for Herman Melville, if we except his masterpiece. *Moby Dick* was just too out-there for readers expecting another sea yarn in the mode of *Omoo* and *Typee*.

Did it work, indeed.

So what happened? Why would the modernists reject and even vilify such a sweet arrangement? In part, the economics changed. The great Victorian journals—*Blackwood's, The Edinburgh Review*—lost their hold on the reading public. Without them, the serial novel became less viable. But beyond that, how many times can you write the same novel? The late Argentinean writer Jorge Luis Borges said he would never undertake a novel because the nineteenth-century English writers had done it so magnificently that they left nothing to do. And he meant Robert Louis Stevenson!

Naturally, the economic shift wasn't the only change. Stuff was happening. The Victorian novel was exquisitely suited to the Victorian world, but it was wildly ill suited to this new epoch. Consider the changes in human thought that occurred in the last years of the old century and the first years of the new one: Sigmund Freud, Friedrich Nietzsche, William James, Henri Bergson, Karl Marx, Albert Einstein, and Max Planck all produced seminal work before 1910. Dickens and Eliot never read any of them. Their novels were matched to the pace of a horse-and-buggy society. But Henry Ford mass-produced the Model T, moving us into a thirty-mile-an-hour reality. *Everything* was moving faster. Novels, too, had to find a new pace. Writers, and no doubt readers as well, grew impatient with the conventional novel. Maybe there's something, they began to think, that novels can do besides plot. As a result, the extremely conventional Victorian-era novel is replaced by the wildly experimental modernist novel. Not right away, but soon. The Edwardian era— those first several years of the century when King Edward VII was monarch—produced a lot of fairly conventional fiction by people such as Arnold Bennett and John Galsworthy, whose names would almost immediately become synonymous among younger writers with the most ancient of old hats.

Soon, very soon, though, the experiments began. By 1920 many of the major modernists—James Joyce, D. H. Lawrence, Virginia Woolf, Joseph Conrad, and Ford Madox Ford (in England and Ireland); Gertrude Stein (the United States); Thomas Mann and Franz Kafka (Germany); and Marcel Proust (France)—had made complete hash out of whatever the conventions had been. And why not? When time (Bergson), the mind (Freud and Jung), reality (Einstein and Bohr and Heisenberg), and even ethics (Nietzsche) have changed utterly, when men fly and pictures move and sound travels through air, what can you do but try something new?

And new it was. Stein wrote strange, repeating, stair-step prose that seemed to come from someone who had not quite mastered English—or any other human language. In novels like *Three Lives* (1909) and *The Making of Americans* (1925), she defamiliarized language, making it strange to native speakers so that they must reconsider their relation to it. Small wonder it took her eighteen years to find a publisher for the latter book, a nine-hundred-page behemoth. Kafka did her one better and, in dozens of stories and three novels, made the entirety of existence unfamiliar. Most readers are acquainted, at least by reputation, with his story "The Metamorphosis," in which a young man awakens one morning to find himself changed into a gigantic insect. The tale takes a common enough figurative expression of alienation and makes it literal, thereby rendering it bizarre and, indeed, alienating in its own right. Less well known are his book-length fictions, which do much the same thing. In the posthumously published *The Trial* (1925), the main character, Joseph K., finds himself accused of a vague crime that he's fairly sure he didn't commit. The crime itself, the circumstances surrounding it, and the legal authority under which the prosecution is to take place are never revealed. Nonetheless, he submits himself to the process of the law, which ultimately results in his trial, conviction, and execution. *The Castle* (1926) features a similarly absurd situation, in which a surveyor, also named K. (Kafka's all-purpose, autobiographical initial for the put-upon), has arrived in a town to conduct work authorized, allegedly, by the ruling castle of the title. When there appears to have been a mix-up and his services are not required, he attempts to reach someone in charge in the shadowing castle, which the villagers accept as the absolute authority and dare never approach or question. Answers are never forthcoming, accusations are made based on spurious information, and bureaucratic errors abound despite the castle's insistence on, and the villagers' belief in, infallibility. K. himself has been brought to the village because of a bureaucratic blunder that he never manages to straighten out. Like Stein, Kafka offers a radical new possibility for what the novel can accomplish. Her arena is language; his, plot and premise. But each takes fiction to a place it has never gone before.

When we speak of modernist fiction, of course, the phrase that immediately springs to mind is stream of consciousness. And indeed, several of the stars of the era—Joyce, Woolf, and Faulkner, in particular—worked in something we could call stream of consciousness, although they themselves did not inevitably subscribe to the term. What we can say with certainty, though, is that the exploration and presentation of consciousness is an ongoing preoccupation. Even those like D. H. Lawrence with little patience with the practices of Woolf or Dorothy Richardson spent a great deal of energy attempting to render the inner lives of their characters. There is a great deal of action and drama on the surface of *Women in Love* (1920), for instance, but the book's energies are directed at the sharper drama of the four major characters' interior lives: How do I feel about this friend, this lover, this antagonist? What is this person demanding of my psyche, and am I willing to comply or resist? What does it mean to be autonomous? Connected? Conscious? Can I survive? Do I want to?

That insistence on interiority is in many ways one of the hallmarks of modernist fiction. Here's a passage about, ostensibly, food.

> *No sooner had the warm liquid, and the crumbs with it, touched my palate than a shudder ran through my whole body, and I stopped, intent upon the extraordinary changes that were taking place. An exquisite pleasure had invaded my senses, but individual, detached, with no suggestion of its origin. And at once the vicissitudes of life had become indifferent to me, its disasters innocuous, its brevity illusory—this new sensation having had on me the effect which love has of filling me with a precious essence; or rather this essence was not in me, it was myself. I had ceased now to feel mediocre, accidental, mortal. Whence could it have come to me, this all-powerful joy? I was conscious that it was connected with the taste of tea and cake, but that it infinitely transcended those savours, could not, indeed, be of the same nature as theirs. Whence did it come? What did it signify? How could I seize upon and define it?*

This is the response to the most famous morsel in literature, the *petite madeleine* dipped in tea that gives rise to seven volumes of memory in Marcel Proust's *À la recherche du temps perdu*, which translator C. Scott Moncrieff renders not very precisely into English as *Remembrance of Things Past* (1913/1922). What's the action here? A guy takes a bite of a cake. In the old days, the action wouldn't even register unless it was connected to some other, larger action. In William Dean Howells, for instance, the only response would be to take another bite, or perhaps disgrace himself in company by talking with his mouth full or something. Not here, though. No, sirree. I have it on excellent authority that, strange as it may seem, Proust never even read Howells. Can you imagine? Marcel, the narrator, will himself take another bite, but not before this bit of mental rumination. The action is all interior: sensation overwhelms him, followed by unaccountable emotion (the joy he alludes to), and then the questions about the origin and meaning of this emotion. His entire life, in other words, comes flooding back in that spoonful of soggy cake. Yes, he will "seize upon and define it," but it will take him about a million words.

Not everyone in modernism went on at such length, although there were numerous multivolume novels, but a great many of them focused their efforts—and their narratives—inside characters' heads. Writers as diverse as Joyce, Hemingway, Djuna Barnes, Willa Cather, and E. M. Forster go spelunking in the caves of consciousness. Indeed, what marks Forster's *A Passage to India* as more particularly modern than his novels of the century's first decade, *A Room with a View* or even *Howards End*, is not the attitude or the form but the emphasis on the *problem* of consciousness, on how characters perceive, process, and respond at the most private levels to the stimuli of their surroundings. And what happens when you can't go any further inside consciousness? *Finnegans Wake.* The book no one has read. And that may include its writer. Actually, I have read the *Wake*, if not all at one time, and have enjoyed much of it, although I won't make any great claims to understanding. Not that there's any real mystery to it:

riverrun, past Eve and Adam's, from swerve of shore to bend of bay, brings us by a commodius vicus of recirculation back to Howth Castle and Environs.

Sir Tristram, violer d'amores, fr'over the short sea, had passencore rearrived from North Armorica on this side the scraggy isthmus of Europe Minor to wielderfight his penisolate war: nor had topsawyer's rocks by the stream Oconee exaggerated themselse to Laurens County's gorgios while they went doublin their mumper all the time: nor avoice from afire bellowsed mishe mishe to tauftauf thuartpeatrick not yet, though venissoon after, had a kidscad buttended a bland old isaac: not yet, though all's fair in vanessy, were sosie sesthers wroth with twone nathandjoe. Rot a peck of pa's malt had Jhem or Shen brewed by arclight and rory end to the regginbrow was to be seen ringsome on the aquaface.

Now, how can you not want to read more? That's merely the first two paragraphs. In a curious way, everything you need to understand the novel is there—the puns, the insistent rivers, the northern European legends and word borrowings, the encryptions of family ("gorgios" plays on the name of his son, Giorgio) and hometown ("doublin," although my favorite is "dear dirty dumplin"), the abuse of English spelling and orthography, the circularity ("rearrived," "recirculation," the invocation of the philosopher of historical circularity Giambattista Vico in "commodius vicus," and the sentence fragment to begin the book that seems to complete the one that ends it). On the other hand, for many readers those two paragraphs are all they'll ever want to know about the strangest book in English literature. Maybe one paragraph more than all.

The *Wake* reminds us of the other great hallmark of twentieth-century novels: experimentalism. If Victorianism manifested a resistance to innovation, modernism and postmodernism seem to require it. Not all experimentalism is as extreme as Joyce's, though. Hemingway was himself a great experimenter, but with short, tight sentences and limited vocabulary and how much meaning could be packed into how few words. Most fiction writers will go their whole careers and never construct a sentence as simple and rich as the question with which he ends *The Sun Also Rises*, "Isn't it pretty to think so?" There are volumes in that seemingly innocuous sentence, which, in another context, could be the epitome of emptiness. He did that in his first novel. Jack Kerouac went the opposite way, constructing sentences in his first novel that are overcaffeinated, hyped-up, jazzed-up, charging, driving attempts to capture the entire giddy, sad, ecstatic, Beat world.

> *There was the Pacific, a few more foothills away, blue and vast and with a great wall of white advancing from the legendary potato patch where Frisco fogs are born. Another hour it would come streaming through the Golden Gate to shroud the romantic city in white, and a young man would hold his girl by the hand and climb slowly up a long white sidewalk with a bottle of Tokay in his pocket. That was Frisco; and beautiful women standing in white doorways, waiting for their men; and Coit Tower, and the Embarcadero, and Market Street, and the eleven teeming hills.*

Now, *that's* a passage Jane Austen never wrote. Kerouac strives to capture the rhythms of a new, postwar America zooming along highways at breakneck speeds in the enforced solitude of the automobile, revved up on jazz clubs and all-night coffee shops, moving away from the war years as fast as it could. What a sound, what a voice! If, like Hemingway, he proves easy to parody and in his later work sometimes seems to parody himself, it's because that voice is so distinctive and original.

Experimentalism comes in every shape and form, even to undoing the shape and form of the novel itself. The French so-called New Novelists, Alain Robbe-Grillet and Marguerite Duras and Claude Simon and Nathalie Sarraute, did away with most of the things we associate with the novel: plot, character, theme, action, and narrative. What replaced them, often, would be objects and sensations, the same scene from various perspectives or sometimes the same perspective again and again. In *Jealousy*, the signature novel of the movement, Robbe-Grillet's tormented hero watches obsessively for evidence of his wife's alleged affair with a neighbor. The husband calls his wife only by a letter and ellipsis, "A . . ." and scrupulously avoids mentioning his own presence, eschewing the first-person pronoun and often avoiding placing himself at scenes where he is clearly present. The New Novel has had later adherents as well, most notably perhaps David Markson, whose books always shy away from the conventional and expected. *Wittgenstein's Mistress* (1988) is presented as a series of very small statements about the world she experiences and her responses to it by a woman believing herself to be the last person in that world.

> *One has a fairly acute inkling as to when Cassandra may be having her period, for instance.*
>
> *Cassandra is feeling out of sorts again, one can even imagine Troilus or certain other Trojans now and again saying.*
>
> *Then again, Helen could be having hers even when she still possesses that radiant dignity, being Helen.*
>
> *My own generally makes my face puffy.*

One is next to positive that Sappho would have never beaten around the bush about any of this, on the other hand.

Which could well explain why certain of her poems were used as the stuffing for mummies, even before the friars got their hands on those that were left.

Well, one can hardly expect conventional on that tale, can one? His books have become progressively less reliant on the traditional constituent elements of narrative and more dependent on moments of consciousness and perception. These, too, are traditional elements, of course, but they have rarely been foregrounded as they are in Markson.

Every era has its literary ethos, sometimes more than one. The twentieth century's, for the most part, centers around one of a few related battle cries: "Out with the old," "Down with convention," "Make it new," or "You don't know until you try it." That urge to experiment and make it new has taken many forms, many times rejecting the innovations of the last bunch of rebels. That's one version, at least, of being modern. Or post.

But back to that Victorian novel. Let me ask again: so what happened? Nothing. The nineteenth-century novel never really left us. That mode of fiction—linear narrative, clearly delineated good and bad characters, and the rest—may have fallen from favor among "literary" writers, but it stayed and stayed and stayed in popular fiction. You can find it in much genre fiction, romance or horror or thriller. Open a Hollywood saga by Sidney Sheldon or Jackie Collins, a "read" by Judith Krantz or Maeve Binchy, a historical saga by James A. Michener or John Jakes or Edward Rutherford, and you'll find the descendant of *A Mill on the Floss* or *The Egoist*. You may have a hard time recognizing it with all the sex and profanity, all the bedroom shenanigans that never appeared in (or maybe occurred to) George Eliot or Howells. The late twentieth century even produced some great Victorian novelists of its own, perhaps most notably that magnificent Canadian, Robertson Davies. Davies, who didn't start publishing novels until his late thirties, produced three and two-thirds trilogies before his death at age eighty-two. His novels would fit uncomfortably into the 1870s or 1880s because of his greater frankness, but in terms of form and sensibility, he's one of Them. In *What's Bred in the Bone* (1985) he even asks the question, what is an artist born out of his right time supposed to do? The answer, in this as in the rest of his novels, is to produce the art he was born to make. Literary history and fashion are artificial constructs, and a Victorian should be a Victorian, whatever his era. And he was.

Which brings us, by a commodius vicus of recirculation, back to our point. Every age has experimentalists and traditionalists. Form breakers and form followers. You can call them radicals and reactionaries if you like, but their aesthetic stances don't inevitably follow their political views. Some ages tend one way and some another, but within them there are always writers out of step with their own time. There are rebels and rebels against rebellion. That's why every literary history is a lie, including this one. They're overly simplistic, failing to capture the vast complexity of men and women doing their own thing in their historical moment, whether that thing comports with those of other writers or not. Mere reporting can't capture all the facets and all the nuances of the fiction of a given year, much less of all the years, in the dizzying multiplicity of what James called the "house of fiction." Who can possibly keep up? Your head, it simply swirls.

1

Pickup Lines and Open(ing) Seductions, or Why Novels Have First Pages

EVER WATCH PEOPLE IN bookstores? They pull a book from a shelf, read the cover, then the back cover, then the benefits page (that little number with all the blurbs on it, if it's a paperback), and then . . . what? You know this one. Hardly anyone I've ever noticed has leapt into the middle of Chapter 23, so that first page had better deliver the goods. Otherwise, the book goes back on the shelf. You can't read 'em all.

We need first pages—and so do novelists. Right from the top, a novel begins working its magic on readers. Perhaps more remarkably, readers also begin working their magic on the novel. The beginning of a novel is, variously, a social contract negotiation, an invitation to a dance, a list of rules of the game, and a fairly complex seduction. I know, I know—seduction? Seems extreme, doesn't it?

But that's what's going on at the beginning of a novel. We're being asked to commit a lot of time and energy to an enterprise with very little in the way of guarantee of what's in it for us. That's where the seduction comes in. And it wants to tell us what it thinks is important, so much so that it can't wait to get started. Perhaps more importantly, it wants us to get involved. When it's over, we may feel wooed, adored, appreciated, or abused, but it will have been an affair to remember. The opening of a novel is an invitation to come inside and play. The first page, in this context, is not so much a guarantee as a promissory note: "Hey," it says, "I've got something good here. You'll like it. You can trust me. Give me a whirl." And that's why the very first line is so important. Try a few of these on for size.

- ✐ "What's it going to be, then?"
- ✐ "Mrs. Dalloway said she would buy the flowers herself."
- ✐ "This is the saddest story I ever heard."
- ✐ "Many years later, as he faced the firing squad, Colonel Aureliano Buendía was to remember that distant afternoon when his father took him to discover ice."
- ✐ "It is a truth universally acknowledged, that a man in possession of a fortune must be in want of a wife."
- ✐ "At an age when most young Scotsmen were lifting skirts, plowing furrows and spreading seed, Mungo Park was displaying his bare buttocks to al-haj' Ali Ibu Fatoudi, Emir of Ludamar."

Now how can you not want to read those novels? They pique the interest. What flowers? Why saddest? And for heaven's sake, who is Mungo Park and what's with the bare buttocks? Those were the first words many of us ever read from a writer who then called himself T. Coraghessan Boyle but has since mercifully shortened the middle name to its initial consonant, in a novel called *Water Music*. The book proved to be just as wild as the opening promised, full of outrageous events, exuberant language, astonishing surprises, and zany humor. Boyle's subsequent novels and stories have shown equal panache in the matter of first pages.

Is the first page the whole novel? Of course not. I once asked in class what group had the best hooks in rock music. The response, not from a burly guy but from a surprisingly demure-looking woman, was AC/DC. Works for me. Now, that doesn't make the lads from down under the best rock group ever, any more than writing the best hooks since Chuck Berry makes Angus Young another Mozart. But his hooks sure are catchy. So are Boyle's. And hooks get novels started. Get readers started. Offer insights into coming attractions. Make us want to read and begin teaching us how to read it.

Say what? We can even make a general proposition here, the Law of Getting Started: The opening is the first lesson in how to read the novel. We have to learn to read every new novel, so the novel must be a series of lessons on how to read this one. Unconvinced? Think about it. Is a Spenser mystery by Robert B. Parker anything like *The Sound and the Fury*? Aside from both having lots of words and justi-fied right margins? But the big things—narrative style, method of character presentation, revelation of consciousness, dialogue, plot? You can make a lot of claims for old Bill Faulkner, but compelling plotting and zingy dialogue aren't among them. Now you might think this means Faulkner is hard to read and any knucklehead can read Parker, but it's not so simple. Parker gives Spenser a certain mind-set that we have to learn, a certain rhythm to his narration, friends and associates who take some getting used to. Lots more people may enjoy reading him than Faulkner, but there's still a learning process we go through when we open his book. The other difference between what's often called genre or category fiction and the "literary sort" is the amount of change from one novel to the next. Parker's lessons carry over pretty well from book to book, so if you've read *Looking for Rachel Wallace* you can manage *A Catskill Eagle* pretty well. Faulkner, on the other hand, rarely does quite the same thing twice, so while some strategies we learn reading *The Sound and the Fury* will help if we open *Light in August* or *Absalom, Absalom!*, each new book will present new and different challenges. And we'll notice the changes on the first page. That's where the new lesson begins.

Take, for instance, that first sentence from Gabriel García Márquez's *One Hundred Years of Solitude*, the one about the colonel, the firing squad, and the ice. Almost everything we need to know about reading this novel is present in this first sentence. It establishes the main family of the novel and the turbulent times in which they live, as evidenced by the firing squad. It emphasizes the importance of marvels, not in the ice but in the verb "discover," which suggests how miraculous this substance must have been to the child in, as we shortly discover, a pre-electrified equatorial Colombia. We know what sort of voice is telling the story, how it manages information, what sorts of words it chooses—and plenty more follows in the next two paragraphs. And it's not just fabulous novels by South American Nobel laureates that accomplish this sort of feat. Robert Parker mysteries, Anita Shreve domestic dramas, Dan Brown thrillers, and this month's Harlequin romances, as well as classics by Hardy, Hawthorne, and Hemingway, do the same thing: tell us how to go about reading them. They can't help it, really. Whatever a novel tells us first is information—about who, what, where, when, how, why. About intent. About irony. About what the writer is up to this time.

That first page, sometimes the first paragraph, even the first sentence, can give you everything you need to know to read the novel. How? By conveying some or all of the eighteen things the first page can tell you. First pages convey information without half trying, but they're always trying.

Yeah, but . . . *eighteen?* I mean, five or six, or even seven, but eighteen? Conservatively. There are probably many other things we can glean from a first page, but here are eighteen beauties.

1. **Style.** Short or long sentences? Simple or complex? Rushed or leisurely? How many modifiers—adjectives and adverbs and such? The first page of any Hemingway novel will impress us with short declarative sentences and a strong sense that the writer was badly frightened in infancy by words ending in "ly." Any first page by an American detective novelist—John D. or Ross Macdonald, say, or Raymond Chandler or Mickey Spillane or even Linda Barnes—will convince us that the writer has read Hemingway. In Spillane's case, with no great comprehension.

2. **Tone.** Every book has a tone. Is it elegiac, or matter-of-fact, or ironic? That opening from Jane Austen's *Pride and Prejudice*, "It is a truth universally acknowledged, that a man in possession of a fortune must be in want of a wife," is a tonal masterpiece. It distances the speaker from the source of the "truth" while giving her permission to trot out an ironic statement about wives running through husbands' fortunes and wealthy men being more desirable than poor ones. "In want of" cuts two ways at least.

3. **Mood.** Similar to tone but not quite the same. The previous item is about how the voice sounds; this one is about how it feels about what it's telling. However we describe the tone of *The Great Gatsby*, the mood of the narration, in Nick Carraway's person, is one of regret, guilt, and even anger, all

of which sneak in between his overly reasonable-sounding statements about mulling over advice from his father and the disparities of privilege. So what is it, we wonder at once, that he's not quite saying here?

4. **Diction.** What kinds of words does the novel use? Are they common or rare? Friendly or challenging? Are the sentences whole or fractured, and if the latter, on purpose or accidentally? Anthony Burgess's *A Clockwork Orange*—which begins with the deceptively simple query, "What's it going to be, then?"—has the most remarkable diction of any novel I know. His narrator, the barely educated young thug Alex, speaks with an Elizabethan elaboration worthy of Shakespeare and his contemporaries. His insults are colorful and baffling to his adversaries, his descriptions and praise effusive, his curses wonders of invention, and his language shot through with a made-up teen slang, Nadsat, based largely on Slavic words. And we get the first inklings of his linguistic temperament in the novel's opening passages. This is merely the extreme example; every novel has its own diction, and every word chosen details it further.

5. **Point of view.** The first issue isn't *who* is telling the story in terms of identity. Indeed, for most of the novels we'll ever read, there is no "who" in that sense. But who relative to the story and its characters—that we can learn straight off. Is this a "he/she" story or an "I" story? When "I" shows up we expect to meet a character, major or minor, and we immediately have our suspicions aroused. That discussion, however, can wait. If the narrative employs "he" and "she" for persons in the story, with no "I" in sight, we can be fairly safe in assuming this is a more distant, third-person nar-

ration. If the narration employs "you," all bets are off and we head for shelter. Happily, second-person narrations are rare, but they are, like Italo Calvino's experimental *If on a Winter's Night a Traveler* and Tom Robbins's *Half Asleep in Frog Pajamas*, very likely to be strange experiences. We can get fooled in all this; as with all literary rules, this one exists to be broken. Sometimes a character-narrator will hide culpability behind a mock third-person viewpoint, or an outside narrator will employ "I" as a narrative gambit. Even with such tricky business, though, we sometimes get hints in the first paragraphs.

6. **Narrative presence.** Now we can speak of that other who. Is this voice disembodied or possessed by a personage, inside or outside the story? Is it a servant talking about her masters, a victim talking about his persecutors, a perpetrator speaking of his victims? They often give us hints right away. With first-person narrators, the "presence" is pretty clear. Hemingway's Jake Barnes (*The Sun Also Rises*) and Fredric Henry (*A Farewell to Arms*) make themselves known right away; their personality imprints itself on the text from sentence one. But what about third-person narrators? In the eighteenth century, narrators were often full of personality, genial companions who, like ourselves (so went the conceit), were men and women of the world, who understood what people were like, who were amused by the foibles of their neighbors. We see such poses in Henry Fielding's *Tom Jones* or Austen's *Pride and Prejudice*. In the following era, Charles Dickens's storytelling presence insinuates his way into *Our Mutual Friend* in the first five words, "In these times of ours," announcing that the narrator will be a very

involved participant in the tale, a passionate observer and commentator. By the time we get to the twentieth century, that third-person narrator is often impersonal, detached, cool, as in Hemingway or Anita Brookner. Compare that Dickens opening to this one you probably read at school: "He was an old man who fished alone in a skiff in the Gulf Stream and he had gone eighty-four days now without taking a fish." This voice is more aloof, less likely to get in there and mix it up emotionally than his Victorian counterpart.

7. **Narrative attitude** toward characters and events. How does the narrator feel about the people and action in the novel? Austen's narrators are generally amused, slightly aloof, a little superior. Dickens's tend to be earnest, involved, direct (if third-person); naïve, earnest, fond (if first-person). Flaubert's narrator in *Madame Bovary* is famously cool and impersonal, largely in reaction to the overheated involvement of narrators in the previous romantic era. In rejecting the extant cliché, Flaubert created the narrative cliché that would predominate for much of the next century.

8. **Time frame.** When is all this happening? Contemporaneously or a long time ago? How can we tell? Does the novel cover a lot of time or a little? In what part of the narrator's life, if she's a character? That "many years later" of the García Márquez opening is magical. It says, first of all, that this novel will cover a great deal of time, enough for a small child holding his father's hand to rise to power and fall from it. But it also says something else magical: "once upon a time." This is a kind of fairy tale, it says, about an exotic place and time, neither of which exists anymore (nowhere can be that backward, he hints), that were special in their

own time. Any novelist who isn't jealous about those three words alone isn't very serious about craft.

9. **Time management.** Will time go fast or slow in this novel? Is it being told in or near the now of the story or long after? Nicholson Baker's little gem, *The Mezzanine* takes place—all of it—during the time it takes its narrator to ride an escalator from the first floor to the aforementioned destination. In order to pull off that stunt, the writer must elongate time to the extreme, relying on flashbacks and digressions, and that strategy shows up right away, as it must.

10. **Place.** Okay, setting, but also more than mere setting. Place is a sense of things, a mode of thought, a way of seeing. Take that T. C. Boyle opening I quote above. In the second paragraph, we learn that Mungo Park, a Scotsman, is an explorer looking for the Niger River who has taken a serious wrong turn. Place here is both locale and story. This—the tent, the continent, the country—is where he is, to be sure. But this is also where he's an outsider, the leading edge of nascent imperial intentions, and a blunderer who keeps finding himself in variations of his current humiliating situation. In that sense, place, the immediate place, becomes motif: time after time we will see Mungo blunder into disastrous situations through total ignorance of the nature, culture, and geography—in other words, of place. Which leads us to . . .

11. **Motif.** Stuff that happens again and again. Sorry about the technical jargon, but that's what it is. Motif can be image, action, language pattern, anything that happens again and again. Like Mungo and his recurrent disasters based on cultural arrogance. Like miracles and the colonel's narrow

escapes in *One Hundred Years of Solitude*. Like the flowers in *Mrs. Dalloway*.

12. **Theme.** Stop groaning—there won't be a test. Theme is the bane of all tenth-grade English students, but it's also about, well, aboutness. Story is what gets a novel going and what we focus on, but theme is one of the things that makes it worthwhile. Theme is, roughly speaking, the idea content of the novel. Sometimes that content is simple: most mysteries share the theme that crime will be found out, that no one gets away with it, that order will prevail. Often, it's more subtle than that. Agatha Christie often has a secondary theme concerning the decadence of the aristocracy. Ever notice with her how many bad eggs there are in manor houses? Or how inept, corrupt, or stupid they are? Think that's accidental? Sometimes theme overlaps with motif, as those recurrences serve to reinforce a key idea. One of *Mrs. Dalloway*'s main ideas, the presence of the past, shows up on the first page, as Clarissa's plunge into the beautiful June day in 1923 launches her back to a similar day when she was eighteen. Throughout the novel, those old days keep showing up in the form of memories and persons, and it all starts right away.

13. **Irony.** Or not—some novels are in dead earnest. The entire nineteenth century springs to mind. Okay, maybe not Mark Twain. Oh, and Gustave Flaubert. But you know what I mean. Others are ironic on any number of levels—verbal, dramatic, comic, situational—and often that shows up right away. This is one of Parker's Spenser novels, *A Catskill Eagle*, getting rolling: "It was midnight and I was just getting home from detecting. I had followed an embezzler around

on a warm day in early summer trying to observe him spending his ill-gotten gain. The best I'd been able to do was catch him eating a veal cutlet in a sub shop in Danvers Square across from the Security National Bank. It wasn't much, but it was as close as you could get to sin in Danvers." Now Spenser is utterly earnest about what he does when he's doing it; he never expresses doubt or irony while shooting someone, for instance, but he's plenty ironic when he talks about it. He knows that his chosen trade, "professional thug" as he calls it in another book, is morally dubious. And that awareness makes its way into the books in phrases like "getting home from detecting." He may, moreover, want to distance his "real" or "private" self from the actions of his professional self: "I'm the sensitive lover and excellent cook who likes wine with dinner and not merely the hired tough guy who threatens and shoots people," he seems to say with this strategy. And he also knows full well that you can find plenty of sin in Danvers or any other sleepy burg; that's just frustration talking. Throughout the novel, then, he'll veer between hard-charging action—lots of bodies fall in this one—and ironic, distanced commentary.

14. **Rhythm.** Of one sort. There are two levels of rhythm in a novel: prose and narrative. Narrative rhythm will take a while to establish, but the prose starts showing up at once. Better, it often suggests how the larger narrative's rhythm will work. Rhythm is related to diction, which we discussed earlier, but with this difference: diction has to do with the words a writer uses, rhythm with how they're deployed in sentences. In practice, they're largely inseparable, as prose rhythm depends a good deal on the words chosen while

also coloring how those words sound. Everything in narrative is related to everything else on some level. Does the writer blurt out information or withhold it? State it directly or bury it inside a tangle of clauses? Cause words to tumble over one another or meander along? Here's the beginning of Barbara Kingsolver's *The Poisonwood Bible.*

Imagine a ruin so strange it must never have happened.

First, picture the forest. I want you to be its conscience, the eyes in the trees. The trees are columns of slick, brindled bark like muscular animals overgrown beyond all reason. Every space is filled with life: delicate, poisonous frogs war-painted like skeletons, clutched in copulation, secreting their precious eggs onto dripping leaves. Vines strangling their own kin in the everlasting wrestle for sunlight. The breathing of monkeys. A glide of snake belly on branch.

How's that for rhythm? It's calm, measured, almost leisurely, yet every detail is a warning or a peril. Why "conscience" rather than the more neutral "awareness" or "delicate" to describe the poisonous frogs? That's masterful—tranquil danger. You are free to like or dislike me, the novel says, but at least you know what you're getting yourself into.

15. **Pace.** How fast do we go? Consider this opening, from Henry James's *The Portrait of a Lady.*

Under certain circumstances there are few hours in life more agreeable than the hour dedicated to the ceremony known as afternoon tea. There are circumstances in which, whether you partake of the tea or not—some people of course never do—the situation is in itself delightful. Those that I have in mind in beginning to unfold this simple history offered an admirable setting to an innocent pastime. The implements of the little feast had been disposed upon the lawn of an old English country-house, in what I should call the perfect middle of a splendid summer afternoon.

This is not going to be a hundred-yard dash. Everything about the passage says "leisurely"—the long, abstract words, the embedded "some people never do," the sense that this should be no more rushed than the event, if you can call it that, that it describes. Know what? Get used to it. James is never frantic, never in a hurry. The things he values in narrative, like psychological insight and interior drama, just can't be rushed.

16. **Expectations.** Of the writer, of the reader. Wait—of the *reader*? Yep, I know what you're thinking: he's lost his mind. But your expectations are there on page one. This is the most interactive space on the first page, or any other. The writer gets to announce his expectations. Does the novelist expect, like George Eliot, someone with time and patience, or like Thomas Pynchon, someone hip and savvy who's unafraid of the wacky and unconventional, or like Wodehouse, a relaxed, jaunty companion? How hard does the novel expect us to work? How much information should we bring to the novel? What sort of attitude is the ideal reader supposed to have? That's all well and good, but this is one place where we get a say. Do we want to read that novel? Do we approve of the word choice? Are we that hip? More? What do we want the novel to do? The first page is the beginning of

a negotiation, or collaboration, between writer and reader. The writer brings a great deal to the process, but so do we. The reader's expectations—this is what I want from a novel today—matter as much as the writer's—this is what I need from a reader. Page one is where we have our first meeting of the minds. And where we find out if there will be a page two.

17. **Character.** Not always on page one, but more often than not. And more often than not, the main character. "Protagonist" comes from the Greek for "first agent," and trotting out your star attraction first works in twenty-first-century novels just as well as it did in fifth-century BCE plays. Naturally, in first-person narratives, we meet someone very like a character right away, as with Huck Finn or Mike Hammer or Humbert Humbert, even if we don't know his name or how he features in the tale. But he's there. And so he or she is in many third-person novels. Mrs. Dalloway is mentioned in the first two words of her novel. James Joyce begins *Ulysses* with "Stately, plump Buck Mulligan"—not the main character but his nemesis. And of course, Aureliano Buendía is one of the leading characters of his family's hundred-year saga. The bottom line: people are helpful to start a novel.

18. **Instructions on how to read the novel.** All of these previously mentioned elements go into teaching us how the novel *wants* to be read. Whether we read it that way or not is, naturally, our call. But every novel wants to be read in a certain way. Try this opening on for size.

As I sat in the bath-tub, soaping a meditative foot and singing, if I remember correctly, "Pale Hands I Loved Beside the Shali-

mar," it would be deceiving my public to say that I was feeling boomps-a-daisy. The evening that lay before me promised to be one of those sticky evenings, no good to man or beast. My Aunt Dahlia, writing from her country residence, Brinkley Court down in Worcestershire, had asked me as a personal favor to take some acquaintances of hers out to dinner, a couple of the name of Trotter.

Well, "Aunt Dahlia" pretty much gives the game away as a Bertie Wooster, but for anyone who has ever read a P. G. Wodehouse Wooster-and-Jeeves story before, it was already game over. Only one narrator I've ever come across is capable of having a "meditative foot," only one character capable of singing something as insipid as a song with that title must needs be, and reporting it proudly, in a digression. "Boomps-a-daisy," moreover, has Bertie Wooster written all over it, as does the "no good to man or beast" characterization of the evening. For those new to Wodehouse, it merely promises good, clean, comic fun, but it's a masterpiece of reader indoctrination. The paragraph is chock-full of information—about character, narrative attitudes, style, diction (he favors the goofier sorts of Edwardian slang), improbable turns of phrase, feelings about his aunt, class and social set, as well as musical taste. Nearly everything one needs to know to read this novel, which is *Jeeves and the Feudal Spirit*, is present in the first paragraph except the character's name and the all-important Jeeves, but even he can be deduced. A character this vapid will surely need a handler. And the most important thing we learn? This won't be Dostoevsky. That's always a relief. All that from one paragraph.

Whew! It's worth noting that we won't get all of those features in every first page, but most of them will show up, and even a mere dozen will stand as a pretty fair assemblage of information. That's a lot of work for a single page to handle. Is it the whole novel? Of course not. Otherwise, we wouldn't need the other hundred thousand words. And in any case, all of those elements are only beginning to be articulated in a first paragraph. There's plenty more to be accomplished, but for that, we'll have to turn the page.

2

You Can't Breathe Where the Air Is Clear

QUICK, WHAT DO THESE have in common: Middle-earth, Macondo, West Egg, Yoknapatawpha County, San Narcisso, and Narnia? They're places you (and I) have never lived, and never will. They're not fit for human habitation. And no matter how scrupulously detailed or sumptuously furnished, they can't be our towns and cities and farms. Not Joyce's Dublin nor Farrell's Chicago nor Roddy Doyle's Barrytown nor Carlos Fuentes's Mexico City (since I've abused his title here). Don't get me wrong—I like them. They're great places for fiction to take us; often they are quite similar to the real deal, occasionally even better. They are, however, not the real deal.

One thing I insist on with my students is that we understand the essential artifice of the novel. It is a made-up work about made-up people in a made-up place. All of which is very real. We are asked to believe in and treat as potentially real a space that is manifestly imaginary. Headaches are guaranteed.

Consider this, on June 16, 1954, five men undertook a lugubrious trip round Dublin. The occasion was the fiftieth anniversary of Bloomsday, the day on which Joyce's *Ulysses* (1922) is set. The group included a cousin, Tom Joyce, the poet Patrick Kavanagh, the young writer Anthony Cronin, the painter and publican John Ryan, and Brian O'Nolan, who wrote the celebrated newspaper column "Cruiskeen Lawn" under the pen name Myles na gCopaleen and had published a novel, *At Swim-Two-Birds* (on which, more later), under the name Flann O'Brien. Their goal was to recreate the wanderings of the characters in the novel. O'Nolan at least had the spirit of the thing right; although they convened in midmorning, he was already drunk, as was his wont. Each member of the little party was assigned a character from the novel that he would enact as they proceeded. Their goal was to arrive at each of the celebrated landmarks of the novel at the hour assigned by the book. They had skipped the morning's first site, 7 Eccles Street, where main character Leopold Bloom fries himself a pork kidney. Eventually, the trip bogged down, quite sensibly, it seems to me, at Ryan's pub. It was a project doomed to failure, of course, and for more reasons than the difficulties of trundling the sodden O'Nolan into and out of cabs. At the same time, it proved a smashing success in ways none of the principals could have foreseen or, likely, would have wished.

In the half century that followed, Bloomsday became big business, literally, providing an annual tourism bonanza. All those Americans smitten by the master must be housed, fed, and guided around the stations of their Bloom-worship. The industry had grown so large by the 1990s that Bartholomew Gill turned the occasion into a mystery, *Death of a Joyce Scholar*, in which a lecherous and rapacious Joycean meets a brutal but not entirely undeserved end. And for the centennial, on June 16, 2004, Dublin hosted a celebration of Bloomsday, complete with breakfast for ten thousand on Grafton

Street. I don't know how accurate the bill of fare was that day, but the mere thought of thousands of sautéing kidneys put me right off my oatmeal. But here's the thing: those later celebrations are just as doomed to failure, on the literary level, as that first desultory attempt. I'm sure the chamber of commerce sees things differently, and while I felicitate the city with seizing the day, as it were (this is the place that held its millennium celebration in successive years rather than settle a dispute over the actual date of the Viking landing), I am unmoved on literary grounds.

Here's my point. Even if you have street addresses, and with Joyce we do, you can't walk where Stephen Dedalus and Bloom and Buck Mulligan and the rest walked. They're not actual streets. Rather, they're representations of streets. Joyce, who lived in self-imposed exile, was famous for hitting up friends and relatives for every bit of documentary evidence about his home city and the time period that interested him—old playbills, city directories, advertising circulars, newspaper cuttings, racing forms, any scrap of paper that might advance the cause of verisimilitude. He was notorious for stealing bits of conversation he picked up while eavesdropping on his father and his friends in pubs. Needless to say, he was not the most popular of John Joyce's children among the elder's cronies. You can think of him as a dutiful and slightly obsessive biographer. Yet he differs from biographers in that he turns all that material inward. If the goal of a biography or history is to recreate the objective reality of its subject, the novel's goal is to create the subjective reality of its object. Joyce says he wants to create the conscience of his race, yet veers to the fictive when he invents characters to inhabit his simulacrum of Dublin rather than tracing the activity of real persons. He openly rejects the documentary options—biography, history, journalism—in favor of the made-up world of Bloom and Molly and Stephen. His interest isn't truly in recreating *the* Dublin but in creating *a* Dublin, which his characters can inhabit. What he does is to trick the eye, to offer enough detail to cause readers to believe that they can see this Dublin, or rather, to offer enough detail that readers will supply the rest. He manages this nifty trick, as most writers do, with numerous specifics, in his case, street names, actual shops, genuine addresses, the National Library. It's pretty convincing, even if short on hard description. We experience that "reality" subjectively, from inside characters' thoughts. Stephen hears the stones crunching under his boots as he walks along the strand in the Proteus episode; the men in the office feel the wind rush through in Aeolus; Bloom sees and hears the fireworks display while watching young Gerty McDowell in Nausicaa. Yet by definition it can't be a complete rendering of the city. Such a thing would get in the way of our focus on the people in the novel. You will process more sensory information about your own town in a ten-minute walk than you can about Dublin by read-ing the entire 768 pages of *Ulysses*.

It's all rather like Marianne Moore's line about poetry creating "imaginary gardens with real toads in them." Novelists create imagi-nary cities and imaginary persons with real crises, real issues, real problems.

The nurse will now dispense aspirin to all who feel overcome.

How imaginary? How much do you want?

Take the obvious situation. We know, for instance, that there is no Middle-earth. You can scour the real earth and not find the Shire or Rivendell or Isengard or Mordor. Many apologists for the novel will say the Shire stands for England and Mordor for Germany, the whole geography representing the struggle against Nazi domination in World War II. This is undoubtedly true. J. R. R. Tolkien has drawn a world strongly suggestive of his own. The important thing here, however, is that it is not his own. That world is not anyone's except the characters' in the novels.

So, what, it doesn't count?

Not at all. In fact, it's entirely what does matter. The responsibility of setting is to the characters in the story. Their world doesn't have to be ours, but it absolutely has to be theirs. Consider Manhattan filled with hobbits, wizards, fairies, and fighting Uruk-hai. Orcs swarming up Wall Street, dwarves in the basements of skyscrapers. Now, that's just stupid. Sounds like the cheesiest kind of horror movie, where you laugh all the way. Or in the cornfields of Nebraska. No, Frodo, Gandalf, and company need their own landscapes, their own geography. Epic romance needs mythic space. On the other hand, that same mythic landscape would look preposterous inhabited by Henry James characters. Isabel Archer in Isingard? Milly Theale in Mordor? I think not. On the other hand, Saruman in Isingard is just right. Or Sauron in Mordor. Here's the description of the entrance to that bleak land.

> *Across the mouth of the pass, from cliff to cliff, the Dark Lord had built a rampart of stone. In it there was a single gate of iron, and upon its battlements sentinels paced unceasingly. Beneath the hills on either side the rock was bored into a hundred caves and maggot-holes; there a host of orcs lurked, ready at a signal to issue forth like black ants going to war. None could pass the Teeth of Mordor and not feel their bite, unless they were summoned by Sauron, or knew the secret passwords that would open the Morannon, the black gate of his land.*

That ought to be forbidding enough for anyone. Notice the signs of rigidity, militarism, and destruction: mouth, Teeth, bite, maggot-holes, orcs, black ants, battlements, sentinels, army, host, Dark Lord, black gate. And in just one paragraph! This is a place of death-in-life, a place without freedom or individuality or, evidently, humanity. Tolkien doesn't miss a trick, nor should he. As a scholar of ancient languages, he is intimately familiar with both the larger structures and the nuances of the epic romance, the really big story of great events and great heroes. In the *Ring* trilogy, he harnesses every one of them, including, as here, the aura of complete evil surrounding the Other, the Enemy. Now this is clearly not a description of setting that can work in very many types of novel, but it does have its special use. Frodo and Sam have to have the bejeebers scared out of them at the enormity of the task confronting them, and readers need to grasp the hopelessness and peril of their attempt. From this one glimpse alone, and there are a number more to follow, all parties get the message.

So, imaginary, even if borrowed from real life, whatever that is. But also functional in their own context. Sounds like we're closing in on a maxim, doesn't it? Here, then, is the Law of Bogus Locales: Places in a work of fiction are never real but must behave as if real.

And just what are the implications of this law? First, the made-upness. Any setting in a work of fiction is an imaginative construct and distinct from any actual place, even when it looks just like it. Novelists, if they use real places as models, select, limit, add to, modify, and sometimes just plain falsify those places. They don't include whole towns, whole streets, just as they are. Why? For one thing, the volume of information would prove overwhelming for readers. Novels would be three times longer, and nobody wants that. Some writers, chiefly the great realists and naturalists, pride themselves on the use of exact details of real locales. Gustave Flaubert, for instance, in *L'éducation sentimentale*, intends for readers to experience specifically the Paris he knows—the sights, the sounds, the smells of a real city. Joyce follows his example with his Dublin in *Ulysses*. Neither, however, is the real city, the whole city, and nothing but the city. The selection of details—including these, excluding those—turns these "actual" cities into artistic constructs. Good thing, too. Almost no one, even its greatest admirers (I speak as one), would wish *Ulysses* longer than it is.

Besides, with indiscriminate detail comes loss of focus. If Fitzgerald included everything on the drive in from West Egg to New York, our attention wouldn't be drawn to the three things that matter: the ash heaps, Wilson's garage, and the eyes of Dr. T. J. Eckleburg. Those three items matter; the rest does not.

And second, internal reality. One of the requirements of a work of literature, if it is to be aesthetically satisfying, is wholeness. That comes from St. Thomas Aquinas, and pretty much everyone who has offered a comment since him has been onboard. Part of wholeness is having appropriate places for characters to exist and to undertake actions. In general, fabulous characters and experiences are best suited to fabulous landscapes. When the children in C. S. Lewis's *The Lion, the Witch and the Wardrobe* slip through the wardrobe into Narnia, they have effectively left the world of the mundane (if Nazi bombing raids forcing them to leave their home can be considered mundane) for the fantastic. Witches? Talking lions? Centaurs? Only on the far side of the wardrobe. On the other hand, the wholly mundane nature of the American prairie suits the characters and actions of Willa Cather's novels. The very nature of the stories she wants to tell requires places that are not merely ordinary but very specific in nature. The tale of the passing of the West that she tells so economically in *A Lost Lady*, for instance, requires farmland and a small town on what was once the frontier. When she moves her tale farther west to New Mexico in *Death Comes for the Archbishop*, the type of narrative changes to one of larger scope both geographically and historically. Those places in either Cather or Lewis work because they offer an internal consistency, a wholeness, within the reality of the novel.

In part, their "reality" is our doing. Readers participate in the creation of these fictional worlds, filling in the gaps in description, seizing on details, making the possible world actual in imagination, agreeing, for a little while, to inhabit the uninhabitable. I've spoken elsewhere of reading as an interaction between two imaginations, that of the writer and that of the reader. Nowhere is this more important than in settings. Novelists cannot possibly provide every detail of their imagined worlds, nor would readers thank them if they did. So readers are obliged—and undertake willingly—to accept the realities on offer, even enriching them when necessary. We have our limits, of course. We won't accept shoddily made imaginary worlds or logical inconsistencies that occur through error or authorial laziness. But give us a well-made world with laws we can understand, even if they aren't our laws, and we're a pretty happy bunch. After all, those worlds take us out of our own for a few hours, and then bring us back again—and isn't that what we're seeking?

3

Who's in Charge Here?

So, you know how there are two things nobody can avoid? Novelists have four. Death and taxes, same as the rest of us. Plus first pages and narrators. Can't live with 'em, can't live without 'em. And usually, they hang out together.

Perhaps the novelist's hardest task is deciding who should tell the story. Main character? Secondary character? And what's his attitude toward others in the tale and the events therein? Is she speaking from within the events as they happen or long after? An outside voice? Limited to a single character or omniscient? Telling all or holding back? Amused, bemused, deeply involved, or bored with it all? It is sometimes said that a change of viewpoint is a change of religion, that an age without firm belief in an all-powerful God cannot utilize the omniscient narrator. While that may or may not be true, this is: the course of the novel is set once the viewpoint is established. Moreover, readers' relationships to the action and characters of the book rest on this critical decision. We cannot imagine a *Gatsby* narrated by anyone but Nick Carraway, a *Moby Dick* without the voice of Ishmael, or a *The Fellowship of the Ring* told by Frodo. We will be spending anywhere from thirty thousand to two hundred thousand words with this voice, this creature; some of us will even share our bed. Small wonder that the choice of narrator and point of view is never undertaken lightly.

And all this angst over a very small range of possibilities. Here's pretty much the whole list.

- **Third person omniscient** (sometimes listed as simply "omniscient"). This is the "godlike" option of immense popularity in the nineteenth century. This narrator can be everywhere in his creation at once, so he always knows what everyone is thinking and doing. The Victorian versions often had loads of personality, but it existed outside the story; if they used "I," it was in the context of talking directly to the reader.

- **Third person limited.** Like the omniscient narrator, this one is an outsider to the action, usually unidentified as anything other than a voice. This one, however, only identifies with one character, going where she goes and seeing what she sees, as well as recording her thoughts. It provides a fairly one-sided view of the action, although this is not the impediment it might seem.

- **Third person objective.** This one sees everything from the outside, thereby offering only external hints at the characters' interior lives. Since this is pretty much the state we find ourselves in regarding everyone we know, it's not all that inviting. I don't need a book to be clueless about other people, thanks.

- ✍ **Stream of consciousness.** Not exactly a narrator at all, more an extractor that goes into characters' heads to pull out their own narration of their existence. More anon, in a separate chapter.
- ✍ **Second person.** A true rare bird. You can count the novels you'll encounter in second-person in a normal reading life on one hand, not use the thumb, and still have digits left free.
- ✍ **First person central.** The main character makes his own excuses. Think of Huck Finn or David Copperfield. Proba-bly more popular in novels of growing up than in any other subgenre, with the possible exception of hard-boiled detec-tive novels.
- ✍ **First person secondary.** Oh, like you need me to explain this one to you. The sidekick, the second banana, the mi-nor player, the guy standing right next to the hero when he took the bullet—you get the idea. The levels of subtlety and subterfuge are almost limitless here, which explains its perennial popularity with novelists.

That's the lot. Doesn't seem like such a big deal, does it? Of course, there are endless combinatory possibilities when the novelist starts dragging in reports, depositions, letters, statements from the involved, and birthday cards from Aunt Maude, but they still fall under one or another of these few headings.

On the other hand, maybe the scarcity of options is precisely why the choice is a big deal: in such a limited universe, how can I make *my* novel stand out? Will my Bildungsroman (a German jaw-breaker applied to those novels about growing up from childhood to adulthood) look like every other Bildungsroman if I use a first-person central narration? On the other hand, will it be recognizable as what it is if I don't tell the story that way? After all, every novel ever written helps to define the universe of the Novel, and sometimes definition involves limitation. It's hard to write a novel about a fraud who comes to a bad end for a phony dream in the first-person secondary without seeming to ape *The Great Gatsby*.

I don't, however, think that's the main issue. Certainly novelists are aware of how their new creation may fit into that universe, but concern over narrative viewpoint is more basic than that. It will determine everything, from how well we know the main character to how much we can trust what we're told to how long the book winds up being.

Everything?

Just about. Consider this: what are the longest novels you've ever read? *Vanity Fair. Middlemarch. Bleak House. Tom Jones. The Bonfire of the Vanities.* What element do those eight-hundred-page monstrosities have in common, aside from chest-crushing weight? Omniscience. Third-person omniscient narration is uniquely well suited to novels of great length. Indeed, it almost invariably causes them. Why? Nowhere to hide. If the novelist plays fair, and if he sets up a universe in which his narrator can know everything, then that figure must show what he knows. He can't have someone moving surreptitiously in the shadows in another part of town and pretend not to know who is moving, what they're doing, and why they're doing it. He's omniscient, for crying out loud. All-knowing. Can't very well say, simply because it serves his purpose, oh, I don't know this one thing. That's not playing the game. That's also why you don't see a lot of omniscience in mysteries. They require secrets. And narrators who can see into everyone's mind can't pretend there are secrets.

So what does work for a mystery? Third person limited or objective shows up a good bit. Either we only know the detective's thoughts or we know no one's. First person is good. British mystery novels incline more toward first person secondary, American toward first person central. Why? Because of the stories being told. British mysteries tend to be ratiocinative (from the Latin, meaning having to do with working things out by means of reason). They rely on the brilliance of the detective. If he tells the story, we'll see where his brilliance is taking us and lose all surprise. So instead, the story is told by someone who is, well, slightly dim. Sherlock Holmes has his Dr. Watson, Hercule Poirot his Captain Hastings (sometimes) or another, delegated-just-for-this-once civilian. These narrators aren't stupid, or no more so than ourselves, and we're not stupid. But they're only ordinarily intelligent, whereas Holmes or Poirot are brilliant in a way that's not entirely human. American mysteries, on the other hand, tend toward the hard-boiled (from the American, meaning I'm tougher than you and will beat or shoot my way to the truth). The detectives aren't particularly brilliant, but they are tough, tenacious, cocky, and often good company. So they tell their own stories, from Raymond Chandler's Philip Marlowe to Mickey Spillane's Mike Hammer to Sue Grafton's Kinsey Millhone. For people in a tight-lipped line of work, they prove to be surprisingly loquacious, joking and threatening their way through life. The choice of first-person narration helps establish their personality, particularly when, as in the case of Linda Barnes's Carlotta Carlyle or Millhone, they ironically undercut their position with self-effacing wisecracks. The other really useful thing this viewpoint accomplishes in these novels is to let the main character make mistakes. One of the hallmarks of the American hard-boiled detective story is that periodically the baddies get the upper hand and the hero gets captured, misled, beaten up, shot, or otherwise snookered. When this happens in a third-person narration, as when Sam Spade gets drugged in *The Maltese Falcon*, it seems like he's letting down the side. After all, we spend most of the novel watching him be nearly infallible, and then *this* happens. Incredible. On the flip side, Kinsey Millhone splits her time between telling us how professional she is and noting her shortcomings, so we're not surprised when she gets herself in a pickle.

Okay, then, so what can first-person narration do and what else is it good for? It creates the illusion of immediacy. And we might as well stop here for a digression on illusion and reality. None of this is real, right? There is no boy Tom Sawyer, no Becky Thatcher he's sweet on, no pal named Huck. They're all built up out of words to trick the mind into believing, if just for a little while, that they exist. The mind, for its part, has to play along, not only believing (or at least not disbelieving) but actively taking the elements and adding to them in ways that render a more complete portrait than the one that actually exists on the page. But also, and this is key, no narrator. That creature who talks to us for all those pages is no more *real* than the rest of the fiction. In fact, it's a general truth; there is something like the Law of Look Who's Talking: The narrator of a fictional work is an imaginative and linguistic construct, every bit as much as the characters or events. The "omniscience" of omniscient narration is not that of God but of a godlike fictional construct, and the "person" of first- or third-person narration is not the author but a made-up entity into which the author sends a voice. (I have made a career of studying ephemera and shadows and things not really there; I could just as well be an economist.) So when we talk about what effects a certain technique produces, we're really speaking of creating certain sorts of illusion. There, I'm glad I got that off my chest.

NOW THEN, THE PROBLEM with first-person narration: here are the disadvantages that make it thorny.

1. The narrator can't know what other people think.
2. The narrator can't go where other people go when he's not around.
3. He's frequently mistaken about other people.
4. He's frequently mistaken about himself.
5. He can never get more than a partial grasp on objective truth.
6. He may be hiding something.

Given those limitations, why would a writer choose to employ such a shaky point of view? Consider the advantages.

1. The narrator can't know what other people think.
2. The narrator can't go where other people go when he's not around.
3. He's frequently mistaken about other people.
4. He's frequently mistaken about himself.
5. He can never get more than a partial grasp on objective truth.
6. He may be hiding something.

So what are the effects and functions of the first person? First, immediacy. If you want readers to feel close to a character, let her speak for herself. It is good for those growing-up stories because they need us to identify with Pip or David or Huck. That sort of identification is also useful in the picaresque, the narrative version of *The Rake's Progress*. The pícaro (the term comes from Spanish) is a rogue or rake who makes his way through the world adventure by adventure, never scrupling too much about common ideas of right and wrong or even about the law, except to keep it off his neck. The scoundrel can be rendered more sympathetic by letting him—or someone very close to him—tell his story, as in the case of Saul Bellow's *The Adventures of Augie March* (1953) or Jack Kerouac's *On the Road* (1957). Okay, pretty much any Kerouac. We like Augie because he's charming and witty and direct, Sal Paradise because he's brooding and wistful and joyous by turns, and both of them because they talk to us.

You can push that identification-equals-sympathy equation one more step and use first-person narration to write about really awful creatures. There are a significant number of novels in which the main character is a monster, usually figuratively but once in a while literally, but in any case some being who in any other sort of book would be the villain. Think about it: would you be friends with Alex, from *A Clockwork Orange* (1962)? Would you even want to *know* him? The thing that makes most people lose sleep at night is the thought that there might be an Alex in their county—amoral, murderous, delighting in the aesthetics of violence, waiting for opportunity. But the thing is, in print, in his own voice, Alex is a charmer. Intelligent. Handy with a phrase. Witty. Clever. Sympathetic. Now how do you get from "amoral" and "murderous" to "sympathetic"? Words. Alex—or rather, his creator, Anthony Burgess—spins a web of words to ensnare us in the more attractive elements of his personality while shielding us from a too-direct view of his more heinous actions. And "spinning a web of words" is exactly how the eponymous antihero of John Gardner's *Grendel* describes his self-conscious movement through the world. Gardner's task is even tougher than Burgess's: the teenage thug is a fairly recent development, but Grendel has been the byword for evil for more than a millennium. Nor does the novelist want to rehabilitate him or make him cute and cuddly. He's still a monster, still eats people, still revels in mayhem and blood. Not exactly best-buddy material. What Gardner wants to do is something trickier and more challenging, to keep him a monster and nevertheless make him sympathetic. So he makes him a good deal like us (except for the people-eating part): witty, observant, interested in language and what it can do for good or ill, interested in and critical of the shortcomings of the human society around him, alienated, aggrieved, and a little bit sorry for himself. As a result, readers are able to see the necessity of Beowulf's ultimate triumph while regretting the loss of Grendel's remarkable voice. And if you can do that for a twelve-hundred-year-old monster, you've really done something.

Now, the fact that there are only six options, and more like four for all intents and purposes, doesn't really limit the way stories are told very much. Novelists can mix and match, adjust, vary, and just plain abuse the options they're presented with. In his masterful *Snow*, Orhan Pamuk employs a kaleidoscopic point of view that seems for much of the novel to be nearly omniscient, then limited, and finally first person as a narrator from outside the story proper, called Orhan just to confuse the issue, reveals that he has been assembling this tale from documents left by the main character, a poet named Ka, as well as statements made about the now-deceased writer by friends and acquaintances. Both the apparent omniscience and objectivity are illusory; as a friend, Orhan is moved by feelings of loyalty and confusion in recounting the events of Ka's final trip home to Turkey. And here's the problem with categories: they're often fairly crude devices. *Snow* is a remarkably subtle narrative performance. Is it "first-person secondary"? Well, yes, sort of. That is, the narrator turns out to be a named character who interacts with others in the story. Yet he's also a chameleon who imitates the devices of various third-person points of view. The definition doesn't really account for the changes a writer of Pamuk's ability can bring.

And if that's a problematic first-person novel, try John Fowles's *The French Lieutenant's Woman* (1969), in which the third-person narrator actually appears. Twice. The book takes the form of a Victorian novel, exploiting its conventions of omniscience (when it suits the narrative purpose) and reader-narrator intimacy. Two times, however, a person resembling Fowles himself (in different guises) turns up, once in a railway carriage where he observes the main character and once toward the end, when he sets his watch back fifteen minutes, thereby allowing for the book's famous two endings. There is only one person who can reset time in a novel, and he's not a character inside the story. Moreover, Fowles frequently uses "I" to refer to the narrator, although he never interacts with anyone or anything in the story. Even his ride on the train and walk outside the residence of Dante Gabriel Rossetti have a kind of stage artifice about them, suggesting he is metaphorically, rather than literally, present. So then, first person? Third? Third, pretty clearly, since the narrator isn't really a character in the novel, but like *Snow*, Fowles's book is far more subtle and sinuous in its use of point of view than any mere definition can ever hope to be.

So what? Why should we care about narrative POV? Does it really matter if it's first or third—or that the definitions don't always get the job done?

Well, yes and no. First, the no. You can get through most novels satisfactorily without paying much attention to who's doing the telling. You'll get the general drift of almost every novel, and everything there is to get with a lot of them. But also, yes. Who narrates matters in terms of trust. In general, third-person narration can be relied upon to be accurate. Narratives with "I"—as we shall see shortly—not so much. Real people lie. Misremember. Get confused. In one of history's most famous writers' tiffs, Mary McCarthy said of her former friend Lillian Hellman that "every word she says is a lie, and that includes 'and' and 'the.'" If persons in the real world have a tenuous connection to veracity, why should we expect those in made-up stories to be more truthful?

But differences can matter in other ways, too. What's our relationship to the story told? How far removed are we from it? How immersed in it? How are we being manipulated to see events one way or another? These things are often dictated by the choice of narrator. So we just might want to notice who that elusive creature is.

4

Never Trust a Narrator with a Speaking Part

QUESTION: HOW CAN YOU tell if a lawyer is lying?

Don't trample each other racing to answer.

We encounter lies in many forms: half-truths, outright false-hoods, self-deception, word parsing, political spin, press conferences, and yes, trial summations. The novel, by definition, is a lie, and many novelists follow Twain's lead in embracing the role of liar-by-trade. But knowing the novel is untrue isn't all that helpful; we know that going in. Within the form there are layers of veracity, things that are "true" or not within the demonstrably false world of the made-up story. How's that headache now?

Here's one sentence you know is a lie: this story isn't about me. Of course it is; otherwise, there'd be no need for the disclaimer. The person who says it is not to be trusted. You know what he is, right? Someone telling a story. About someone else. Hardly any connection at all. Nick Carraway says it, but goes further: "I don't think my psychology matters at all." Now there's a guy running from responsibility as fast as he can go. Fortunately, by the time he makes this statement (and it's still very early), we already know he's lying. We knew earlier. Much, much earlier. When? The first word of the novel. And what word can possibly tell you all by itself that the narrator is unreliable? A very short, tall, skinny word. Here's the Law of Narrative Unreliability: Stop believing the narrator when you see the word "I." Yes, even if it is the first word in the novel. He's toast. Given the game away.

Wait a minute. Do I mean he's a bad person, a conscious spreader of falsehood and deceit? Quite possibly. Not necessarily, though. He may simply be deluded. Naïve. Mistaken. Uninformed. Feeling guilty. Not in complete possession of the facts. Or he may be lying through his teeth. In any case, he—or she—is not to be trusted.

Why? Because, in the words of John Lennon, "Everybody's got something to hide except me and my monkey." And just how are first-person narrators unreliable? Let us count the ways.

Oftentimes character-narrators simply don't know what's going on or can't fully process what they see. That would be the case with child narrators. The great ones, Huck Finn, Pip, David Copperfield, even Holden Caulfield, tell us more than they understand precisely because they *don't* understand. When Huck says the Shepherdsons and the Grangerfords are fine, upstanding people upholding a noble code, it's because that's what they tell themselves, and him. But they aren't figures in some noble, medieval, dynastic struggle. They're cheap backwoods murderers. We can see that, but Huck can't, which is Twain's point, really. Huck is Twain's Candide, the wide-eyed innocent moving through the world that threatens to sully him and drag him down to its level. But we don't want him destroyed that way. If he were older, sixteen or seventeen, he would understand more of what he sees and be made cynical by that understanding. Pretty soon, he'd be saying, "And then I encountered the next mountebank, charlatan, brute, thief, or crook in a long series." Then he would be forced to offer criticism or judgments of their conduct. Now seriously, where's the fun in that? Such a Huck would be a drag. Part of the pleasure readers can take is that *we see* that these creatures are mountebanks, charlatans, all-around villains, but he does not. He's just innocent enough, standing on the threshold of adolescence, to miss the full measure of their viciousness. So we get to pass judgment and render the moral verdicts, a job we perform with relish. But most important, Huck has to be innocent for the novel to work. When he decides to tear up the note revealing the runaway slave Jim's whereabouts, it has to hurt him, and it does.

> *I studied a minute, sort of holding my breath, and then says to myself:*
>
> *"All right, then, I'll go to hell"—and tore it up.*
>
> *It was awful thoughts, and awful words, but they was said. And I let them stay said; and never thought no more about re-forming.*

It's the most moral moment in American literature. No other even comes close. But the thing is, dramatically, Huck can't understand that. The scene only works if he really believes he's going to hell, that he's rejecting not merely the law, but the good and upright people he knows and, by extension, the God they've foisted on him, a God who would support the enslavement of one person by another. For that to be meaningful, he can't see through them. If he thinks, even a little, that their sea of righteousness is actually the putrid ethical swamp that it is, then the entire moral force of his decision is lost.

And, of course, if we can't see that his "damnation" is really his salvation, then woe to us. Happily, we can and he can't, so everything is cool.

Huck is quite a representative figure of the underage narrator. More often than not, the child narrator's task is to provide the Martian perspective. Craig Raine has a poem called "A Martian Sends a Postcard Home" (1979), in which the extraterrestrial visitor attempts to describe such everyday "novelties" as telephones, automobiles, books, and bathrooms—all things he can't understand because he has no frame of reference for them. There's no room for Martians, of course, in most novels, so that otherworldly view must be provided by someone closer to home yet still unfamiliar with common aspects. Have you ever noticed, by the way, that children look slightly, well, alien? The child narrator observes but can't always comprehend and also allows a sort of clear-eyed honesty not always available to the novelist with other narrators.

Even when the narrator has left childhood behind, looking back through his younger eyes affords the novelist this same *defamiliarization* of the ordinary, adult world. Charles Dickens uses Pip in *Great Expectations* (1861), for instance, to critique the notion of gentility as broadly understood in Victorian England. The Russian critic Viktor Schlovsky gives us the term "defamiliarization," by which he means "making strange," or turning the familiar and ordinary into something strange and wondrous. This magic, he says, is what literature does for us, thereby making us reexamine what we thought we knew. The child Pip can aspire, as he is instructed to do, to values regarding wealth, idleness, smugness, and class consciousness that readers recognize as not merely worthless, but actively evil. Pip cruelly turns his back on his greatest supporter, his brother-in-law Joe Gargery, because Joe's peasant ways embarrass the upstart young "gentleman." He accepts Miss Havisham's imperatives because he can't see that her values are as decayed as her wedding feast. And he desires the imperious, cruel Estella, whose abuse seems to prove superiority. Naturally, the child can articulate none of this; in fact, his inability to register all that is wrong in his world provides much of the tension in the narrative and much of the satisfaction readers ultimately derive. It's not a child doing the talking, exactly, but a slightly older edition of him. Still, the narrative strategy is for the slightly older Pip not to reveal what he knows, so we're limited by his immature self's ability to process the world.

Okay, so that's what a juvenile narrator can do for you. But that won't explain all the grown-ups. What's their story?

Got a lifetime? The reasons for employing first-person narrators are nearly as numerous as the novels that employ them, but they tend to fall into one of a handful of categories. Here they are.

- **Stories about characters who just don't get it.** There are aspects of every life that remain mysterious to the central figure. We all have blind spots, incomplete understanding, faulty self-knowledge. But the main characters in the clue-less novel are real corkers.
- **Stories about people who are hiding something.** Again, not atypical. Everybody's got secrets.
- **Stories about several people with competing versions of the same events.**
- **Stories about people who are picking up the pieces.** This category is more fun if seen from the inside.
- **Stories about the multiplicity of reality or where reality is up for grabs.**
- **Stories about really, really, really bad people and the odd monster.** This category is so rich that it warrants its

own chapter, but it's worth mentioning in the context of this chapter, just to show the continuum of possibilities.

What's the common thread of all these narrative types? In each one, the narrator-character tells the story while laboring under a significant handicap: he or she is estranged in some way or other from the truth. All right, if you're going to get picky, truth is always up for grabs, but in these novels truth is playing hide-and-seek with the narrator, who is generally losing.

Examples? Let's say your wife has died. Let's say your best friend has died, too. One of them is the person you admired most in the entire world. And just for chuckles, let's say they had been having an affair for eleven years, carried on not merely under your very nose but with your express, if blithely unaware, assistance. And for those eleven years you had not a whiff of impropriety. They knew, of course. So did the other wronged spouse. Only you operated in the dark. Because, for various reasons, they conspired to keep you ignorant and, when they might have told, you dissuaded them. Clever fellow. Now you know there's only one person on Earth who can tell that story and do it justice, and it's not the other surviving spouse. That's what Ford Madox Ford decided when he penned his masterpiece, *The Good Soldier* (1915).

Or maybe you had given your life in service to an unworthy master, sacrificing happiness, love, personal fulfillment, only to find the cause of that sacrifice vilified, and quite rightly. Perhaps you can't even bear to admit how much you gave up, can't openly acknowledge that you let the love of your life slip away or even that she was the love of your life. You were so caught up in your role as the perfect butler that you forgot to have feelings, to live, to be human. Then, when everything you might have had was behind you, your master turned out to be a Nazi sympathizer, and even then you couldn't denounce him, couldn't detach from him, because he was all the identity you had. Well, you'd just have to tell your own pathetic story, wouldn't you? Kazuo Ishiguro thought so when he wrote *The Remains of the Day* (1989). In both of these novels, the drama is in the self-discovery; to view that process from the outside would drain from the story everything that makes them worth reading. And they are very much worth reading.

Or maybe the first-person narrator knows the truth full well. Maybe he (or, again, she, since we don't want anyone to be left out of the dishonesty sweepstakes) would really rather we didn't know the truth. Agatha Christie often employs Captain Hastings or some other slightly dim character as a narrator whose failure to perceive detail, or ability to seize upon the wrong detail, can mislead readers and make Hercule Poirot the more brilliant. And in one very celebrated novel whose title I omit for obvious reasons, the narrator just happens to omit the small fact that he is, when the truth is revealed, the murderer. First-person narration, by and large, is the perfect vehicle for offering something less than the whole truth and nothing but the truth.

Sometimes, of course, the truth is not only elusive, but painful. Darley, the principal narrator of Lawrence Durrell's *Alexandria Quartet*, has a lot to sort through. He describes himself as a shattered man. Everything he thought he had going has managed to slip away. His lover, Melissa, to whom he was not very nice, has died of a combination of consumption and emotional neglect (how often they go together in literature). His illicit lover, the Justine who gives her name to the first novel of the series, has vanished, leaving more mysteries than solutions. Worst of all, the Alexandria he presumed to know, a seedy warren of decadence and privilege, has vanished with her. In its place is something alien and hostile, so he retreats to an island with a small child who is Melissa's but not his, hoping to beat this unformed mass of event and emotion into some shape that will be aesthetically, if not ethically, manageable. Through three of the four novels (he does not feature in the third, *Mountolive*, the only one of the four told in the third person), he tells what he knew, finds out much that he did not know, and learns that much of what he knew was illusory. So then, he's looking back on the train wreck of his life, discovering his mistakes, finding out how deluded he has been, and trying to move toward a more solid moral basis for his existence. How could Durrell possibly have anyone but Darley tell that story? The answer, of course, is that he couldn't. Only Darley can tell the story, at least in its initial incarnation, since its success depends on his particular combination of vanity, lust, and incomprehension.

You know those dressing-room mirrors, not much in evidence in today's department stores, where three panels stand at angles to one another so the customer can get the full effect of the new ensemble? Multiply those panels be a factor of, oh, half a dozen, and you have the fiction of Louise Erdrich, who has made a substantial career writing about life on and around an Ojibwa reservation in North Dakota. From her first novel, *Love Medicine*, she has exploited the collision of competing personalities and memories. Her novels are typically composed of more or less independent short stories that link into larger narratives, and those short stories allow her to vary the narrative viewpoint within a single novel. In that first novel, for instance, we have third-person narration that is sympathetic to June Morrisey Kashpaw, Albertine Johnson, Gordie Kashpaw, Bev Lamartine, and Henry Lamartine Jr., as well as first-person narrations by Albertine, Nector Kashpaw, Marie Kashpaw, Lulu Lamartine, Lyman Lamartine, and Lipsha Morrisey. Needless to say, these various tellings rarely agree on motivations, perceptions, or even the main facts of their tangled lives. Jealousy, resentment, self-deception, misinformation, superstition, and inspired insight, sometimes with supernatural intervention, predominate. This is a novel about identity on so many levels, well beyond the chief question of Lipsha's parentage, that it's hardly surprising to find so many aspects of identity involved in the narrative strategy itself. All of the character-narrators struggle with questions of who they are both personally and within the larger tribal structure, what their purpose is, what they need and what they merely want. Of course the stories they tell are biased, selfish, short-sighted, envious, generous, needy, wise, confused, outrageous, and amazing.

This may sound strange, but first-person narrative is just the ticket for dealing with the possibly insane. Sometimes the character doing the talking doesn't know what's really going on, and moreover doesn't know that he doesn't know. Sometimes you just can't tell about reality. That's the case in Nabokov's *Pale Fire*, in which we're never entirely sure what reality is, except that it's not what the narrator, Charles Kinbote, claims it to be. The only "facts" of which we can be reasonably certain in the novel are the 999-line poem that shares its title with the book and the murder of its author, John Shade. Kinbote, the self-anointed editor and commentator of the poem, provides the bulk of the novel's narrative in the form of a foreword, a commentary, and an index. All well and good, except that the critical "apparatus" has nothing to do with either the poem or its creator. Kinbote either is or believes himself to be the deposed king—Charles Xavier Vseslav, Charles II, or Charles the Beloved—of a small northern European country, Zembla, who is being hunted down by the assassin Gradus. And even though Shade's poem contains no mention of Zembla, Kinbote, Charles the Beloved, or Gradus, nearly all of Kinbote's commentaries and glosses invent connections to his story. He believes, for instance, that Shade's killer, Jack Grey, is Gradus and shot Shade while intending to assassinate Kinbote. This despite the fact that Grey is an escapee from an asylum for the criminally insane, sentenced there by Judge Goldsmith, whose house Kinbote rents and who physically resembles the victim. Small details such as these cannot impede a mind such as Kinbote's, however, and he takes it all in his demented stride. Confused yet? Well you might be. The novel never resolves its mysteries, so that Kinbote may be correct, as unlikely as that seems; insane and inventing the entire tale; an alter ego of a difficult Russian colleague of Shade's, Professor V. Botkin; or a literary device made up by Shade, who has faked his own death and contrived the narrative surrounding his poem as a cover. This last theory was developed by readers and critics over a number of years following the book's publication. The point of the first-person narration in this case is that the free-floating "I" eliminates the possibility of certainty or objectivity. Even if Kinbote is representing things accurately, his insistence on himself as the center of the universe displays a certain derangement; megalomania always makes us nervous.

And sometimes you can tell. Maybe. Eventually. In Flann O'Brien's *The Third Policeman*, a bad man meets a bad fate and doesn't know it. The unnamed narrator, a devotee of a deranged scientist-philosopher named de Selby, has participated in a murder and robbery. When he goes to retrieve the money, at the behest of his accomplice, something goes awry and he finds himself in a surreal parallel universe that looks like Ireland but seems to have a logic and natural laws of its own. The policemen he encounters (and he encounters almost no one but policemen) promulgate crackpot theories of existence, physics, and bicycles, and they are almost never of any help with his particular problem. Indeed, he seems to be talking at cross-purposes with the inhabitants of this familiar-yet-strange world. Only when, near the end of the novel, he visits his old accomplice, John Divney, now well set up in life, does the truth become clear. Divney, shouting that the narrator must be dead because the black box contained not the loot but a bomb, drops dead of a heart attack and then joins the narrator on his walk through what, despite the absence of brimstone, is clearly hell. Since the narrator has no memory of what has gone before, however, he is clearly doomed to repeat the experience endlessly. For reasons logical and theological, of course, the narrator does not realize where he is. He no longer even knows his name, so what are the chances he can make sense of his new home?

Okay, then: if you want to deal with the slippery business of reality, truth, perception, and delusion, let a character tell your story. That would seem to describe every novel in the world, wouldn't it? But I think not. They are enough, however, to give you the general idea about character-narrators and the mischief they can create. And what do all these have in common? In every case, the innate drama of the situation would be compromised by an objective view.

Oh, right, the lawyer. Well, were his lips moving?

5

A Still, Small Voice
(or a Great, Galumphing One)

NARRATORS ARE LIKE CATS. They may talk about other people, but the world is mostly about them. Even the omniscient sort tend to be smugly self-involved, for all their appearance as dispassionate observers. Point of view is about which cat is telling the story and whether he's looking at the world from on top of the rock or under it. Voice is about what sort of cat he is. It's about word choice and word order, about dropped endings and distance from Her Majesty's English.

It's what makes novels worth reading. Or sometimes not.

A few observations need to be made, even if they may seem self-evident. First, you can have more than one voice in the narration of the novel. Figured that one out for yourself already, did you? Then why is it so rarely on display in story anthologies and primers on studying fiction? They tend to speak of "point of view" as if there were only one on display in any given work. We know this to be false, that a novel can have many narrators, that something like Emily Brontë's *Wuthering Heights*, ostensibly told by Mr. Lockwood, who has arrived on the scene after the events detailed in the novel, is of necessity handed off to Nelly Dean, the only remaining witness to the turbulent times that are the basis for the novel, who can then cite others' testimony to her. This is hardly a new phenomenon. Brontë has been gone for some little time. It is in the way of tale telling that additional assistance is sometimes required, so from the earliest days of novels, multiple narrators appear, often in quotation marks, as they tell their story to the main narrator.

You see the problem, at least the potential problem? Confusion. Which leads to self-evident point number two: if you're going to employ multiple voices in a novel, you simply must keep them sorted out. Seems like a no-brainer, doesn't it? But try it sometime and you'll find that it's not that easy to sound like anyone but yourself. And the more voices, the more differentiation required.

One of the more spectacular instances of voice differentiation is Barbara Kingsolver's *Poisonwood Bible*, in which there are five voices that matter, the four Price sisters—Rachel, Leah, Adah, and Ruth May—who offer the principal narration of events, and their mother, Orleanna, whose troubled, mournful recollections frame the sections of the novel that are then told by the daughters.

> *Ripe fruits, acrid sweat, urine, flowers, dark spices, and other things I've never seen—I can't say what goes into the composition or why it rises up to confront me as I round some corner hastily, unsuspecting. It has found me here on this island, in our little town, in a back alley where sleek boys smoke in a stairwell amidst the day's uncollected refuse.*

We can sense, even in this short passage, that Orleanna's description is also a commentary on something else, something that did not stay put in the past, something dangerous, alien, hostile, something that hunts—and haunts—her still. The signs are everywhere: "acrid," "urine," "dark," "things I've never seen," "a back alley," "uncollected refuse." She herself is "unsuspecting" as she moves "hastily" in her "little town," where this huge thing tracks her down, sneaks up on her unaware. Suppose those words tell us anything?

Your honor, it goes to the state of mind of the witness.

Exactly. What we may want to make of that state of mind, what all those words of peril signify, readers will want to decide for themselves, but their presence throughout her narration, in number, is undeniable.

The girls all come from the same place, Georgia in 1959, before arriving in the Congo on their parents' mad evangelical mission, yet they are distinct because of differences in age and outlook. Even the twins speak quite differently despite being fairly well matched in terms of raw intelligence, largely due to Adah's physical damage. The hemiplegia she suffered at birth has left her with a damaged leg and a disinclination to speak. In turn, her disability provides her with distance from her obsessed father, unlike Leah, whose identification with him is nearly all-consuming. It has also resulted in some interesting linguistic traits; she is a brilliant thinker with a knack for palindromes and other inversions at both the letter and word level.

Wonk ton o dew.

The things we do not know, independently and in unison as a family, would fill two separate baskets, each with a large hole in the bottom.

The initial inversion of "we do not know" is pure Adah: surprising, almost like language but just off, with no allegiance to the orthography of the original. She breaks words as she will, inserts or removes punctuation to suit her purpose, as in her take on William Carlos Williams's "The Red Wheelbarrow": "Chickens white beside standing water rain, with glazed wheelbarrow. Red on! Depends much. So?" She omits the articles "a" and "the" without apology and inserts "standing," not in the original. Her version has a kind of weird logic to it that does not rely on its source material. In her village, for instance, there is red on everything from the soil and the ubiquitous dust, as nearly all the girls comment at one time or another. Her narration differs from Leah's well-marshaled, conventional prose not by being disorderly but by being intentionally *dis*ordered. For Adah, the world is without plan or Planner, the rule-obsessed God of her father, and her response is to offer up language in kind. Yet the seeming chaos of her narration is, ironically, a product of a highly ordered and careful intelligence. The seeming leaps in logic or connection manifest great method in their arranging.

Rachel, at fifteen, is a compendium of teenage slang and malapropisms.

> *I screamed and kicked the furniture until one whole leg came off the table and threw a hissy fit they could probably hear all the way to Egypt. Listen, what else can a girl do but try? Stay here? When everybody else gets to go home and do the bunny hop and drink Cokes? It's a sheer tapestry of justice.*

There is, of course, a good deal of comedy in Rachel's narrations, since she's easily the shallowest of the girls and the most likely to suffer linguistic misadventures of the "tapestry of justice" sort. Yet she is more than the sum of her parts, and here, too, her voice is a reminder. The seemingly generic teenage idiom she employs reminds us of just what has been taken from her when she is ripped away from the high school experience she had expected, like so many others of her generation, to be her birthright. From her, we are reminded of the cruelty and heartlessness of her father's religious mania, which admits of no personal aspirations or interests except his own.

Ruth May, at five, only understands the things she can touch or can compare to what she already knows. She calls spearmint gum "Experiment gum" and is endearing in her lack of vocabulary.

When I am grown my mother will still have my shoes. She aims to turn them into brown shiny metal and keep them on a table in Georgia with my baby picture. She did it for all the others, even Adah and her one foot's no-count; it curls up on one side and makes the shoe wear out funny. Even that bad sideways-worn-out shoe Mama saved, so she'll save mine.

The limitations of a child's intelligence allow a certain innocent charm to slip into Ruth May's voice: lacking the word "bronze," she manages, as best she can, "brown shiny metal" for the baby shoes her mother has bronzed. Yet she is more than a stereotype of the small child, and that shows through, too. She has a kind of direct-ness and bossiness that her sisters all acknowledge. It is Ruth May who breaks the ice with the native children and organizes games and other forms of play, and it is sometimes she who speaks the truths that make the others uncomfortable, as when she remarks quite ca-sually on their father's violence. These qualities of being forthright and determined come through in her narrative not only with events but with her sometimes brutal honesty. She becomes the spy, as it were, because her age renders her invisible. Comparing herself to the deadly green mamba that can slither along tree branches and remain unseen, she declares that she can go unnoticed and therefore remain out of sight when her parents are having discussions that the other girls would be forbidden to hear.

These five voices, six actually, since a distinctly new one shows up at the end of the novel, share experiences and traits yet remain highly differentiated as speakers grow and mature. Kingsolver reminds us even without saying so outright that we experience life subjectively, that people who live through the same events under the same roof will still have individual responses and recollections, will still be their own persons with their own outlooks. The interplay of the storytelling voices is fascinating in this novel, which no one character could possibly narrate on her own. Even collectively things are left unsaid; not every perspective can be covered. One perspective that is, significantly, not covered is the divine one, and for good reason. The godlike, omniscient narrator would know too much, would reduce sympathy for the individual suffering of the five females in the Price household, and would violate the scale of the novel—for, even with all the vastness of the place and the overwhelming scale of events, this is a profoundly human, private story. Tragedies always are.

The voices we tend to notice are those attached to characters, often the big, boisterous sorts like Bellow's Augie March or Henderson. We remember Augie's brassiness, the enthusiasm and sadness of Kerouac's Sal Paradise, the tight-lipped control and irony of Hemingway's Jake Barnes. Every novel, however, no matter what the point of view, has a voice—at least one. Omniscience may be the godlike perspective, but that doesn't mean its voice is that of God. Here's one such example.

Women, to their glory be it spoken, are more generally capable of the violent and disinterested passion of love, which seeks only the good of its object, than men. Mrs. Waters, therefore, was no sooner apprised of the danger to which her lover was exposed, than she lost every consideration besides that of his safety; and this being a matter equally agreeable to the gentleman, it became the immediate subject of debate between them.

All right, class, discuss. So what sort of person is behind this voice? Slightly old-fashioned (or just old, maybe), given phrases like "being a matter equally agreeable to the gentleman." Who writes that now? Someone sounding as if they're not from now, right? Well, what else? He seems pretty well amused. The line about "to their glory be it spoken" seems first of all like something a man would say, so I would posit a male identity, and it seems secondly mildly ironic and jocular. So, too, does the reversal in the last line, where, since the situation was agreeable to both, "it became the immediate subject of debate between them." Now, that's just funny. It says, in essence, I'm a man of the world and have seen a few things, and this is one of those sillinesses men and women get up to now and again. If it's folly, it's mild, he seems to suggest, and we can forgive it, being men (and women) of the world.

This voice would be just the right sort to a funny and slightly outrageous tale of minor misconduct, something like *Tom Jones*. Which it is. Henry Fielding chooses this as the voice for telling his masterpiece. It has the advantage of being much like himself, a man who was witty and often cutting in his remarks but with an eye to the public good. Besides being a novelist, playwright, and satirist, Fielding made a career in law, rising to the rank of chief magistrate of London, from which perch he got to observe a good deal of human folly. The novel's voice captures that view from on high, along with amusement at the foolishness of his fellow mortals. More importantly, however, that voice is the right one for an uproarious tale of improbability and more than a little mischief, and that is what really matters. It's important that we keep separate the two beings involved in this transaction, the author and the narrative presence he creates. The author is the guy who gets up in the morning and puts brown sugar on his oatmeal. The other is a fictional construct. To help with sorting these two out, Wayne C. Booth in *The Rhetoric of Fiction* (1961) offers the notion of the *implied author*, a creature the real author has chosen to stage-manage the proceedings of a work of fiction. We generally speak of Fielding as "saying" this or that, but it would be more accurate to indicate that Fielding's implied author says those things. And what his implied author has to say is a hoot.

A hoot, though, is not the right timbre for every voice. Suppose you want to write a very simple fable, a story with a moral and a fairy-tale atmosphere. Fielding's wordly-wise, lightly amused persona is not your inevitable first choice. Paulo Coelho, in *The Alchemist*, accordingly strives for a much different sound.

> *There, in the sand of the plaza of that small city, the boy read the names of his father and his mother and the name of the seminary he had attended. He read the name of the merchant's daughter, which he hadn't even known, and he read things he had never told anyone.*

This passage is, of course, Alan R. Clarke's translation and not Coelho's Portuguese original. Even so, we can glean from it the essentials of the style. The language is very plain. Both nouns and verbs tend to be simple and unadorned by adjectives, adverbs, or figures of speech. Places and people alike tend not to have proper names or, if they do, to have them employed.

We often encounter this plain style in service of overtly moral teaching in fiction, as in the fables of Aesop or La Fontaine or *The Little Prince* or E. L. Doctorow's *Ragtime* (1975).

> *In 1902 Father built a house at the crest of Broadview Avenue hill in New Rochelle, New York. It was a three-story brown shingle with dormers, bay windows and a screened porch. Striped awnings shaded the windows. The family took possession of this stout manse on a sunny day in June and it seemed for some years thereafter that all their days would be warm and fair. The best part of Father's income was derived from the manufacture of flags and buntings and other accoutrements of patriotism, including fireworks.*

Again, we see the simplicity of the language, although this is not quite as stripped down as Coelho's. The house is as generic as a description could be. No real specifics are offered beyond the color or the "screened porch." How many dormers or bay windows? We don't know. It's a "stout manse," but that doesn't really say much, does it? Doctorow doesn't want us to become lost in surface detail, so he makes it as nonbusy as possible. He is capable of much more elaborate writing and a far richer vocabulary than he utilizes here, so we must consider the strategy that makes him embrace this minimal level of diction. This plain style is appropriate to the fable or parable, since its purpose is to convey story without getting in the way or calling attention to itself. Its simplicity is a ruse, of course, no more automatic or untutored than any other.

Writers are tricky, and never more so than when they appear to be playing no tricks at all. Here, then, is a way of thinking about how writers use voice, the Law of Hearing Voices: The narrative voice in a novel is a device invented by the writer. Always. Everything about a novel is made up, even when based on reality. A main character may look and act like the novelist's brother, but it is not his brother. The narrative voice may sound like the author or like someone she knew. It is, nevertheless, a creation selected to best tell the story. The writers may not even have to think about it. The stories they make up may flow so smoothly from the available voices that little conscious planning is required. Such happy coincidence, however, doesn't change the fact that the voice, like the story, is invention. It only means that invention is pretty close at hand for this writer with this book.

You will notice, for instance, that many writers sound pretty similar from book to book. Henry James in *The Portrait of a Lady* (1881) is not that far removed from the James of *The Wings of the Dove* (1902). D. H. Lawrence's narrative voice varies little from book to book, perhaps only becoming more hectoring in the later novels of the 1920s. On the other hand, even when similarities are strong, writers sometimes display considerable range. *Light in August* (1932) and *Absalom, Absalom!* (1936) are both clearly by William Faulkner, for instance, yet they sound quite distinct from one another. The former book is much more open, much less crabbed than the latter, whose narrative voice falls all over itself in a torrent of verbiage.

The man apparently hunting out situations in order to flaunt and fling the apelike body of his charcoal companion in the faces of all and any who would retaliate: stevedores and deckhands on steamboats or in city honky-tonks who thought he was a white man and believed it only the more strongly when he denied it; the

*white men who, when he said he was a Negro, believed he said it
to save his skin, or worse: from sheer sexual perversion; in either
case the result the same: the man with body and limbs almost as
light and delicate as a girl's giving the first blow, usually unarmed
and heedless of the numbers opposed to him, with that same fury
and implacability and imperviousness to pain and punishment,
neither cursing nor panting, but laughing.*

This is the voice not of the third-person narrator but of Rosa
Coldfield, who becomes the principal narrator of the story. The impersonal narrator is equally voluble, with phrases like "augmenting
and defunctive twilight" and "retroactive overcoming of primary
inertia" arranged in a tumble of clauses and phrases, although he
is less emotional. Rosa, in addition to being unthinkingly racist in
the way of her time and place, as in the "apelike body" description, is living through events from many years earlier as if they just
happened, and their vividness gives her narration a slightly hysteri-
cal tone. The verbs—"flaunt," "fling," "retaliate," "cursing," "panting," "laughing"—are active and sharp, the nouns frequently long
and Latinate—"implacability," "imperviousness"—but also strong
and clear, as in "stevedores," "deckhands," and "honky-tonks." And
the punctuation! What punctuation! There's a reason Hemingway
so rarely resorts to colons and semicolons: Faulkner took them all.
And one other thing you might notice here is sentence structure.
Hand this in to your freshman writing teacher and expect to get it
back marked "fragment—see me." Faulkner writes the world's longest sentence fragments (in fact, this one isn't close to his record),
sentences that eschew a main verb altogether or opt for a participle
("hunting," in this case) where the main verb should be.

It also goes the other way, though. A few writers can sound incredibly different from one book to the next, even within books. Jane Smiley creates a host of voices in *Ten Days in the Hills* (2007), her recreation of Boccaccio's *Decameron*. In addition to the third-person narrator, the novel features ten characters telling a phalanx of stories over ten days, a veritable orgy of narrative to go with the other orgy in the narrative. She's like Boccaccio in that as well. In such a structure, it is absolutely necessary to make every voice distinctive. Her characters, although largely drawn from the same class, differ by age, gender, race, national origin, and region, and their language differs by vocabulary, sentence structure, rhythm, and tone. They each, in other words, have their own sound. Edna O'Brien accomplishes much the same thing in her searing *In the Forest* (2002), a tale following the case of three horrific murders, which could be called, after Wallace Stevens, *Thirteen Ways of Looking at a Murderer*. A central narrative presence periodically hands the story off to various characters, including one of the victims and the killer himself, who come from very different backgrounds and psychological places. From the beginning of her career, in *The Country Girls* (1960), O'Brien has specialized in finding distinctive and appropriate narrators to carry her storylines, and this late novel makes perhaps the finest use of varied voices, because of the communal nature of the tragedy, of any of her works. These two writers go a bit beyond *Wuthering Heights* perhaps, in the number of speakers combining on a narrative, but the impetus is largely the same, to find the best way of telling a story and the best voices to carry it along.

So why should we care about all this?

Depends. Does it matter to you with whom you spend the next sixty or eighty or two hundred thousand words? Sometimes at the bookstore, you'll open a novel, read a page or so, and decide, right then and there, that this narrator is not for you. Too erudite, too low-brow, too smarmy, whatever. You just can't take that voice for five hundred pages. Or you find yourself absolutely mesmerized by a voice in the first paragraph and you have to have that novel. Ever had that happen? I have. Both ways.

But here's a more significant reason: voice is meaning. What a narrator says and how he says it changes the story being told. Can you imagine *Huckleberry Finn* without Huck telling it? Might as well ask if you can imagine the book without him in it. Or *Pride and Prejudice* without that knowing, arch, amused narrative intelligence. Austen could have told the book with a straight face, no smirk, but I don't believe we would still be talking about it. The stories writers tell are important, but just as important are the means they find of telling them. And that's plenty of reason to care.

6

Men (and Women) Made out of Words, or My Pip Ain't Like Your Pip

PICTURE THIS: IT'S 1841 and the new issue of *Master Humphrey's Clock* containing this week's installment of *The Old Curiosity Shop* by Mr. Dickens has appeared. And that sound you hear is weeping. In streets, in parlors and kitchens, in maids' rooms under the eaves and masters' bedrooms, even on the docks of New York where citizens, incapable of waiting until copies hit the booksellers' stands, have turned up to ask sailors the important question: "Is Little Nell dead?" The answer prompts many tears. In one of the most affecting scenes in literature, poor Nell has died, after spending the week since the last installment hovering between this world and the next.

This is the famous story, and it's fine as far as it goes. Child heroine, set upon by villains (Dickens never stints on villainy), devoted grandfather bereft at his loss, tens of thousands of readers distraught at death in one so young. All makes sense, right? Except for one thing.

It never happened. There never was a Little Nell. Never an Old Curiosity Shop. No grandfather, no villains, no death. We know this going in. Every novel comes with a virtual warning at the out-set: "Caution: what follows is made up and only ever happened in the mind of the writer and, should you continue, in your mind as well." Readers know this going in, even if we tend to ignore it en route. So then, why the weeping?

I really hate to bring this up, but there is no Huck. No Bilbo Baggins. No, not even a Scarlett O'Hara. The most *real* character who has ever existed in a novel is merely a linguistic construction, a house made not out of cards but of words. So why do we celebrate when they triumph? Suffer when they suffer? Because words matter. Because those word houses take on a life of their own. Because we, dedicated and inventive and slightly gullible readers, take those words and bring our imagination to bear on them, so that mere words become living beings. There are consequences, naturally. We help to imagine characters. So that's why no one agrees on what characters are like.

By way of explanation of this peculiar phenomenon, we turn not to a novelist but a poet. Samuel Taylor Coleridge, early in the nineteenth century, gave us the very helpful phrase "willing suspension of disbelief" for the trick of the mind that readers and viewers perform to allow imaginative works to, well, work imaginatively. If, at every moment of watching a play or reading a novel, we consciously insist on what we know to be true, namely, that this thing is not true, we'll never reach the end. Instead, we'll be out of the theater at intermission, never returning for act two. We'll put down the "untrue" novel in favor of a history or a farm price report. But we don't do that; rather, we accept fictions as fictions, as things that *might* be true in their world, if not quite in ours.

Does this mean we accept everything in a work of fiction, that we have to tolerate everything that occurs without a murmur of dissent? Of course not. The novel may or may not obey the laws of our universe, but it must certainly obey the laws of its own. If we're reading a novel by, say, Henry James, and a hobbit turns up, we're not buying. The psychological realism of the Jamesian novel simply does not admit of fabulous creatures. Even very short ones. There are undoubtedly readers who feel *Portrait of a Lady* would be improved by the odd hobbit, but his presence would prove too jarring. When a hobbit turns up in a work by J. R. R. Tolkien, on the other hand, we're not surprised in the least. Middle-earth is just where he belongs. Internal consistency, then, is one of the main things an audience demands of a literary work. Whatever rules we start with, we expect to apply throughout.

In general, though, we check our incredulity at the door. There's a social contract between novelist and reader: we agree to accept the novel's premises and to believe in people and events we know not to exist in the real world. We even agree to respond to them as if they were real. Novelists, for their part, agree to live within the rules they establish for this particular narrative. And for the most part, everybody behaves reasonably well. Except the villains. Naturally.

Why does this contract matter? Why does the novel need its readers to comply with authorial wishes? Simply put, because the novelist didn't finish the job. I don't mean that he's deliberately shirked, looked at his watch and said, "Well, that's all the time I have for character development." Rather, he's obeyed the laws of his craft, which dictate that characters be incomplete. Some are more complete than others, of course, but all of them are seriously lacking in some way or other.

You doubt? Take any novel you like. It needn't be a classic, but it can be. Now, start asking yourself what you *really* know about the characters—looks, life experiences, attitudes toward government, the lot. You'll find there's considerably less there than you had thought.

Let's take one you probably read under protest. Tell me everything you know about Jordan Baker. You remember her, right? The cheating golfer and sometime romantic interest of Nick Carraway in *The Great Gatsby*. Here's the first part of the exercise: close your eyes and picture her. No problem. If you've ever read the novel, you have an image of Jordan, who doesn't look much like Lois Chiles, the actress who played her in the 1973 train wreck of an adaptation. Beyond that initial description I gave—sport, dishonesty, attractiveness—what do we know? Not much. She lounges rather determinedly with Daisy, exhibiting a distinctly supine modernity. She's attractive, but Fitzgerald doesn't cause Nick to spend too much time on the details. Her hair is the yellow of autumn leaves, her movements restless and athletic, her poses often struck theatrically with her chin "jauntily" raised. There are a few more specifics, but she's a long way from a whole person physically or psychologically. You can do the same with any of the minor characters: Klipspringer, Meyer Wolfsheim, either Wilson, even Tom Buchanan.

Okay, why?

Because that's all we need. Jordan is part plot device, part stage property, part thematic articulation. She helps things happen, gives the joint a certain look, and, through her personal dishonesty, embodies the more general corruption. Beyond that, we don't care. In fact, beyond that, we don't want to know. The Law of the Conservation of Character states: Thou shalt not burden the punters with needless character development. Meaning what? If fiction writers are any good, they only tell you as much as you absolutely need to know. Minor characters like these require minimal development since they (a) are only on stage briefly and (b) have very specific roles to play.

Aha! Minor players! But what about the major ones? Very well, then: Daisy, Nick, and Gatsby. This all gets back to E. M. Forster's theory of flat and round characters. Minor characters tend to be flat—that is, two-dimensional cardboard cutouts rather than fully developed, complete persons. Major characters, by comparison, are more fully fleshed out, more three-dimensional or "rounded." It's true. Sort of. They are more fully, but not fully, fleshed out.

Why? Because characters aren't built like pickup trucks—chassis, engine, transmission, seats, body, skin, windows. They're sketched, which is why many of them are pretty sketchy. Moreover, they aren't typically described in huge detail or analyzed by the narrator. These are novels, not essays or biographies. Rather, characters are presented, and what is presented of them are actions and statements. What do they do and what do they say? Those are the questions the novelist pursues.

Analysis of those deeds and words falls to another party entirely. That would be us. What kind of analysis? Biological? Chemical? Not likely. Psychological? It's sometimes tried, with mixed results. No, the principal form of analysis we employ with characters is linguistic. We look at the words, because that's all there is. Look around you at the people you meet. Flesh and blood, every single one of them. Something a character can never be. The best, most vivid, most fully realized character in all of literature is exactly the same as one who is only a name and walks through a novel a single time in a single sentence: each is a verbal construct. Nothing more. And nothing less. Whatever you think you know about Pip or Frodo or Dumbledore or Emma (Bovary or Woodhouse), you can't touch them or smell them or see them, except as words on a page. Language, pure and simple.

Now you've gone and spoiled the illusion.

Not me, Bub. Writers have been doing that for years. Besides, you knew it already. You've read them but never met them, right? Can you picture them? Literally, now. Assuming you had the ability (a big assumption, if you've ever seen me draw), could you create a picture of your favorite character? Didn't think so. It's okay, not your fault; you lack data. Here's a word picture of a main character.

He was an inch, perhaps two, under six feet, powerfully built, and he advanced straight at you with a slight stoop of the shoulders, head forward, and a fixed from-under stare which made you think of a charging bull. His voice was deep, loud, and his manner displayed a kind of dogged self-assertion which had nothing aggressive in it. It seemed a necessity, and it was directed apparently as much at himself as at anybody else. He was spotlessly neat, apparelled in immaculate white from shoes to hat, and in the various Eastern ports where he got his living as ship-chandler's water-clerk he was very popular.

This is shocking for two reasons. First, it is the very first paragraph of its novel, a masterpiece from 1900. We don't normally meet someone in this much detail in the first sentences of a novel. And second, it is so direct in its presentation of physical characteristics. Like the man described, it comes straight at you, no punches pulled or holds barred. But you know what? That's almost it for the novel. Oh, we hear a time or two that he's fair or that he has pale eyes or a reddish complexion, but out of ninety thousand words or so, the description of the main character is only a hundred words altogether—a bull of a man in a white suit.

That's what Jim looks like made out of words. And here's where

we discover the difference between characters as linguistic constructs and characters as cinematic embodiments. He looks almost
nothing, the man in this paragraph, like Peter O'Toole. Hardly
the most powerfully built bullish figure in the barnyard. Yet that's
who starred in the film version of *Lord Jim*. It's okay that he doesn't
look exactly like Conrad's conception; what matters with an actor is
capturing the essence of the character—his attitudes and postures,
his motivation, his needs. And that O'Toole can do like nobody's
business. You can't always get an actor who physically resembles the
person on the page; there might be lots of us who look like Jim, but
most of us can't act. O'Toole can—and how. In fact, he can act as
if he looks the way he's supposed to, and we believe him. Mostly,
that's about behaving the right way to be Jim. His task is made easier
since Jim is famously uncommunicative about his motivations. He
leaves a lot of room for interpretation, which is why Marlow has a
job, narratively speaking.

There is a large set of conventions for establishing character, and
strangely enough, less is generally better. Beginning fiction writers
almost always err on the side of excessive detail, offering lengthy
descriptions, character histories, explanations of drives and desires.
But this is one place where Hemingway's iceberg theory—the savvy
novelist keeps the vast majority of what he knows about his characters and situations buried under the surface—really comes into play.
In fact, the ratio of one part above the surface to four parts below
may actually be too generous in favor of the exposed part.

So less is more. How does that work?

How it works is that character creation is outsourced. To you. To
me. Writers give us enough to begin to form a picture of a character,
but not so much that it will overwhelm us with detail. We supply
what else we might need from our own storehouse of information

about how people look in the real world. There are exceptions of course. If how a character looks will carry enormous weight, or if elaborate visual detail is evidence of another character (usually the narrator) obsessing on the one described, then the writer will supply a lot of specifics. From there, appearance generally matters less and action, both word and deed, takes over. Even with actions, however, readers must supply interpretation, since the novelists supply plenty of material but very little elaboration or rationale. In fact, narrative explication is more often than not misleading or consciously false, since it tends to come from first-person narrators who, as we know, are untrustworthy. Since I've invoked Hemingway and his iceberg theory, consider his characters. The only character Jake describes in detail is Robert Cohn, and that description has more to do with exhibiting Jake's obsessive loathing of Cohn than with Cohn's importance. Of his own appearance, Jake says virtually nothing. And Brett Ashley is curvy and short-haired, but otherwise, not much information is forthcoming. Much the same is true of motivations. Why does Brett go off with Cohn? Or with Romero, the matador? Can her explanation of her motives for either the affairs or the breakups be trusted, except as further evidence of her duplicitous (or possibly multivalent) personality? I have my ideas, but I'll almost guarantee they're not all like yours.

That's how it is with characters and readers. Do you think we all have the same Brett? Or Ahab? Or Pip? I don't. I've seen character analysis in action too many times. We each bring a great deal of our own lives, our own perspective, our own reading of other works, to each new novel that we'll never see the same things. Your Pip can never be quite like mine, and not because I'm special. You and I know too many different things, entertain too many different thoughts, hold too many different beliefs to see Pip—or any character—in quite the same way. Same words, same pages. Different us. Sometimes, different me. I find that my Pip today is not my Pip of yesterday. As I've changed over the years, I find that my thinking about characters has changed as well. I'm much more generous, for instance, toward youthful folly now than I was in my youth; probably I was more threatened by it, having so much of it myself. Now that I have an abundance of other folly, and no youth, the youthful sort has a certain charm. That's how it goes. Characters live, dear reader, because we do.

7

When Very Bad People Happen to Good Novels

I THINK MOST READERS are basically law-abiding. I, for instance, do not wish to be Humbert Humbert, Nabokov's molester of young girls. Nor John Gardner's Grendel, however charming he may be; there's no real attraction in a career path that involves eating Vikings. And certainly not Anthony Burgess's young thug Alex, with his droogies in tow. We may chafe at rules, but we follow them. Well, mostly. But in fiction we get to transgress, or at least watch from nearby while others transgress. We can watch others in the movies, too, but film is essentially a voyeuristic medium in which we observe passively. Fiction puts us into the action, allowing us to identify with the characters in very personal ways. We can, if we choose, work our way into the terror of being a child pickpocket in Victorian London, the elation of the old ultraviolence, the thrill of breaking every rule of civilized society or even of Hogwarts, the outrage and anger of Ned Kelly on his crime spree, all while safely ensconced in our Barcalounger.

Once upon a time, there was a good guy and a bad guy. The story was about the good guy. The bad guy was only let into the story—on parole, as it were—because things needed to happen to the hero, things he couldn't make befall him on his own. Don Quixote de la Mancha may be delusional, but his heart's in the right place. Tom Jones? Bit of a rake, but a definite good guy. David Copperfield, Oliver Twist? Why, they're just kids. What could they have done wrong? And boy, do they have villains. Fagan, Bill Sikes, Uriah Heep, nasty schoolmasters and scheming rivals. Dickens's heroes may be a bit fey, his heroines idealized cardboard, but what great scoundrels! The thing that really fired his imagination was wickedness. Protagonists may have been naughty or misguided on occasion—Huck Finn is no saint, and Hardy's heroes are clearly works-in-progress—but they were essentially good.

Then something went very badly wrong.

In the twentieth century, we begin to meet genuinely evil central characters, such as Robert Musil's Moosbrugger in his novel *The Man Without Qualities* (1930, 1942). Moosbrugger was famously characterized by the Hungarian Marxist critic Georg Lukacs as "a mentally-retarded sexual pervert with homicidal tendencies." These characters, who occupy the role traditionally held by the hero but who lack nearly all his qualities—or embody his opposites—are often called "anti-heroes." This term is vague to the point of uselessness, yet, as with so many literary terms, it's what we have. The critic Ihab Hassan, who wrote an early book, *Radical Innocence* (1961), on the phenomenon, prefers the term "rebel-victim," although that, too, may miss the mark, since it ignores the narrative centrality that "anti-hero" captures. Whatever we may call it, this new development marks a shift: Oilcan Harry has muscled Mighty Mouse out of the center of the frame and made the story be about him. Where once the protagonist was the good if flawed star of the show, while the villain was consigned to the story's margins, in the modern age, often there is no good guy and the protagonist is deeply blemished, if perhaps possessing one or two endearing qualities.

Nice work if you can get it.

Okay, so a lot of anti-heroes are basically misguided souls looking to do a little better, like Updike's Rabbit Angstrom or Bellow's Augie March. Or Henderson. Or pretty much any Bellow main character. The point is, while they may screw up on a pretty regular basis, they aren't really evildoers. Often, as with Peter Carey's Ned Kelly in *The True History of the Kelly Gang*, they may be outlaws, but they nevertheless compel our sympathy But then there is the fringe element. Real bad actors hogging the spotlight.

Let's say you were going to write a novel. Consider the attributes you would want your main character to have. Now consider the ones that are unthinkable. He lies. He's heartless. He is sexually obsessed with young girls. He likes it that way. He's cruel. He is without conscience. He molests an adolescent. He thinks that's all right. He marries a woman he does not love in order to get close to her daughter. He drives the poor woman to her death. He transports his victim across many state lines—and every moral boundary—for immoral purposes. He actively murders another human being. He believes himself justified in having done so. At this point, if you have any common sense, you run the other direction. There's no way you can write that novel.

Nabokov could. And did. *Lolita* may have outraged them in the hinterlands, but it proved a *succès de scandale* of the first order. Only a genius could write this novel and get away with it. Nabokov's friends told him he was crazy to attempt it, that it would never be published, that it could even result in criminal charges. No American publisher would touch it. After the Olympia Press in Paris published it and

Graham Greene called it one of the best novels of 1954, the British banned the book, with the French following suit. So of course, its fame was made. When it was finally published in the United States four years later, it was a huge success. Many people read it, and many of them misread it, of whom more than a few were, evidently, pornographers. Newspapers in the 1960s were filled with ads for movies called *Teenage Lolitas* (which strikes one as redundant), *More Teenage Lolitas*, and *Lots More Teenage Lolitas*. Terribly highbrow stuff, no doubt. Even on the legitimate side of the street, "Lolita" became code for a certain type of sexual misconduct, as well as for a certain kind of dirty book, which only goes to show that not only purveyors of smut have trouble with irony. For irony is one of the weapons Nabokov uses to manage his materials, including his very bad protagonist. The author despises his creation, but he never tells us so, never says, "This is one bad hombre," not even, "Don't try this at home." He lets Humbert Humbert rhapsodize about the desirability of his nymphet, about what the ideal measurements and appearance of body parts are for a not yet sexually ripe female, about his own obsessions, while never inserting his authorial scowl—or smirk—into the mix. Lets him, in other words, hang himself with his own words. And hang himself he does, because of those words.

You see, Humbert is an addict. No, not of young girls. Though ugly, appalling, and stomach-turning, that's ultimately a mere obsession. But the thing he's addicted to, the thing that gets Nabokov off the hook, is language. The guy's besotted with words. He never met a pun he didn't like. He loves double entendres, anagrams, tricky reversals of linguistic expectation, false names. Now all of these features can be found in most Nabokovian narratives, but here the author makes special use of them by handing them over to his character.

Lolita, light of my life, fire of my loins. My sin, my soul. Lo-lee-ta: the tip of the tongue taking a trip of three steps down the palate to tap, at three, on the teeth. Lo. Lee. Ta.

She was Lo, plain Lo, in the morning, standing four feet ten in one sock. She was Lola in slacks. She was Dolly at school. She was Dolores on the dotted line. But in my arms she was always Lolita.

If he'll go that far in the paragraphs where we first meet him, there can be no limits. The manic alliteration of the two consonants of her nickname, the obscene description of the formation of her name in the mouth (one feels one's tongue deserves a severe cleansing after that sentence), the many ways he finds to emphasize her youth and smallness—all this is the work of an obsessive personality. He is often artful and coy in revealing his revolting conduct, as when he says he "deceived [Charlotte] with one of Lolita's anklets" or when he describes in terms of beauty and the beast (the beast being not the entire Humbert but only that portion being gratified) a masturbatory session of rubbing against the child that culminates in "the last throb of the longest ecstasy man or monster had ever known." Reveal it he does, though, because the lure of words is too strong for him. He seems to think his beautiful narrative justifies his hideous behavior, that lovely words spruce up a moral dung-heap. His creator, of course, knows this assumption to be false but keeps that knowledge to himself. Instead, he lets Humbert keep talking.

To be sure, all that talking demonstrates that the speaker is a tolerably bad individual. But it also shows him to be brilliant, insightful, linguistically gifted, and charming. A bit disconcerting, being charmed by a snake? Yes, but there it is. That's a lot of how we can put up with him, knowing what we do. He's good company. And that's the point. He has to be something. It's written in the Law of Bad Actors: We will follow the exploits of villain-heroes, but only if they give us something in return. In Humbert's case, that something is charm.

Same thing with Alex. Same thing with Grendel. They're amusing, witty, verbally clever, and—strange to say of monstrous beings—ingratiating. Burgess imbues Alex with an Elizabethan sensibility; his wordplay is worthy of a Shakespeare hero—intricate, formal, quick, sharp, and full of aggression. Grendel's charm lies in his anachronisms: he knows things about the world, like cinematic jump-cuts, that no human of his time could possibly know. He seems to have access to the major schools of philosophical thought, none of which will exist for several hundred years after he ceases to. And then, he's surprisingly personable for someone who could, quite literally, bite your head off. Grendel's also able to make his case as a misunderstood victim: he didn't choose to be a monster, didn't get to select his mother, had no say in the irrational terror humans feel at his mere appearance. This approach has the advantage of being true, mostly, although we have to ignore his predations against their livestock and the tremendous strength that allows him to dispatch a bullock with a single blow to the spine. Oh, and the atrocious table manners, including some very untidy blood guzzling. Still, murderer or no, he is a victim.

Murderers have often made good company. John Banville won acclaim and prizes for *The Book of Evidence* (1989), a novel that follows the life of a confessed murderer, Freddie Montgomery. The novel is less a crime tale than a confession in the classic sense; Freddie writes his narrative not to exculpate his crime but to indict his life. The brutal murder of a maid in the course of robbery is less important than his inability or refusal to imagine her as having a life worth living separate from his own reality. Tough claim to make when the manner of the killing involves repeated strikes with a hammer. Even so, the argument has resonance: if one denies the autonomy or inherent value of other persons, nearly any level of violence becomes possible. Like Alex, like Humbert, Freddie wins readers over with his mix of sharpness and verbal ability.

So there's one approach—let the bad actor have the microphone. He can talk his way into readers' hearts, use that charm to win us over. But what about when he lacks that charm? Or is missing all the sympathy markers we've come to know and love? What, in a word, if he's Michael O'Kane? Edna O'Brien took readers in a new and immensely disturbing direction in her novel *In the Forest* (2002), based on the real-life case of Brendan O'Donnell, who in 1994 kidnapped and murdered a young mother and her son as well as a priest. O'Kane is a victim of circumstance and biology, to be sure, but he's also a genuinely frightening figure, a "Kindershrek," one who— quite properly in his case—frightens young children. (Adults, too, if they've any sense.) Throughout his life he has suffered loss and humiliation. His mother died when he was small, although he could never process that information, insisting that "they" had smothered her by burying her alive. The men in his life all either failed him or actively abused him, and his treatment in a juvenile detention center with the Kafkaesque name the Castle was beyond criminal. From his earliest days he was invariably scapegoated for any crime in the vicinity.

And yet, and yet. He is without redeeming qualities. There's no remorse in him, nothing but anger and resentment. His violence is not artful; it's ugly, irrational, terrifying. He is utterly without charm. His linguistic abilities are quite limited. He's no Humbert, no Alex, no Grendel. From a human standpoint, he's an appalling specimen; from a novelist's perspective, an intriguing problem. In almost any other age, he would be a villain, held at arm's length from the narrative. Going back to the gothic novel, we find characters who are abundantly villainous, yet they require very little of the reader emotionally or even intellectually. Ann Radcliffe's *The Mysteries of Udolfo* and Matthew Gregory Lewis's *The Monk* supply baddies aplenty, especially the latter with its depraved clerics and Gestapo-quality inquisitors. Those villains, however, are cardboard cutouts, frightening because of their actions rather than their proximity to reality, which is roughly that of Dracula, Bram Stoker's gothic nightmare figure. Romanticism gave us the Byronic hero and Heathcliff, but Emily Brontë imbues her hero with more torment than malice; her aim is pity rather than revulsion. O'Brien, it seems to me, is after something different. And riskier.

But what? Sympathy is out of the question, given O'Kane's loathsome conduct. Even in early childhood, when readers might be tempted to feel sorry for him given the terrible things that befall him, Michen, as he is known, is difficult, unresponsive, and slightly alien. His responses never square with our expectations of an approximately normal human being. As he matures and his relationship with the world becomes increasingly strained, his behavior more bizarre, we find ourselves more and more estranged. Well, what then? If an emotional response, or at least a sympathetic one, seems unavailable, then what is O'Brien's purpose in telling this terrible story? The novel's long suit has always been emotional identification. That's why readers wept at the death of Little Nell and sent character suggestions on who should marry whom to Thackeray midserialization. It's why we're so conflicted about Gatsby and Heathcliff.

Long suit, but not only suit. The novel has always proved itself capable of multiple uses, one of which is analysis or intellection. It can be a vehicle for sympathy or dread, but also for rational understanding. In this case, we're asked to make rational sense of an irrational being, to stand at the edge and peer into the abyss. O'Brien never makes excuses for Michen's behavior or asks that he be let off the hook. Even as we're tempted to feel sorry for him, she reminds us that he's not that special, that other children have come through difficult early lives without committing horrific acts of violence. Instead, she gives what sympathy the novel bestows to his victims, Eily Ryan and her child, Maddie, and the priest who offers him sympathy, Father John. Their only qualifications for their roles seem to be that they overlap with O'Kane's memories and psychotic fantasies. To think about the unthinkable: that's one possible explanation.

There's another prospect, though, a source much older than novels. Here's a hint: *Michael O'Kane*. Though he's called Michen, the name most reviewers and reporters have used in referring to him, we forget his proper name at our peril. The archangel Michael, of course, is the great enemy of Satan and his legion, having defeated them, according to the book of Revelation, in the battle that dropped them from heaven. Ironic that the scourge of evil gives his name to a monster? Perhaps. But that monster also bears a homonym of the first murderer. To be sure, "Kane" isn't "Cain," but it's close enough for government work. And as the heavenly being sometimes credited as the voice in the burning bush who spoke to Moses, Michael may be appropriate for someone who acts because he hears voices. The forest of the title, moreover, reminds us that the wilderness has stood since biblical times as a place of temptation and danger, a place where the devil operates. Something vile certainly operates in Cloosh Wood, where the murders take place. Wild speculation on my part? Perhaps. A bit obvious? Contrived? Maybe. But it has a purpose. O'Brien is investigating, as much as anything, the problem of evil: how is it that terrible things happen in our world, that people can go so badly astray? Not surprisingly, her answer has little to do with either angels or demons. Though she draws on Judeo-Christian imagery, as she often does in her work, her view of evil is profoundly earthbound. A human being enacted these horrors, and other human beings influenced his development, either through visiting awful actions upon him or, like the townspeople, standing idly by and doing nothing to stop him. With such creatures in the everyday world, she suggests, who needs supernatural explanations?

Well, then, are we simply gulls, able to be manipulated at an author's whim? I don't think so. We won't embrace just any horrible person; he (or she, to be fair) has to be a very special horrible person. And presented just right. It seems to me that what this phenomenon expresses is the tremendous curiosity and capacity for intellectual understanding of readers and writers alike. We can comprehend what revolts us. We can begin to understand how awful people exist and commit terrible crimes, without being implicated or sullied by those crimes. We respond, we feel, we may even mourn, but we do not become the thing we read. There's always a distance there that makes the situation, however terrible, bearable. That distance is the novel's—and our—saving grace.

8

Wrinkles in Time,
or Chapters Just Might Matter

YOU PICK UP A novel, open to page one, and your heart sinks. Why? No number, no title. In other words, no chapters. You're facing the bleak prospect of life without breaks, the long, long slog through an untrammeled narrative wilderness. Does it matter, having or not having chapters? Sure, in ways both trivial and profound. Without chapter breaks, when do you turn off the lamp and go to sleep? When do you reward yourself with a cookie or a hot chocolate? When do you feel that you've got somewhere? But chapter breaks—and the text that separates them—are more than mere rest areas on the reading interstate. Done right, they tell us that something significant has happened, that a certain interval of time or unified activity or narrative unit has passed. Done badly, of course, they can just mean that 3,987 words have elapsed since the last white space in the text. Ideally, though, chapters exist to contain a meaningful block of story. They sometimes have clever titles explaining their contents. They may have beginnings, middles, and ends. Sometimes, in recent novels, they're even freestanding stories that may or may not seem like parts of a single narrative body. Whatever their shape or external features, all chapters have some aim involving readers and meaning, some reason for looking the way they do.

Once upon a time, chapters fell into disrepute. That was during the modernist period, and the disdain the moderns—Joyce, Woolf, Faulkner, and company—show toward the chapter was really an expression of their disdain toward all things Victorian. The Victorians, you see, had perfected the chapter as the key element in their perfection of linear narrative. Nineteenth-century British novels go from A to Z with a smoothness and regularity that you couldn't improve upon if you wrote a thousand novels. They move like clockwork, or rather, like calendar work. They were linear because they were serial, their appearance spread out over time. We'll come back to how and why all that happened in a few chapters.

The shape of the Victorian novel, from a plot standpoint, was a series of exaggerated smiley-faces hooked together. Each episode started from the high of the previous cliff-hanger, then slacked off in intensity to conduct the business of these two or three chapters, then a kick-up at the end into another cliff-hanger. And chapters are an integral part of this episodic structure. The writer couldn't hope to maintain that high intensity of last month's closing spike, so he had to bring the reader down slowly—nobody likes a crash landing—to a level that was manageable, a level of only modest intensity. That's where most of the chapters would take place. Often, there would be a small upward spike at the end of a chapter in the middle of the episode, then a big spike in the chapter that ended the installment.

You can go through almost any Victorian novel and figure out exactly where the installments ended. That will be where the big stuff happens: kidnappings, mysterious appearances or disappearances, the discovery of a corpse, the letter revealing (a) inheritance, (b) loss of the inheritance, (c) true paternity, or (d) some combination thereof. If the novel had a regular publication history, those moments will be at the end of even-numbered chapters, since many novels followed the two-chapter-per-installment formula. Not all, though, so it can be a little tricky. But you'll be able to tell. They were good at this stuff. They had to be, as an economic imperative and as an expression of narrative art.

Chapters in traditional novels can sport a lot of different looks, with titles or roman numerals or arabic numerals or some other delineating sign, but they all fulfill one basic, common function: they break a vast narrative down into some sort of meaningful unit. In Chapter LVIII (I believe that would be fifty-eight but don't entirely trust my roman numerology) of the decidedly pre-Victorian *Pride and Prejudice*, Austen brings together Elizabeth Bennet and Mr. Darcy on a walk alone where, for the first time, they can frankly discuss their previous actions, explain their motives, ask for and receive forgiveness, and reveal their love for each other. The chapter begins and ends with the walk, and by the time they part in the hall, everything is explained to the satisfaction of both, and naturally they will marry. It is a miracle of economy. Everything one might want addressed in the chapter is present; nothing extraneous dares intrude.

Dickens prefers titles for his chapters. So do I. Titles give you something to work with from the start. "In Chancery" says a lot more than "I" or even "Chapter 1" ever could. It is, in fact, the opening chapter of *Bleak House*, and one of the greatest first chapters ever written.

London. Michaelmas Term lately over, and the Lord Chancellor sitting in Lincoln's Inn Hall. Implacable November weather. As much mud in the streets as if the waters had but newly retired from the face of the earth, and it would not be wonderful to meet a Megalosaurus, forty feet long or so, waddling like an elephantine lizard up Holborn Hill. Smoke lowering down from chimney-pots, making a soft black drizzle, with flakes of soot in it as big as full-grown snow-flakes—gone into mourning, one might imagine, for the death of the sun. Dogs, undistinguishable in mire. Horses, scarcely better; splashed to their very blinkers. Foot passengers, jostling one another's umbrellas in a general infection of ill-temper, and losing their foot-hold at street-corners, where tens of thousands of other foot passengers have been slipping and sliding since the day broke (if the day ever broke), adding new deposits to the crust upon crust of mud, sticking at those points tenaciously to the pavement, and accumulating at compound interest.

How can you not want to read what's coming? The answer is, you can't. That's why he was a huge bestseller in his day. What kind of story must follow from such an opening paragraph? This is a place that's almost mythic in its wretchedness and misery. And then there's the fog, which he introduces in the next paragraph:

Fog everywhere. Fog up the river, where it flows among green aits and meadows; fog down the river, where it rolls defiled among the tiers of shipping and the waterside pollutions of a great (and dirty) city. Fog on the Essex marshes, fog on the Kentish heights. Fog creeping into the cabooses of collier-brigs; fog lying out on the yards, and hovering in the rigging of great ships; fog drooping on the gunwales of barges and small boats. Fog in the eyes and throats of ancient Greenwich pensioners, wheezing by the firesides of their wards; fog in the stem and bowl of the afternoon pipe of the wrathful skipper, down in his close cabin; fog cruelly pinching the toes and fingers of his shivering little 'prentice boy on deck. Chance people on the bridges peeping over the parapets into a nether sky of fog, with fog all round them, as if they were up in a balloon, and hanging in the misty clouds.

So just like that, we have a motif, a recurrent element—in this case an image, the fog—that will hang around to remind us of a central problem in the story. Before the chapter's over, motif will become theme, an idea or attitude about things, as the fog turns out to be not merely at large in the atmosphere but in the Court of Chancery (like an American probate court, minus expeditiousness): in the solicitors and the clerk and the Chancellor as well as in the air of the place, a miasma of confusion and indolence, of claim and counterclaim, of unresolved cases hovering like ghosts, like bad dreams, for generations.

Somehow, again miraculously, all this happens in the space of five pages. Without introducing any of the principals involved in his novel, Dickens manages to lay out a problem, a location, the particular case (Jarndyce and Jarndyce), a mood, a theme, and a very compelling image. It's so good, we practically don't need the next 660 pages. At the very least we're primed for the introduction of a main character or two. And we will get them pronto.

This is what chapters do, by convention: achieve small structures in support of the large structure of the book. A traditional chapter has a beginning, a middle, and an end. It offers readers something: a small story within the larger one, a scene that develops a theme or idea, a shift in the direction of the plot attributable to a single event or accident (accidents are great narrative devices in traditional novels).

What's that you say? Those are just moldy oldies? What about newer books? Sure. If you want convention observed, look at genre novels. Chapter 53 of Robert B. Parker's *A Catskill Eagle* shows us the chapter as endgame. Spenser, the detective-hero, finds his way into the enemy lair, confronts the bad guy, kills him, settles his personal account with another character, and escapes from a place swarming with security guards and other armed types. All very tidy, except for the blood. This isn't terribly high-brow writing—the subtitle could be "Spenser and Hawk Go Cross-Country and Shoot People"—but it's *efficient* writing. Every chapter has business to accomplish, and it does. Beginning-middle-end. Mini-narratives. Plot twists. Punchy finishes.

Then, not too many years after the death of Queen Victoria herself, things changed. Along with linear narrative, hard-driving plot structures, exaggerated minor characters, and buttoned-up morality, the moderns gave chapters the ax. In a great many modern novels, chapters are vague affairs, if they appear at all. Joyce's *A Portrait of the Artist as a Young Man*, for instance, has only five numbered sections. Those aren't chapters, whatever they may be. Stages of development of the character and narrative, perhaps. His *Ulysses* contains eighteen untitled, unnumbered episodes corresponding more or less to episodes from his Homeric model, *The Odyssey*. Those episodes, however, are less chapters than occasions to change the technical devices of the narrative. Woolf has no chapters in *Mrs. Dalloway*, rather loose, numbered sections in *To the Lighthouse* that are more centers of consciousness than narrative structures, and sections named for speakers in *The Waves*. None of these novels could be accused of being heavily plotted, of course, and in Woolf's case they tend to move any direction but in a straight chronological line.

Woolf was friends with E. M. Forster, who was just a few years older but miles away in sensibility. His *A Room with a View* offers a Victorian approach to chapters—very linear narratively, almost substories within the main body of narrative, and with catchy titles like "In Santa Croce with No Baedeker" or "How Miss Bartlett's Boiler Was So Tiresome." This novel appeared in 1908, just a few years before Woolf began publishing her work. Her novels of the teens share many conventional aspects with Forster's work. By the time she gets to *To the Lighthouse* (1927), though, she is using individual consciousness, what she calls "moments of being," as her organizing principle. Her narration is less about events than about how we experience and process events subjectively. As one might expect, her "chapters" are moments within, typically, a single consciousness. The book is divided into three sections, "The Window," "Time Passes," and "The Lighthouse," the first and third each comprising a single day, the middle one covering roughly ten years. In Chapter 9 of "The Window," we follow the thoughts of William Bankes, a friend and summer guest of the Ramsay family, as he ruminates on Mr. Ramsay, then "passes" the narration to another guest, Lily Briscoe, who thinks about William and about Mrs. Ramsay and about the picture Lily is trying to paint, and then they "share" the narration to complete the experience of a moment. Nothing *happens* in the ordinary sense; two people merely see the world around them. And yet, something has happened. When Mrs. Ramsay thinks, later in the evening, that Lily and William must marry, the idea strikes her like a thunderbolt. Yet it's wrongheaded on one level, superfluous on another. While Lily and William are ill-suited to a permanent life together, they have already achieved a matching of minds, if only in the transitory realm. Most of the chapters of the novel's first and third sections act in this way, as the consciousnesses of one or more persons gather around the small events of a moment.

So then, are they chapters? As with most things literary, you'll get debate. Traditionalists may well say that these aren't chapters because they don't go anywhere, that they lack shape or direction. But they have exactly the right shape for the novel they inhabit, and their narrative direction, if it can be called that, is a small version of the novel's larger narrative direction. They're not Dickens chapters, nor James, Fielding, Austen, or Eliot chapters. But I would argue that they're just what we want, here, in this novel. In fact, I would argue that they illustrate the Law of Chapter and Verse: A chapter, as a section that makes sense for its particular novel, follows no rules but its own.

Only the reader, finally, can decide if a chapter does indeed make sense in the context of its novel. They can be straightforward or subtle, logical or mystifying, transparent or opaque. They can be, as in Helen Fielding's Bridget Jones novels, diary entries for single days or, as in the openings of some James A. Michener novels, records of geological time. None of that matters. What does matter is that *somehow*, and that how is pretty variable, the chapter must work for the novel that houses it.

I started thinking seriously about chapters a couple of decades ago when I read one called "Oh, Mama, Can This Really Be the End?" Two things were going on when I saw the title. First, like every other person of my generation, I could complete the couplet: "to be stuck inside of Mobile with the Memphis Blues again." It's Bob Dylan, of course. No one else could or would write those lines. The second thing I noticed was that the context had absolutely nothing to do with Dylan or Memphis or Mobile or even America, except that its author had, like me, first heard the song when it was new, in his youth. He's T. Coraghessan Boyle, whose nom de plume (his birth name is Thomas John Boyle) ranks among my absolute favorites with Petroleum V. Nasby and Sparse Grey Hackle. And the novel is *Water Music*, a wily mix of genres set in the late eighteenth and very early nineteenth centuries and centered on the discovery and early exploration of the River Niger. The novel bounces between dueling storylines, one an adventure, or possibly misadventure, yarn involving the historical discoverer of the Niger, Mungo Park. The other is a picaresque romp featuring the entirely fictitious and wonderfully named Ned Rise, a ne'er-do-well who manages to scuffle his way from one calamity to another yet keep on scuffling. This being a contemporary novel, the reader knows which character will, as it were, rise to the top by novel's end. Indeed, the relative fortunes of the high- and low-born protagonists constitutes one of Boyle's main critiques of the traditional novel. And the lengthy Dylan quotation relative to a very short (only about a page) chapter reminds readers, were they ever in doubt, that this is a postmodern novel. The anachronism, the cheeky attitude, the element of parody that is present throughout all announce a take on the world and the novel that is less than earnest, that is an attack on earnestness. That's a lot for a tiny chapter and its unwieldy title to accomplish.

When you see something like Boyle's chapter, you have to consider the function of chapters, or at least I do. And it turns out they can be anything. They can be solid narratives, complete in themselves. They can even be freestanding stories that make sense out of the context of their novel. They can focus on single events or on chains of occurrences. They can be impressionistic renderings or subjective responses to the events of the novel. They can be, in short, whatever the novelist wants them to be.

So who benefits from chapters? Almost anyone whose stories are heavily plot-driven. I already mentioned the great Victorians. But also mystery novelists, writers of historical romances (or every other kind) or westerns or horror novels. All those mini-endings allow for upticks in tension, suspense, or revelation. That part's pretty obvious, right? But also novelists who don't plot much at all. A writer of impressionistic fiction can indicate the organization of the larger work through the organization of the smaller.

Most of all, readers. Chapters provide us with breaks in the reading. Hey, never discount the dumb stuff. Even when we read straight through huge chunks, those breaks provide moments to consider the implications of what we've just read, to see how things are fitting together. Chapters tell us what's important in the novel, what's important to the novel. How is it constructed? Does it emphasize revelation or the withholding of information? Does it prize external event or internal impression? Is it tight and coherent or loose and rambling? Chapters help teach us how to read the novel. And we'll take all the help we can get.

9

Everywhere Is Just One Place

LET'S SAY YOU'VE HAD your great insight on the human condition. It's about the desire for peace or happiness or tomato soup. Something major, anyway. You want to reach the largest possible audience, but PBS won't give you a special. So you decide to write a novel to, you know, tell everybody a universal truth. Stop! Can't be done. *In the world of the novel, the universal doesn't have a zip code.* If you want to write about everywhere, you'll have to stick to just one place. There are some medieval plays about the human condition, with names like *Everyman* and *Mankind*. Their heroes, whose names are the titles, are earnest representatives of us all—bland, generic, indistinguishable, and undistinguished. There's a reason Stratford, Ontario, has a summer Shakespeare Festival and not a Medieval Morality Play Festival.

There's only one novel with any staying power that is overtly about a generic figure: John Bunyan's *The Pilgrim's Progress* (1678). That's short for *The Pilgrim's Progress from the World to That Which Is to Come*, just so there's no mistaking the didactic intent of the work. It details the journey of its hero, Christian, toward a place called the Celestial City. He's helped on his way by characters called Evangelist and, well, Help, and impeded by Mr. Worldly Wiseman, Obstinate, Pliable, and Hypocrisy, among others. You get the drift. The problem, from a reader's perspective, is that it's an allegory. These aren't characters or places but types, and not very interesting types, either. The names have had more lasting appeal than the things or persons to which they're attached: Vanity Fair, the Slough of Despond, Doubter's Castle, Giant Despair. As allegory, I suppose it does what Bunyan wanted it to do. As a novel, it just doesn't get it. The characters lack depth or complexity, so the achievement of the journey and the places and people encountered are the only points of genuine interest. If you want tales of individual humans wrestling with their faith and with issues of right and wrong, you'll find much more satisfying reading in Nathaniel Hawthorne's *The House of the Seven Gables* (1851) or *The Scarlet Letter* (1850). Hawthorne sometimes veers perilously close to allegory, but his people feel like real humans rather than cardboard cutouts, his ethical dilemmas genuinely troubling.

And there's the trouble with allegory: dull, stiff, two-dimensional. The allegorist means well, and he doesn't want us to miss *the point*. The point, however, is usually all there is. The novel needs to be more dynamic if it wants to engage our attention and our emotions. It needs to present characters as rich and complex as those we believe ourselves to be, and they need to struggle with problems worth their effort—and ours. This richness, complexity, and individuation is what the novel's best at. Yet novelists do sometimes want to write about "the human condition" or "the problem of the past" or any number of vexatious big themes. So, then, what to do?

First of all, get a handle on the problem. Understand the twin, sometimes opposing, pulls of the local and the general. Here's the Law of Universal Specificity: You can't write about everywhere or everyone, only about one person or one place. If you want to write about everybody, start with one person, in one place, doing one real thing. Bellow's Augie March, now there's a guy—American, hustling, morally suspect, energetic, hopeful, a little out of control at times. Representative? You bet. But individuated, not quite like anybody else. You want to show the disillusionment and loss of World War I veterans? Jake Barnes. You want a place that stands for everyplace? Joyce's Dublin. Faulkner's Yoknapatawpha. Erdrich's reservation. Bellow's Chicago. Melville's ship. If you get the local and particular right, the universal will take care of itself.

Partly, this is a no-brainer. You can't describe *everywhere*. Where would you begin? How would it look? How many millions of pages is your novel, anyway? And what does *everyone* look like? So obviously the novelist can't go in that direction and maintain anything like verisimilitude. Beyond that clear-cut problem, though, lurks a trickier one: how can you convey universality to your reader? How can you make sure that your characters stand for something like all of us?

You can't. Don't even try. Don't even think about it. And yet, it happens. *Vive le paradoxe!* And yet, as with most paradoxes, this one can be understood. I'll let you think about it for a bit. (Hint: the answer's not in the book.)

Meanwhile, an example. Let's say you want to write about a big event. A really big, earth-changing event. Something like, oh, Indian independence. At midnight on August 15, 1947, something on the order of half a billion people achieved their freedom from colonial rule. Now that's big. Might even be worth writing about. Here's the catch, though: how do you write about half a billion people? You don't. You can't. Even just saying the names would take thousands of pages. But you can write about one person. You can even give that one person a special trait, maybe connect him (it is a him) to a few others who share that trait. You could even have him be born on August 15, 1947. At midnight. He could be telepathically connected to others who share the moment of birth with him and the newly formed countries of India and Pakistan. That's the conceit of Salman Rushdie's brilliant evocation of the emerging nations in *Midnight's Children*. His novel is a sprawling tragicomedy centered around Saleem Sinai, whose life and tangled fate parallels that of his country. The strategy proves a winner. Why? In part, we can follow the ups and downs of Saleem's fate far better than those of a whole nation. Partly, too, by using Saleem, Rushdie can select those aspects of India's entry into nationhood he wishes to emphasize; an individual life, however messy, is far tidier than the whole history of a country. Even if that history is very short. And finally, he tells a great story.

The novel, because of its magical realist elements, is often compared to the work of Gabriel García Márquez. The greatest similarity between the two, however, is this localizing strategy, which also places them close to William Faulkner. Faulkner spoke repeatedly of his "little postage-stamp of ground," Yoknapatawpha County, Mississippi. Like Rushdie, like García Márquez, Faulkner grappled with history, in his case one even more gnarled and thorny than theirs, entwined as it was with guilt, failure, pride, sin, and the inheritance of slavery. But he was too savvy to attempt to write about the entire South, or even the entire state. Rather, he whittled his concerns down to a single county, based on Lafayette County, where he lived in Oxford, the county seat and home of the University of Mississippi. Here, in *The Sound and the Fury* (1929), he created the

Compsons, an aristocratic family on a downward spiral from the social prominence of the plantation and General Compson to grandsons Quentin, who commits suicide while a freshman at Harvard, and Benjy, the thirty-three-year-old with the mind of a small child. In *Go Down, Moses* (1942), he tells the story of the McCaslins, descendants of a slaveholding family, and their long-unacknowledged black cousins, the Beauchamps. In his Snopes trilogy, *The Hamlet* (1940), *The Town* (1957), and *The Mansion* (1959), he creates a far-flung family of ne'er-do-wells who actually do pretty well, winding up, sometimes in spite of themselves, owning pretty much the whole town. They seem to support a Faulknerian beatitude that the rascals shall inherit the earth. In novel after novel, he explores various aspects of Southern inheritance, always focusing on this one small parcel of land.

García Márquez does much the same thing in *One Hundred Years of Solitude* (1967), using the fictional coastal town of Macondo as a microcosm of postcolonial South America. Many events of the novel—civil war, the prevalence of the military, corrupt leadership, assassinations and massacres, the dominance of foreign companies (in this case, a multinational banana company)—resonate as elements of the history of many Latin American countries, yet it is the spectacular and singular nature of the town and its main family, the Buendías, that make the novel a permanent feature of readers' memories. Everything about them is prodigious, from the tremendous age of the matriarch, Ursula, to Colonel Aureliano's miraculous ability to escape death at the hands of others and even himself, to his brother José Arcadio's male member, remarkable for its size and the fabulous tattoos with which it is adorned. Even the gypsy, Melquíades, who sets the family on the path to greatness and dissolution, is a figure of outsized accomplishments, claiming to have come back to life because death bored him. You've got to love a family like this one. Except that there is no family like this one. Part of García Márquez's program is to create a family like no other.

So how do we get from there to a pattern of experience that can stand for the whole of postcolonial Latin America? Ah, our paradox again. The solution, dear Brutus, lies not in our stars but in ourselves. The business of universality can't be found in the text. If the writer tries to place it there, the work will almost automatically sound contrived. The writer's job is to provide a story that engages, fascinates, provokes, and above all registers as unique. Robert McLiam Wilson subtitles his novel *Eureka Street* "A Novel of Ireland Like No Other." That's what every novel aspires to be, a work of fiction about *x* like no other. The novelist gets to create his story and to make it specific, particular, singular. Then he's done. We readers get to decide on significance. We may decide that it's genuinely universal in its depictions or themes, or that it's not, or that it's so poorly done that we don't care one way or the other, or any of a hundred other determinations on many topics.

To come back to *Midnight's Children*, Saleem Sinai has to be, above all else, himself. Rushdie can supply hints or suggestions of a broader set of connections, as he does starting with the coincidence of Saleem's birth. What he can't do is make readers take those connections seriously. We decide that for ourselves. Does he represent some aspects of modern India? Which ones? In what ways?

Do all novels aspire to universal themes?

I don't think so. There may be representative elements in character or situation, but a lot of novels are happy merely to tell their story. In fact, every novel needs first of all to be happy telling its story. If it doesn't do that well, there's not much chance it can speak to broader themes. But many novels do not seek to go beyond their story. The obvious but by no means only works here would be category or genre fiction, as if "literary" fiction didn't belong to categories or genres. What these terms apply to are those novels that fall into one or another of the popular culture genres: mystery, thriller, horror, western, romance, science fiction, fantasy. Dashiell Hammett's Sam Spade or Raymond Chandler's Philip Marlowe, for instance, can't be said to stand for anyone beyond themselves or a sort of wish fulfillment of sure justice. The novels they occupy suggest certain aspects of the world: the prevalence of evil, the murky ethical realm where good guys and bad guys meet, or the improbable ratio of darkness to light even in sunny Los Angeles. Similarly, with horror novels, say, it's tough to generalize from a demented car/canine/caretaker, nor is that really the point. The business of entertainments, after all, is to entertain.

Even so, we can and do learn things from them. Not direct moral lessons, but more general implications about human behavior, the desire for justice, the need to be loved, or right conduct. We can't help it; we are an inference-drawing species. Give us a particular and we'll generalize from it. So almost any novel can teach us, and the novel has one big lesson that lies at its very root: we matter. A human life has value not because it belongs to an owner, a ruler, a collective, or a political party, but because it exists as itself. How is this in the novel form itself? It lies in the subject matter, which has to do with the little guy. Oh, you may find one or two novels that feature kings or princes or dauphins (real ones, not Twain's), but nearly every novel that has ever been written is about an ordinary life, be it middle-class, working-class, or down and out. The people of the novel would have been very minor figures, had they appeared at all, in Homer or Shakespeare—a name to be killed off, a messenger racing to his master, a bit of comic stage business, no one to be taken seriously. And all those novels expect us to take an interest in the lives they present, to hang around till the end just to see what becomes of their chosen person. What's more, we do. Do care, do follow with interest, do hang around to see the finish, big or small. Because they matter, we do. And that's pretty universal.

10

Clarissa's Flowers

WHEN MRS. DALLOWAY SAYS, in her novel's famous opening line, that she will buy the flowers, she sets a day and a novel in motion. More importantly, she gives us a first look at what will become her dominant character emblem. Virginia Woolf used *The Hours* as a working title (but happily left it for Michael Cunningham), but she might just as easily have called the book *The Flowers*. Not every character in every novel has an emblem, but many do. We have only to think of Nero Wolfe's orchids, Hemingway's Old Man's Great DiMaggio, Stephen Dedalus's "ashplant" walking stick. Those emblems guide our responses to their characters. Objects, images, and places become associated not merely with characters, but with *ideas* about characters. Some of that is the authors' doing, of course: Woolf puts the flowers in Clarissa's arms. But much of the creation of meaning lies with readers. Ultimately, it falls to us to decide what *we* think it all means.

William Faulkner once said that his favorite among his novels was *As I Lay Dying*. My admittedly limited experience teaching Faulkner is that it is the favorite of students as well. I have better luck getting them through the whole of that novel than the twelve anthology pages of "Barn Burning." And I suspect it's the favorite Faulkner novel of a lot of nonstudents, too. Why? They can get it. On one level, this is a matter of narrative simplicity. *Absalom, Absalom!* is a darned hard slog. Ditto *The Sound and the Fury.* The Bundren saga, on the other hand, is a *slightly* hard slog. A colleague calls it a romp, but I'm not sure I'd go that far. But I don't think that's why so many readers prefer it. I think it's because they can keep the characters straight. No doubt there are a host of reasons why it's easier to sort characters out from one another in *As I Lay Dying* than in his other novels. The names at the heads of each interior-monologue-chapter help. And the names are memorable: Anse, Addie, Darl, Jewel (for a man), Cash, Dewey Dell, Vardaman. Okay, I'm good with that. But there's something else that really helps. Each character has an emblem, some thing or obsession or goal that helps to differentiate him or her from the rest. Anse, in addition to refusing to be "be-holden" to anyone outside the family, keeps thinking about a new set of teeth. Jewel has his horse (and his anger), Cash his carpentry and his desire for a "graphophone," as he transposes the syllables of phonograph, Vardaman the fish he catches and comes to equate with his dead mother, Dewey Dell her pregnancy and desire for an abortion. How do they work? First of all, they're mnemonics. When we see someone obsessing about his horse or reacting with anger beyond what might be called for in the situation, we know that's Jewel. No name necessary after the first time or two. And then there's character structure. Their obsessions provide depth and coloring. Cash uses carpentry to avoid thinking about the reason he's building that particular box.

I made it on the bevel.

1. There is more surface for the nails to grip.

2. There is twice the gripping surface to each seam.

3. The water will have to seep into it on a slant. Water moves easiest up and down or straight across.

4. In a house people are upright two thirds of the time. So the seams are made up-and-down. Because the stress is up-and-down.

And so on, for a total of thirteen items, concluding with the best reason, "It makes a neater job." What's conspicuously absent from his musings is their real source—that is, what "it" is. It's a coffin, of course, and readers know that, but Cash doesn't say it. He does mention graves once, but only in contrast to other dug holes. For all his matter-of-fact tone, he avoids the one fact that matters, namely, that he has built a coffin for his mother. Why? Grief. Or rather, the avoidance of grief. None of the characters properly channel or even acknowledge the grief. Instead, each one plunges into his or her own sphere of interest.

Character mnemonics are extremely important in the Victorian novel, for obvious reasons. Remember, this is the age of the serialized novel. If your copy of *The Edinburgh Review* arrived on, say, the tenth of March with the new novel you've become obsessed with, it might take you four or five days, tops, to read the two chapters of the current installment, leaving twenty-six or -seven days until the April issue and the next two chapters. I don't know about you, but in twenty-six days, I can forget my name. I would need a little authorial help. Meet Silas Wegg, authorial helper. Wegg is a "literary" man and seller of ballads who has a wooden leg (a "wegg"?) and a pal named Mr. Venus, who is an undertaker and "articulator of bones." They're greedy and unscrupulous and, generally, great fun as minor villains. The major villain is Bradley Headstone, a schoolmaster who does pretty much everything except foam at the mouth to indicate his derangement. His mnemonic, like Mr. Venus's, is his name. We're not likely to forget a Bradley Headstone in a month's time, any more than we would any of Dickens's great emblematic names: Jaggers, Miss Havisham, Magwitch, Uriah Heep, Mr. Micawber, Quilp, Skimpole, Pecksniff, or that Christmas favorite, Ebenezer Scrooge. Beyond the names, though, Dickens often provides other emblems. Quilp is a dwarf, Bill Sikes has his growl and his dog, Mr. Venus his bones, Micawber his punch and his belief that "something will turn up." They have limps and prostheses (no writer in history has supplied more characters with wooden legs), facial oddities and peculiarities of hair, sidekicks and talismans. His characters are sometimes described as grotesques, yet it's grotesquery with a purpose. They must remain not only memorable but vivid for readers over the long stretch of months. Nor is he alone among Victorian serialized novelists. A quick glance, if such a thing is possible, at William Makepeace Thackeray or George Meredith or Anthony Trollope or Thomas Hardy or even the comparatively restrained George Eliot reveals a wealth of vivid and occasionally outlandish figures, especially among minor characters.

Even once the historical wheel had turned and left the serialized novel behind, writers continued to use emblems to express character. We may think of Jay Gatsby in terms of the green light, but the things that mark him out are shirts. Nick Carraway can scarcely take his eyes off Gatsby's clothes, so items of apparel show up repeatedly in the description. When he goes to Nick's house to await Daisy's arrival, for instance, he's wearing "a white flannel suit, silver shirt, and gold colored tie." Doesn't exactly take a semiologist to interpret those signs, does it? The real show stopper, however, is the scene when Gatsby, giving Nick and Daisy the tour of his house, pauses to throw shirt after shirt after shirt on a table while telling how he has them tailored in London, until he has created a large, disheveled mound of "stripes and scrolls and plaids in coral and apple-green and lavender and faint orange, with monograms of Indian blue." Daisy, overcome by materialistic fellow feeling, sinks down among the garments in tears, declaring them "such beautiful shirts" that they make her sad. Without any authorial commentary, Fitzgerald manages to convey volumes about both Gatsby and Daisy—not only their individual character traits but a strong sense of what's wrong in the relationship between them. Honestly, can two people get any shallower than these two textile mavens? They're virtually inarticulate about feelings during this meeting that all parties recognize as a disaster, but thank heaven they both speak the language of shirt.

Throughout the modern and postmodern eras, character emblems continue to play a role, although those roles are not always the same. The licorice-flavored Blackjack chewed by the title character in Tim O'Brien's *Going After Cacciato* expresses, along with his dribbling a basketball in his Vietnam foxhole, his childlike and often inappropriate soldierly demeanor. In Hemingway's *The Sun Also Rises*, Jake Barnes's war wound has plot, character, and thematic implications. It renders him incapable of consummating his relationship with Lady Brett Ashley, thwarting their passion for each other and sending them off on their misadventures, and it speaks more generally to the sterility, sexual and otherwise, of society in the wake of the Great War.

Emblems are particularly useful in that signature modern genre, the mystery, where they can be a sort of shorthand, as Agatha Christie certainly understood. Hercule Poirot is a virtual flotilla of signs, including his "moustaches" and his drink of preference, a small tisane, and Miss Marple has her knitting. These items position the characters in a specific way within their worlds. Even when the first Poirot mystery appeared, for instance, his spats were a sign of a rather old-fashioned fashion plate, a sort of fuddy-duddy dandy. That description pretty neatly summarizes Poirot. Nor did Christie invent anything here. This practice goes back at a minimum to Sherlock Holmes, with his deerstalker (which he actually wears infrequently), his meerschaum pipe, and his seven per cent solution of cocaine. Within a generation, detectives and recurring cops all had their personal talismans, from Lord Peter Wimsey's monocle to Nick and Nora Charles's fox terrier, Asta, to Nero Wolfe's orchids and yellow shirt, on down to the cooking of Robert B. Parker's Spenser (and come to think of it, is Hawk—or any sidekick—a character emblem? Is Susan Silverman, his longtime, sometime lady friend?) and the blues recordings (female singers, all) of Linda Barnes's Carlotta Carlyle. On the other hand, if a female detective is 6-foot-1 with flaming red hair, as Carlotta is, does she need any further elaboration?

Sometimes these emblems can form a sort of motif in their repetition. In *A Passage to India*, E. M. Forster develops the character of Dr. Aziz through his conveyances, from the polo pony he rides when we first meet him, to the bicycle he rides to dinner with friends and which is stolen there, to the tonga he has to engage when summoned to the English officers' club (and which is summarily commandeered by a group of English women, forcing him to walk home), to the train he takes for the ill-fated trip into the Malabar Hills, to the police car taking him to jail after his arrest, to the landau he rides in during the celebration of his "victory" in court, and finally to the horses he and Cyril Fielding ride in the novel's last scene. We track Aziz's progress, if it can be called that, through his conveyances. In his first appearance, he bicycles to his friend Hamidullah's, then takes the pony-drawn tonga to the Chandrapore Club when his tire goes flat. To be reminded that the club is whites-only while simultaneously watching English women take his tonga as if by right is to be put in his place quite rudely. Later, after the dismissal of charges, he is swept away by forces quite beyond his control—there's a near-riot in progress—in the relative grandeur of a landau.

Forster works particular magic with a pair of horses. At one point still fairly early, Aziz plays a friendly chukker of polo against a young British subaltern. This aspiration to the middle class as defined by the occupying British defines the delusions under which the young doctor operates. He can never be treated as an equal, even if the subaltern thinks him a fine fellow. It's false from the start. He must borrow a pony from his better-heeled friend Hamidullah to practice in the first place, and although he rides well, he's no natural at the game; rather, he must think his way through it like the outsider he is. The sham camaraderie between Indian physician and English soldier can only exist in the artificial world of the maidan, and only because the two avoid all the differences between them: there is no topic on which they can engage except polo. Aziz again rides a horse at the end of the novel, this time on a sort of farewell outing with his old friend Fielding. They talk; they ride; they quarrel over matters of Indian identity and possible nationhood, topics Aziz could never have discussed with the young subaltern, or with virtually any other English person in the novel. It is precisely because they are friends that they can argue so frankly and even heatedly. Yet the friendship is doomed. In the marvelous final paragraph, the horses answer Fielding's question about why the two can't be friends in the here and now of India.

> *But the horses didn't want it—they swerved apart; the earth didn't want it, sending up rocks through which riders must pass single file; the temples, the tank, the jail, the palace, the birds, the carrion, the Great House, that came into view as they issued through the gap and saw Mau beneath: they didn't want it, they said in their hundred voices, "No, not yet," and the sky said, "No, not there."*

This passage shows the difficulties of genuine friendship, with its missteps and uneven ground, its rocks and impediments, as against the artificially smooth surface and bogus amity of the polo maidan.

These are mere things, conveyances and animals, associated with Aziz, yet they are also the means by which we can evaluate character, explore thematic implications, and gauge the political implications of the narrative. Pretty amazing achievement with just a few modes of travel.

More importantly, look what's avoided. Dull exposition about character traits. Heavy-handed reminders about what's important. Overt message statements from the author. None of which is dramatic in the least. Action is dramatic. A triumphant ride in a landau, a spirited chukker on the maidan, even a simple bicycle ride. They move. They show the character doing something. And in doing, he reveals elements of himself. That's what novels do: they reveal. They're not very good at explicating, at declaiming, or even at essaying. But they're excellent at revealing. It was a poet, William Carlos Williams, who said, "No ideas but in things," but he could just as well have been talking about novels. Here then, is the Law of People and Things: Characters are revealed not only by their actions and their words, but also by the items that surround them. This last element is often overlooked in creative writing texts, which advise the aspiring fictionist to eschew lengthy explanations of character in favor of revelation through actions and words. Sage advice, as far as it goes, but it needs to go a bit beyond. The things—the trinkets and baubles, the essentials and frills, the tools and toys—associated with a character typically reveal aspects of his personality as well as key ingredients of the story: plot, significance, idea, motif, theme.

Okay, so how does that work?

It's a mystery. Seriously. Lots of theories posited but nothing decisive. I put it under the heading of *deflection of meaning*, by which I mean, broadly, the alchemical process by which a literal thing comes to stand in figuratively for some other thing. This bit of magic is the subject of my previous book, *How to Read Literature Like a Professor*, but this is almost the only time I'll employ it here, and only because it is so critical to the business of creating character. T. S. Eliot, in his essay "Hamlet and His Problems" (1922) and elsewhere, gives us a more or less useful term, the "objective correlative," by which he means the external set of objects that stand in for some internal emotion or condition. The objects provide the concrete, tangible images that allow readers or audiences to grasp the necessarily abstract inner workings of a character. Where Eliot goes wrong, to the extent that he does, is in insisting that the result of the objective correlative is to convey one and only one emotion, so that confusion is impossible. I believe that when very young, Eliot was badly frightened by a double meaning, hence his determination to exert absolute authorial control. Rather, the ambiguity is precisely what intrigues in the objective correlative or character emblem. We can forgive his excess as a product of his age; like so many of the so-called New Critics, he was also a writer, in his case a writer first who was also a critic, and so he and they naturally want to cede power in the writer-reader relationship to the writer, to put the *author* in *authority*. What anyone who came of critical age after about 1965 or so will note, however, is that the balance of power has shifted, that readers are the ultimate arbiters of meaning in a work. Besides, the work becomes so much livelier as a space of engagement when the possibilities are more open-ended, when ambiguity, indeterminacy, and irony are all in play.

Consider Stephen's "ashplant." Joyce gives Stephen Dedalus a walking stick made of ashwood, an object he acquires first in *A Portrait of the Artist as a Young Man* and carries through to *Ulysses*. He employs it sometimes in its designed role, as a cane carried by a young man, sometimes as a fashion accessory, sometimes as a mock sword or a punctuator for his rapier wit, sometimes as a weapon, as when he smashes the chandelier in Bella Cohen's brothel during the hallucinatory Circe episode of the later novel. When he is beaten by the soldiers, Stephen has his ashplant, along with his hat, restored to him by Leopold Bloom. So then, class, what does Stephen's ashplant stand for? Oh, it almost certainly has some Freudian possibilities as a phallic symbol, the more so given the character's doubts about his manhood. And it is without question a crutch of sorts, at times. Is it a device for keeping the world at bay? Probably. Will other readers find other possible explanations and interpretations? Indubitably. Whatever Joyce may have intended, the matter, like the ashplant, is out of his hands. The moment the book was published on February 2, 1922, it ceased to be his and became ours. Thanks all the same, Jim, but further assistance is no longer required of the author; we'll make the decisions from here on out. Writers can suggest meaning and significance, but ultimately, readers make the final call.

And how are those calls made? Let's go back to the case(s) of the flowers. At the start of this chapter, I mentioned two characters with emblematic flowers. There are lots more, of course, but two will suffice.

First, Nero Wolfe. Wolfe has many character emblems, so many in fact that I sometimes think the emblems are a substitute for actual characterization. Perhaps this is generally true of fictional detectives; they're almost always less fully developed than main characters in standard novels, yet they seem to have twice as many tics and signs hanging about them. Wolfe has his great size—a fifth of a ton, we're told in more than one novel—as well as his personal chef, Fritz; his bottles of beer, always delivered to him already opened and waiting; his dislike of personal contact; his rare books; and his clothing, especially his invariably yellow shirts. You can do a good deal with any of them. In fact, I once heard the famous literary biographer Leon Edel hold forth for many minutes on the significance of a writer named Rex (Latin for king) Stout having a hero named Nero (as in the emperor), whose stature at four hundred pounds is well beyond *stout*. See the fun you can have with books? But the one emblem that best defines Wolfe is the orchid. He cultivates them in his rooftop greenhouse. Either they or the greenhouse itself figure into the plots of several of the novels and stories. They seem almost anomalous at first, being so delicate and small, so dainty set against his great girth. But both he and they are hothouse creatures. He almost never leaves the brownstone he calls home. Fresh air is anathema to him. Like them, he requires very precise and careful handling in order to bring out his genius. Moreover, they allow him to express his artistic side, to show a passion completely absent in every other area of his existence. When he is troubled or perplexed, he retreats to the greenhouse to commune with his orchids, nearly the only things in his world with which he is never angry. We could learn the things we know about Wolfe without orchids, but they offer a kind of short-cut to that knowledge, both revealing and reinforcing aspects of his character in ways both tangible and vivid.

And what of Clarissa Dalloway? On a purely practical level, she needs flowers for her party that evening: what, after all, is a gather-ing without a bit of floral decoration? Flowers present lead to flow-ers past and memories of being a girl in flower many years earlier. The imagery is more troubled than with Wolfe's orchids, however—perhaps to be expected of a more complex, layered narrative. Cla-rissa collects the flowers at the shop as promised, of course, and their reflection in a window catches the eye of the doomed, fran-tic ex-soldier Septimus Warren Smith when the car backfires in the street. He can't be sure what the reflection is an image of—a tree perhaps, even the tree behind which his dead comrade Evans hides throughout the day—but he is sure the image is fraught with mean-ing especially for him. Or perhaps merely fraught. And there is a fit-ting image of the reader's enterprise: an image that catches our eye, suggesting some secondary thing of whose meaning we can't quite be certain and whose significance is vague at best. We are forced, like Septimus, to invent, to select for ourselves from a catalog of dim possibilities the one or two most likely or most comforting or perhaps least implausible.

The holder of those flowers is herself a fading bloom, brought low to earth in her own autumn by time and hardship (she now has a bad heart as a result of influenza during the epidemic of 1918). Yet she hearkens back to her own springtime, a season marked with flowers, and to other uses of them, particularly to Sally Seton's arrangement of stemless flower heads floating in a bowl of water, a youthful statement that shocked their elders. Are those shocking flowers emblematic of an equally shocking attraction between the two girls, which found its expression in a single kiss Sally gave Clarissa? Is the brevity of floral life emblematic of the transient nature of Clarissa's own or an ironic commentary on the permanence of relationships, since not only the memories of that long-ago time but the persons involved all reappear during Clarissa's day and evening? Is the obvious sexual nature of flowers, which exist after all not for our pleasure but for propagation of the species, a reminder of human sexual nature as embodied by her blooming daughter, Elizabeth, or a commentary on the diminished (and always ambiguous) sexuality of Clarissa, who, past the age of childbearing, now sleeps alone in a "narrow bed"? Woolf isn't telling. She offers, suggests, intimates, but never explains. As with the stocking Mrs. Ramsay knits in *To the Lighthouse*, of which the critic Erich Auerbach made so much in his famous chapter, "The Brown Stocking," in *Mimesis: The Representation of Reality in Western Literature* (1946), where he observed that there is no "authorized" or authorial reality in this modern novel, as there would have been in a traditional work. Instead, external objects and events stand as mere markers for moments in time and as occasions for the characters' internal realities to assert themselves. Indeed, as with the lighthouse itself, or Mr. Ramsay's peripatetic verse recitations, the brown stocking can and does mean many different things, changing from moment to moment and character to character. The same with Clarissa's narrow bed, or Peter Walsh's pocketknife, or Miss Kilman's shabby mackintosh. So what to make of all those flowers? Woolf prudently leaves that to someone else. Any volunteers?

This is why we readers get the big money. From the merest

threads, from hints and allegations, we weave something we believe to be solid and permanent. We find reality in characters who never existed, find internal motivation and emotion from the things they carry, construct whole people from outlines and sketches. It is, in the language of book reviewers, a bravura performance. Maybe we deserve the royalty checks. Just, for safety's sake, don't hold your breath.

11

Met-him-pike-hoses

"O, ROCKS!" THAT'S WHAT she says, "O, rocks." To what? "The trans-migration of souls." Well, isn't that your reaction? Except that's not what she's responding to. The real question, and real annoyance, is about a word. And maybe about her husband. She's Molly Bloom, the female leading figure (one can hardly call her a heroine) of James Joyce's *Ulysses*. Molly is earthy, musical, chiefly uneducated, intuitive, and unfaithful. Very right-brain, except for the infidel-ity, which is probably lobe-independent. She is the source of the world's most famous fictional monologue (we'll exempt Hamlet here as dramatic), but that's not our subject here. Her husband, Leopold, is the more cerebral of the two by far. He's intellectually curious, philosophically inclined, ineffectual, a great reader. Her literary tastes run more to steamy romances with titles like *Sweets of Sin*, and when she encounters a new word, she turns to her hubby. The word in this case is "metempsychosis," a true jawbreaker meaning, yes, the transmigration of souls, the closest to which she can get, or so he later reports, is met-him-pike-hoses. Not all that bad, really.

Bloom defines it, and she offers the interjection with which I started this paragraph, followed by a request: "Tell us in plain words."

And there, friends and neighbors, is about 90 percent of what we need to know about the Bloom marriage.

Since I've already abused Shakespeare, we might as well trot him out again. To his question, "What's in a name?" we might equally ask, what's in a word? Novels are full of words, of course, but they tend to be on offer in bulk. Novelists get paid, sometimes literally, by the word. And sometimes it feels like it. Think I'm kidding? Read some Thackeray and get back to me. Actually, you can still find open by-the-word payment for short fiction, often from the literary magazines, but the rate of payment is so low that it doesn't threaten anyone's amateur status. Besides, we're not really interested in words by the bin here. More in words by ones and twos.

Sometimes the same word in different contexts. A bit earlier in our novel, Joyce tells us that Bloom "ate with relish the inner organs of beasts and fowls." Contrast that with the F. Scott Fitzgerald short story "May Day," published at almost exactly the same time (appearing in *Tales of the Jazz Age*, also in 1922), where the flappers and fraternity men "ate their buckwheat cakes with relish." Ewww. What, they were out of maple syrup? Here we go, then: one word, two, to my mind, very different revelations about the writer. "Relish" is one of those wonderful English words with two very different meanings: you can relish an opportunity but you shouldn't put relish on it. Right? Joyce clearly knows this doubled meaning and exploits it in his sentence, the very first one in which Bloom appears in the novel, right at the beginning of the "Calypso" episode. He's thinking about that secondary meaning involving diced pickles and mustard. Chiefly, he's thinking that he wants the other one clearly predominant, but if a little of the messy relish hangs around, that could be fun, too. Fitzgerald? Not. How can I say that with such certainty? Word placement, for one thing. Joyce situates it right after the thing it's modifying, "ate." Not "organs," not "fowls." After the verb. To *verb* something—do, watch, listen, eat—with relish is to do it with enthusiasm and energy. Bring a noun into the picture, though, and we might just be talking condiment. In "May Day," the operative phrase is "cakes with relish." That's what the eye perceives and the tongue rejects. At least, mine does. Yes, Fitzgerald may mean, in the first instance, that they, too, "ate" with gusto, but the secondary meaning arrives neck and neck in a photo finish with the primary, and the gusto flies right out the window. Conclusion? Someone here is more precise with language than someone else. It need not work to Joyce's credit; you may see him as excessively concerned with detail or anal or something, Fitzgerald as more relaxed, more open to possibility. Or you may simply put it down to work rates, to Joyce's painstaking composition by accretion, adding as he goes, or to Fitzgerald's frantic pace in those early days, cranking out short story after short story. That's not what I see, but it's anyone's call.

All that from a word. Not word choice even. Just sentence position.

So then, maybe words do matter. In works of literature, no less. Who knew?

On one level, this concept is pretty straightforward. Here's something you'll probably never read in a novel unless you work as an acquisitions editor at a publishing house: the novel's set in some past century; for simplicity's sake, we'll say the nineteenth. Okay, then, words: crinoline, gentility, propriety, soot, stain, buggy. If your novel suddenly drops in the observation that some character is "hard-wired" to behave a certain way, the illusion, what the late John

Gardner called "the vivid and continuous dream" that is fiction, is broken. There are words that are appropriate to our own time that have no place in earlier times, unless they are in quotation marks or used either in irony or to deliberately violate the fourth wall and break the illusion. Gardner himself provides an example. His *Grendel* takes as its anti-hero the monster of *Beowulf*; sure, he eats people and breaks bulls' spines with a single blow, and his fur is often messy with blood and entrails, but he's a fun guy. He's also, of course, a medieval guy who has no access to the twentieth century. Except . . . when he does. In one chapter, Gardner peppers his narration with terms from film and physics: "Cut A," "Time-Space cross-section," and so on. In a conventional historical novel set in the murkier part of the Middle Ages, the monster doesn't get to know such things. Gardner, however, never wrote a conventional anything. His novel is a meditation on heroes and villains and the individual's role in society. He could care about historical "authenticity," but that's not the vivid and continuous dream he seeks to maintain. His monster, as a result of his visit with the dragon (the last evil being Beowulf confronts in the original epic), has become unstuck in time. He knows things he couldn't really know. If he were real. Which, of course . . .

Every writer has signature words and ways of stringing them together. Sometimes a single word is enough to identify a writer. Take the word "abnegation." Please. As you know, I have read rather a lot of books, and I have never found the word "abnegation" in any of them except by one writer. And he uses it a lot. That would be William Faulkner, who finds uses for it, usually with "self-" appended, in more works than one would think possible. It's not in every novel, but it turns up rather frequently. Show me that word in a sentence and I'm guessing Mississippi Bill every time. Now, since that word often turns up somewhere in a sentence with 130 friends, whose order is a bit of a jumble, the guesswork is largely taken out, but you get my point. I could be wrong; I've heard rumors of a use by Melville. "Self-abnegation" means self-denial or even self-sacrifice and shows up in military commendations, particularly the sort given posthumously. Faulkner, of course, has a lot of former military persons in his work, what with General Compson and Major de Spain and Colonel Sartoris and so on, and the notion of service and sacrifice runs strong throughout his work, but he also tends toward a very formal and slightly archaic diction, so that characters with sixth-grade educations sound like Daniel Webster with a drawl.

There are lots of words that indicate Faulkner, noble sounding words in odd combinations or lowly places, as in this passage from *Absalom, Absalom!* (1936).

> . . . *and opposite Quentin, Miss Coldfield in the eternal black which she had worn for forty-three years now, whether for sister, father, or nothusband none knew, sitting so bolt upright in the straight and hard chair that was so tall for her that her legs hung straight and rigid as if she had iron shinbones and ankles, clear of the floor with that air of impotent and static rage like children's feet, talking in that grim haggard amazed voice until at last listening would renege and hearing-sense self-confound and the long-dead object of her impotent yet indomitable frustration would appear, as though by outraged recapitulation evoked, quiet and inattentive and harmless, out of the biding and dreamy and victorious dust.*

Be comforted: that sentence did have a main clause and wasn't simply a fragment of massive proportion. But we'll stick to the interesting part. Who is a "nothusband"? Have you ever thought of children's feet as possessing "impotent" or "static" rage? Really? Not even once? Hemingway (don't worry, he's coming) counseled writers to write with nouns and verbs. Sage advice, mostly. Unless you're Faulkner, who writes with adjectives and says the most amazing things. Think about the "biding," "dreamy," "victorious" dust. How is dust ever victorious or biding, to say nothing of dreamy? The answer is, it never was. Until he made it so. Or "*outraged* recapitulation." Just magnificent. And I, for one, would give up large chunks of my career to have written "that grim haggard amazed voice," although I know I would have lacked the courage to have dropped the commas even had the words occurred to me. The thing is, Faulkner requires a special kind of labor from readers, and I'm not talking here about untangling those gargantuan sentences, although that's labor-intensive as well. What, for instance, does that voice *sound* like, all grim and haggard and amazed? In what way is dust victorious or recapitulation outraged? His out-of-the-blue adjectives and obscure, slightly archaic nouns make us sit up in astonishment, but they also remind us of an obligation. We feel the rightness, the aptness of his descriptors, but then we have to go to work.

Hemingway takes a rather different approach, not how much can I pack in here, but how little can I say? For him, the real drama of life lies in what goes unsaid, the meaning behind our conversations. Everyone knows his simple sentences—a handful of words, subject-verb-object-and-get-out, hardly any adjectives, fewer adverbs, nouns and verbs. I want to talk about his adjectives. They're just as amazing as Faulkner's: "good," "fine," "all right," "swell," "nice."

Wait a minute. What's so special about "nice"? It's not "haggard," or even "victorious."

That, my dear Watson, is what is so remarkable. "Nice" is the dog that didn't bark in the night. Consider his debut novel, *The Sun*

Also Rises (1926). First of all, there's the verisimilitude: Hemingway is capturing the speech of a certain set of people at a specific moment in history. Those people, expatriates from America, chiefly, but also England, hanging out in Paris and Spain and trying to forge new lives amid the personal debris after the Great War, are, like the speaker in T. S. Eliot's "The Waste Land," shoring their fragments against the ruins of a crumbling civilization. More often than not, they speak in those same fragments, little snippets designed to reveal as little as possible. These characters are all damaged goods, riddled with injuries physical and psychological, stripped of illusion about the goodness of humanity or the nobility of the cause, too familiar with emotion and suffering. Jake Barnes's severed male member is only the most spectacular—and representative—damage done by the war. Everyone has suffered and lost, whether friends, sanity, or pieces of bodies or psyches. Their speech, accordingly, is designed to suppress feeling, to reveal as little as possible about their inner lives. Robert Cohn, the friend Jake detests, sins against the tribe in various ways. He's privileged (a Princeton graduate), successful among men still struggling to establish themselves, Jewish among Gentiles, left out of the experience of warfare, excessively earnest, insufficiently guarded. Perhaps worst of all, he says too much.

> *We went out into the street again and took a look at the cathedral.*
> *Cohn made some remark about it being a very good example of*
> *something or other, I forget what. It seemed like a nice cathedral,*
> *nice and dim, like Spanish churches.*

Being too specific or knowing too much is unforgivable. The rules of the group are clear, if unstated: say little, and nothing of substance. "Nice" is good, even "nice and dim," but go no further.

Were people talking this way in the years just after the war? Yes, if they were of a certain age, if they had suffered through the war, and if they were disaffected, alienated, rootless, unhappy. It was a big club. The 1920s may have been, as Fitzgerald named them, the jazz age, but the Hemingway decade could have been called the deracinated age. Not quite the same pop, is it? Still, those were his people: uprooted, footloose, aimless, and quite as self-destructive as Fitzgerald's. But there is more than mere historical accuracy here.

What does "nice" mean? It was "a nice cathedral." What is a nice cathedral? What is one that isn't nice? What does it mean when Lady Brett says of Mike, "He's so damned nice and he's so awful"? Bill says that Brett is "nice," Jake that the count is. People they don't like are occasionally "nice." The *rioja alta* is "nice." Probably the Fundador (a Spanish brandy) is "nice." I don't remember any of the bulls being "nice," but I wouldn't rule it out. But why?

Because it doesn't mean anything. Or rather, because it can mean so many things and yet nothing in particular. Or because it is capable of meaning what it says and also its opposite, depending on context, delivery, and inflection. You can't do that with "red," you know. There's simply no inflection you can give to "red" that will make it mean "green," or even "not red." "Nice," on the other hand, can mean pleasant, diverting, pretty, agreeable, rewarding, or even, in a pinch, nice. It can also mean lousy, distasteful, unpleasant, disagreeable, obnoxious, or any of dozens of other not-nice qualities. Why can it do that? Because, unlike "red," it has no firm meaning in the first place. If I tell you the balloon is red, you have a solid idea at least of the range of possible colors for the balloon. But if I say it's nice, then what? Consider this famous, if generally misquoted, statement from that eminent literary critic, Oliver Hardy: "Well, here's another nice mess you've gotten me into." We tend to remember it as "fine mess," but he evidently never actually said that. Do you think he means "nice"? Or is it more like terrible, awful, sticky, vexatious? If you're Stan Laurel and your pudgy pal says this to you, do you believe you've been complimented? I didn't think so. And anyone who has ever been set up with a blind date knows what "nice" means in that context: your guy (or gal) for the evening is not winning any beauty prizes.

That's Hemingway's "nice," or one of them. And his "pretty" and "good," too. They mean what you make them mean. His prose is the art of the unspoken. Readers sometimes mistake his simplicity of style for simplicity of thought. They do so at their peril. Robert Frost, another deceptively "simple" writer, said he wrote his poems "in parable, so the wrong people won't hear them and so be saved." That explanation will cover Hemingway's case very, um, nicely.

Faulkner is a cascade of information and elaboration, Hemingway a trickle of insinuation and understatement. Ultimately, both Hemingway and Faulkner demand that readers conspire in creating meaning. We may not always think of those two writers as belonging to the same party, but on this point they are pretty unified. Is the narrator (or character) being truthful? Simple? Ironic? Sarcastic? How much? What does that mean? You can see the work involved with "nice" easily enough, where it may mean one of eleventy-three things or their opposite. The decisions are just as demanding about a "grim-haggard-amazed" voice or "victorious" dust. What do they sound like, look like?

This is where reading becomes an active element in creating meaning. Yes, the writer puts the words on the page, but that's only half the story. We're not passive receivers of information in this transaction. Rather, we take those words and make something comprehensible of them, teasing out meanings, building up associations, listening for echoes and innuendoes. We can't do that without writers, naturally. But they also can't do it without us. This isn't quite the tree-falls-in-the-forest question. A novel without readers is still a novel. It has meaning, since it has had at least one reader, the person who wrote it. Its range of meanings, however, is quite limited. Add readers, add meanings. Anyone who has ever taught literature knows this. Book groups know it, too, whether the individual members have considered it or not. If a novel could only have the meaning that the author had imprinted on it, then all readers would passively accept that meaning, or as much of it as they could process. There would be no need for literature classes or discussion groups beyond simple remediation: for those of you who missed the meaning, here's what you weren't clever enough to grasp. That is sometimes the view of beginning literature students. They will come to class and ask, in so many words, "But what does it mean?" as if it can only mean one thing or as if my reading is the only authorized version of the text. And of course there would be no scholarly journals or monographs necessary in literary studies. Okay, so perhaps that's not the worst outcome you've ever heard, but you get the idea.

Want to play a game? From a single page of a single novel we get the following phrases: "the daughter of that house had traversed a desert of sordid misery"; "she herself was nothing of a sybarite"; "she elevated daintiness to a religion; her interior shone with superfluous friction, with punctuality, with winter roses"; "she assimilated all delicacies and absorbed all traditions." Okay, name that tune. What would you say about the writer of these phrases? From some century not our own? From some planet not our own? We can be pretty sure no one wrote those phrases after Hemingway, who murdered them. If I came across them cold, I would probably guess the nineteenth century and England. I would be wrong. Slightly. They are indeed from the same page (277 in my old Modern College Library edition) of Henry James's *The Bostonians*. James, of course, was an American, technically. He lived much of his adult life, however, in Britain as an Englishman; there was a quarter of a century, from 1880 to 1905, during which he did not set foot in the United States. But American nevertheless. James is, to my mind, unique, as much in his way as Twain is in his. No one sounds quite like him, no one strings words together in quite his way. Perhaps no one, even those with the benefit of Freud and Jung, investigates the human psyche with quite the same subtlety, and no one does it with such interestingly convoluted sentences. But even before the sentence level, his word choice and phrasing, his *diction*, mark him out as a special case. You need someone who is a better James scholar than I (not a great challenge) to tell you what that special quality consists of, but I know it when I hear it. There's a kind of magic to the play of words in an author, in part because his or her diction is not like anyone else's. James's magic is not Hemingway's or Faulkner's, nor theirs Laurence Sterne's nor Edna O'Brien's. It's always their own.

Sometimes the magic words are names. Here are two from a novel I'm pretty sure you have not read: Veneering and Podsnap. Sound like a slightly demented home and garden store, don't they? Okay, class, name that writer. As I say, you've probably not read this novel (which is not in the top six of his that might be assigned for course study), but if you've read any of those six, you'll get it. You're right. Again. Nobody, and I mean absolutely nobody, even comes close to the artful inventiveness of Dickensian naming practices. Names have an edge to them. We talked about them just a moment ago as emblems of character, but they have qualities of their own. Weight. Feel. Geometry. They're sharp or boxy or roly-poly. They're evocative. You don't need a description to envision Mr. Pumblechook or

Lady Dedlock; you only hope that when the descriptions come, they match the expectations the names have set up. The novel that gives us the Veneerings and Podsnap is *Our Mutual Friend* (1865), the last novel Dickens completed. I first read it as the seventh and final novel in a course on his later, "social" novels (we skipped *A Tale of Two Cities* as being too unlike the others), so after mucking around the fens and the ruined mansion with Pip and the jail in *Little Dorritt* and the miasma of the Court of Chancery in *Bleak House*, when I came upon "Podsnap," I remember thinking, "of course he is." It's simply perfect. Dickens's names, like his characters, are generally a shade grotesque—just a little deformed or a little outside the normal run of things. Dickens sounds like himself in other ways, naturally, but he most resembles himself in those hilarious, alarming, punning, suggestive names he slings around the necks of his characters.

All of which brings us to the Law of Narrative Diction: By their words shall ye know them. Word choice and placement and combination act to define a writer's style, texture, tone, mood. Everyone has the same language; no two people use it the same way. Sometimes writers don't even use it the same way from book to book.

Try this one on for size: "'Wow! Looks swank!' remarked my vulgar darling squinting at the stucco as she crept out into the audible drizzle and with a childish hand tweaked loose the frock-fold that had stuck in the peach-cleft—to quote Robert Browning." We've got ourselves a two-fer—the main speaker, who is the narrator, and the person, the "vulgar darling," who offers the aesthetic statement. What can we discern here? First of all, that the narrator is someone for whom "wow" and "swank" are vulgarisms lying outside his working vocabulary, although they are very much typical of the speech of the other person in this scene, who says them naturally. He, on the other hand, can speak of an "audible drizzle" and employ "peach-cleft" for a different sort of cleft, one that sweaty frocks might hang up in, as well as writing in an alliterative (squinting . . . stucco, frock-fold) and almost cloyingly poetic way. So we might deduce that she is young and relatively unschooled, as evidenced by that bit of 1950s slang, he older, rather more literate and even literary, if not inevitably in ways that are profitable or even particularly attractive. Would it surprise you to find that her name is Lolita? Yes, that fussy narrative diction and hauteur belong to our favorite child-molestor, Humbert Humbert. I've talked about his hideousness elsewhere. For now we want to notice the brilliance of this nonnative speaker, Vladimir Nabokov, in capturing both the diction of an overeducated immigrant to these shores (not hard, perhaps, since English was his third language) but also the argot of the American teenager circa 1955. His brilliance, for many of us, has to do with his ear for language, for the Americanisms most of us rarely notice. In *Pnin* (1957), for instance, the hapless immigrant professor of the title is confronted by all manner of native speakers—hustlers and sycophants, glory grabbers and social climbers—no two of which sound alike. And in *Pale Fire* (1962), which for many readers stands as his masterpiece, he plays off the immigrant voice of the possibly mad, possibly royal Charles Kimbote against the family and acquaintances of the poet John Shade, again with perfect pitch for the things Americans of various stations and generations do to the Mother Tongue. There are many pleasures along with a few frustrations in reading Nabokov. The frustrations have to do with how much smarter the writer is than the average bear, which includes professors of English. The pleasures lie chiefly in what he can do with language, with *our* language, as he makes it his own playground. The games, the puzzles, the puns, the tricks he can make English do—those are all wonderful. Most wonderful of all, however, is how he can make us sound, how he can capture so perfectly the speech of the new and strange people he found when he discovered America.

Speaking of sound: rocks. Not "fiddlesticks" or "humbug" or "phooey." Rocks. More specifically, "O, rocks." That just says volumes about the speaker. Later on, she'll say a mouthful in her closing soliloquy, but for now, two words suffice. She also has a few things to say about Leopold, who knows words like "metempsychosis" but has a few kinks of his own. Here's Molly's own pronouncement on her husband: "well hes beyond everything I declare somebody ought to put him in the budget." You can't say fairer than that.

12

Life Sentences

"I WANTED TO CAPTURE it all," Faulkner said, "in one sentence, between one Cap and one period." Such stylistic bravado, or perhaps hubris, may not always sit well with readers, who may ask in return, "Why can't he just say it simply? Why can't he be more like Hemingway?" What we discover is that if a novelist is any good, he has a reason for the sentences he writes, and in terms of being simple, even Hemingway didn't write like Hemingway. One of the great joys of the novelist's life is the construction of ambitious, outrageous, magnificent, impossibly coherent sentences. From Fielding to Dickens to Hardy to James to Proust to Fowles to Boyle, writers have been having fun with sentences, and readers have indulged them. Of course, not every writer attacks narrative with long, baroque sentences. On simplicity, more anon. But let us start with the basic premise: you can't write a novel without sentences.

Those sentences, moreover, tell us what sort of writer and what sort of story we're dealing with. Hard-boiled detective novels, those by Robert B. Parker, say, or Rex Stout, tell us a lot about the attitude and psyche of the narrator as well as about the pace of storytelling. Stout's wisecracking, tough-talking narrator, Archie Goodwin, often sounds like he belongs in a different sort of mystery from his cultured, orchid-cultivating boss, Nero Wolfe. On the other hand, Archie is the one who goes out in the world, mixes with the high- and low-life, and gets beaten up and threatened, so it makes sense for him to be streetwise and tough. Here he is in the first Wolfe novel, *Fer-de-Lance* (1934).

> *Miss Barstow invited me to lunch.*
>
> *I liked her better than ever. For ten minutes or so I waited for her in the hall which connected the sunroom with other apartments. When she joined me there she wasn't sore, and I could see why: I hadn't pulled Mrs. Barstow's leg for any of that stuff, she had just handed it to me on a platter, and that wasn't my fault. But how many people in Sarah Barstow's place would have stopped to consider that? Not one in a thousand. They would have been sore anyhow, even if they had realized I didn't deserve it and tried not to show it; but she just wasn't sore.*

Archie definitely has a style. He's a 1930s wiseguy, sure of himself, slangy, down-to-earth, direct. The repetition of "sore"—three times for a word in its nonstandard usage—and phrases like "pulled Mrs. Barstow's leg" and "all that stuff" sets a character type, a period of history, a tone, an attitude. This is a modern American can-do person talking. No nonsense about him, and no fooling him. His sentences here say, "I know people" and "I know myself." He may not be the genius detective, but he's a man to reckon with in his own right.

The contemporary American novelist T. Coraghessan Boyle

calls himself a maximalist, largely based on the hyperinclusive, jazzy, careening-almost-but-not-quite-out-of-control sentences he favors. His sentences mirror his overall narrative approach, which is to know—and employ—everything, as in this beauty from *Drop City* (2003).

> *Reba tried to crack the whip, and of course Alfredo had his nose in everything, and the Krishna cat (Tom Krishna, everyone was calling him now) came out of his Krishna funk long enough to show some real skill with a hammer and saw, and the chicks, all of them, kept putting things in boxes like a disaster-relief crew—but still, it looked as if Drop City was going nowhere right up until the moment the county dicks came up the drive in their county dick cars with the little gumball machines whirring on top and the bulldozers swung in off the highway.*

This sentence meanders and loops around like the marijuana smoke of its characters, from quasi-factual ("Reba tried to crack the whip") to impressionistic ("came out of his Krishna funk") to satirical ("little gumball machines whirring on top") to the plain-speak finality of bulldozers swinging in off the highway—all of it soaked in the attitudes and perspectives (for they are several) of the stoners and dropouts and dreamers who populate the Drop City commune. Over and over again Boyle gives his readers sentences that mimic the larger narrative structure: druggy dreams and half-baked actions are crushed by the bulldozers of reality. No one can experience these sentences and be shocked by where the plot ultimately takes us.

That's actually pretty standard with novels. As readers, we typically know by the end of page one what sort of stylist we're dealing with. Especially when there's only one sentence on page one. But the farther we go in a book, the more certain we become about style. Hemingway, since I've brought him up already, never disappoints. The sentences you see in the opening paragraph will still be there on any page of the novel. This is very near the end of *A Farewell to Arms* (1929); Frederic Henry's baby son has died at birth, and will momentarily be followed by his mother.

> *Now Catherine would die. That was what you did. You died. You did not know what it was about. You never had time to learn. They threw you in and told you the rules and the first time they caught you off base they killed you. Or they killed you gratuitously like Aymo. Or gave you syphilis like Rinaldi. But they killed you in the end. You could count on that. Stay around and they would kill you.*

This is so simple that we might at first take it as simpleminded. In lesser hands, it would be. Here, it's the language of a man of action—soldier, lover, deserter, deviser of a separate peace—bringing his accumulated knowledge of the world to bear on a single moment. He knows two things: Catherine, his beloved, will die, and so will the rest of us, usually too soon. His creator knows something else: Frederic Henry is grieving. He won't say it, won't admit to giving in, won't say, "It's unfair that this war has claimed so many young lives, unfair that my lover and baby are being taken from me, that the love of my life has been forced to desert me, that God is a bully who despises human happiness." He would never say that. But it's in there. What he says is that death is like a pickoff play in baseball, where you're thrown out if you lose focus and stray too far from the bag. That we're given some rudimentary guidelines but never enough to figure life out before we're ripped out of it. That random and cruel fates are visited upon the innocent. Aymo doesn't earn his death; it merely comes. Even Rinaldi, who clearly has had a role in acquiring syphilis, doesn't *contract* it; rather, it's a passive thing that *they* "gave" to him. And who are *they*, anyway? It's not the Italian army, not the Germans, not anyone he knows personally. It could be the Fates, but he doesn't mention them. No, *they* can only be *he*, the entity at whom Frederic Henry is angry. But he doesn't say that. He doesn't even say he's angry. Instead, his tone is quite measured, "You could count on that. Stay around and they would kill you." A careless reader could easily miss what's really at stake here. Anyone can read this passage and get the notion that no one gets out of life alive, but there's a lot more than that going on. Henry, who has earlier walked away from the Italian military and the ill-conceived war, is now walking away from the possibility of a benevolent Creator. How do we know? He tells us in the only adverb in the passage: Aymo is killed "gratuitously." A God who kills gratuitously is no God for him. He'll go it alone from here on out.

That's what you can do with really short, simple, declarative sentences. If you're Hemingway. It's terribly difficult, though, which is why there's so much bad imitation Hemingway out there, including a fair bit of later Hemingway. To write in this style and have it mean something beyond the Dick-and-Jane level, you have to be in complete command of tone, you have to understand the implications of everything you do and do not say, and you have to know, as he does, what lies in that huge mass of iceberg below the surface. It's a kind of magic. Think it's simple? Try it sometime.

Sentence magic has always been at the heart of the novel. Opening my copy of Laurence Sterne's *Tristam Shandy* (1760–1767) at something like random (the break in the spine may invalidate randomness) to a two-page spread in Volume III, Chapter XX (my copy of the 1967 Ian Watt text for Houghton Mifflin follows the first edition, and others will show different volume and chapter enumeration), I find one sentence under ten words: "I enter now directly upon the point," itself a joke, since Tristram almost never enters directly upon any point. And the other sentences on that spread? Try this one, just a couple earlier.

> *I hate set dissertations—and above all things in the world, 'tis one of the silliest things in one of them, to darken your hypothesis by placing a number of tall, opake words, one before another, in a right line, betwixt your own and your reader's conception—when in all likelihood, if you had looked about, you might have seen something standing, or hanging up, which would have cleared the point at once—'for what hindrance, hurt, or harm doth the laudable desire of knowledge bring to any man, if even from a sot, a pot, a fool, a stool, a winter-mittain, a truckle for a pully, the lid of a goldsmith's crucible, an oil bottle, an old slipper, or a cane chair?'—I am this moment sitting upon one.*

Now that's more like it. Sterne is playing one of his favorite games, the sentential organic-form game. The novel is a series of digressions, or perhaps a gigantic digression, for it's not clear that, whatever the ostensible purpose of Tristram's narrative, he ever achieves it. He can't even get himself born for several hundred pages, a serious blemish in an "autobiography." The plot of the story is nearly nonexistent, the telling largely backwards or sideways in time, and the resolution a punch line. Sterne's real business is sending up the barely established conventions of this new form, the novel. He is first among novelists to recognize and parody narrative practices, and one of his chief forms of parody is to delay or even deny entirely the fulfillment of readers' expectations. So the sentence interruption acts as a localized form of the interruptions in the larger narrative. Both are goofy, frustrating, intrusive, often irrelevant, and very, very funny.

And that's the point, or at least one point, of style: it should have something to do with the story that's being told. That something may relate to the content or the chosen form or the attitude (or needs) of the narrator, but there should be some sort of relation between the larger narrative design and the design of sentences. Too often, as any creative writing teacher can attest, apprentice writers can't make those connections. Students are saddled with a style that is theirs either by default or by adoption because they're in thrall to some great writer.

I say this as a recovering Lawrentian. As an undergraduate, I read more D. H. Lawrence than is good for anyone. At least I have an excuse: his fiction was my thesis subject. Still, the stylistic effects were pernicious, or at least occasionally obnoxious. All that repetition, all that thumping a point to death. The shrillness, the stridency. Oh well, part of being a student is trying on different masks, even badly fitting or poorly made ones. But here's the real crime in my stylistic slavishness: neither my essays nor my fiction had any *need* of the Lawrence touch. I couldn't have written *Women in Like*, much less *Love*, and without Lawrence's genius, one is best off leaving his style alone. In his creative writing text, *Three Genres*, Stephen Minot employs the term "mock-Faulkner" for a certain kind of overwrought short story that attempts to pack all the action of a Faulkner novel—two murders, incest, rape, a kidnapping, three fires, and several outrageous racist incidents—into twenty-five hundred words, broken into maybe five sentences. Those stories would be comic masterpieces if the writers had any self-awareness of what

they were doing, but they never do. These days it may be Jack Kerouac (a hardy perennial) or Toni Morrison or Alice Walker being
inadvertently mocked, but the most likely inspiration for bad apprentice prose has never changed since about 1927.

Why does Hemingway bring out the worst in so many writers?
And we're not talking just students here. Browse the mystery section
of the local book emporium, and what's the dominant style? Sure, it's
watered down, puffed up, denatured, ineptly managed, loose in the
stays, but you recognize it. There's that tight-lipped, clipped diction,
subject-verb-(maybe)object, seven- to ten-word sentence, over and over
again. Noun and verb and *and*. Very few adjectives and fewer adverbs.
A vocabulary the size of a Dr. Seuss primer. Maybe one out of ten is
worth the bother of reading. Maybe. So what's the problem? I think
it's that Hemingway looks easy: hey, I could write those sentences.
And it's true. I (or you) could write those sentences. They just wouldn't
mean much. Hemingway's sentences typically say very little. Their
meaning, however, speaks volumes. Contradiction, you say? Very well,
then, contradictory it is. His meaning isn't in the words, but in the
silence around them. To accomplish this requires two things most of
us don't have enough of: linguistic sensitivity and great discipline. He
is absolutely scrupulous about what word he uses in any context and
about how many. He pares his language down to the starkest minimum, leaving out everything that doesn't scream to be left in. Most
of us can't do that. We don't have enough self-control.

So, long sentences, short sentences, simple, complex, mixed. They
come in all forms. Which forms are right? The ones that work. The
Law of Novelistic Style: There are no rules for sentence length and
structure except those dictated by the novel in which they're used.
And they generally do. We're happiest when we can make those connections between style and story.

I may have given the wrong impression of writers' involvement with style, since this discussion would seem to suggest that every novelist is a consummate stylist, or is at least consumed with style. Yet I would hazard a guess that the vast majority of novelists have written their sentences under the rubric, *just get on with it*. Certainly the vast majority of novels display a merely serviceable, if that, prose. Not that there's anything wrong with that. We think of Henry James, and rightly, as one of the great innovators of fiction at both the macro and micro levels. But another of his great contemporaries, William Dean Howells, hardly ever wows anyone with the magic of his sentences. This if from *The Rise of Silas Lapham* (1885), again, pulled more or less at random.

> *The next day the head book-keeper, who lunched at the long counter of the same restaurant with Corey, began to talk with him about Lapham. Walker had not apparently got his place by seniority; though with his forehead, bald far up toward the crown, and his round smooth face, one might have taken him for a plump elder, if he had not looked equally like a robust infant. The thick drabbish yellow mustache was what arrested decision in either direction, and the prompt vigor of all his movements was that of a young man of thirty, which was really Walker's age.*

So, you ask, what's wrong with that? Not a thing in the world. It does its job, which is to carry narrative forward, without tripping over itself or otherwise impeding the business at hand. In other words, it is serviceable, which is ever Howells's goal for prose. If it doesn't sing, that's because he doesn't intend it to. Remember, too, that Howells was no slouch: intimate of Mark Twain and Henry James, biographer of Lincoln, U.S. consul to Venice, editor for a decade of *The Atlantic Monthly*, best-selling novelist and all around literary lion. If serviceable is what he wants from his prose, and if, moreover, it's what he gets, who's to squawk?

Or take his near-contemporary Arnold Bennett. Bennett writes of his native England rather than the America of Howells, but the approach is similar.

> *And then, on this last day of the year, the second year of her shame and of her heart's widowhood, Mr. Scales had reappeared. She had gone casually into the shop and found him talking to her mother and Mr. Povey. He had come back to the provincial round and to her. She shook his hand and fled, because she could not have stayed. None had noticed her agitation, for she had held her body as in a vice. She knew the reason neither of his absence nor of his return. She knew nothing.*

Again, nothing defective here, just solid, workmanlike prose. Bennett was a businessman of literature, writing reviews, essays, fiction that would sell, anything that kept the till active. He lived from, rather than for, his art, which made him a natural whipping boy for the modernist hotshots. He's the model for the character in Ezra Pound's "Hugh Selwyn Mauberley" who tells the young man to give up poetry because there's no money in it. And Virginia Woolf excoriates him in her essay "Mr. Bennett and Mrs. Brown" for, well, chiefly for belonging to the immediately prior generation. Even while indicting him, however, for his shortcomings, she admits that he is highly competent (indeed, his competence is part of the indictment—how dare he be a good craftsman?). What she dislikes in him, as in H. G. Wells and John Galsworthy, is that his work lacks the aspiration to rise to the level of art. He's a *materialist* (her word), satisfied with craft. I share her impatience with Bennett's fiction, but I've always suspected that the fault lay in me rather than in him. What we might say is that, on the stylistic level, he seeks the adequate. He wants sentences that will carry his meaning and otherwise stay out of the way. Rarely will readers stop in midchapter to admire a brilliant sentence that has called attention to itself. Bennett doesn't want sentences calling attention to themselves, and that's fine.

In fact, it's better than fine. Bennett and Howells write prose that is *right* for their fiction. Sentences that arrest readers' attention disrupt the narrative flow in ways that run counter to the interest of these novelists. For both of them, the instructions they would give their prose would be, as I suggested earlier, *just get on with it*. Do the business. Don't be showy or ostentatious.

Precisely what a lot of readers want.

I recently had a conversation with a colleague about Julian Barnes and how terrific his sentences can be. Real showstoppers. We both like that in him, but I had to point out that I often find that students disagree. They tend on the whole to prefer a *transparent* style, one they can forget about as they can forget about the glass pane in a modern window. It's much easier to get student readers to like Willa Cather than William Faulkner, and that's largely due to the difficulties of the Faulknerian sentence.

Come to think of it, if I make a list of my novelistic pantheon, two of the things that unite a lot of them would be that they all are, or at least can be, wonderful writers at the sentence level and that most of them can be a tough sell in the classroom: Joyce, Lawrence, Woolf, Faulkner, Hemingway, Hardy, Lawrence Durrell, John Fowles, Gabriel García Márquez, Toni Morrison, Pynchon, Barnes, the Swifts Jonathan and Graham, T. C. Boyle, Flann O'Brien,

Henry Green, Louise Erdrich. Edna O'Brien is one of the great stylists in English, yet I often get the sense from readers that they like her in spite of her prose rather than because of it. It may be in part an American mistrust of showiness or a post-Hemingway slant toward simplicity or merely a wish for the easily digestible—a high style requires a bit of chewing. But a really good style—whether it's Hemingway's or O'Brien's, Pynchon's or Durrell's—is a pleasure in itself. At least for some of us.

This business of high style also points toward what matters for the novelist. It suggests the novel isn't entirely about the story being told, or that the *story*, the stuff that happens, is being enhanced by the manner of the telling, that some elements will matter more than others because of how the thing is told. Hardy's sentences are one of several factors that limit the kinds of stories he can tell, but oh, what he can do with the ones he does tell. Style—sentences, their length and structure and arrangement, paragraphs, word choice, word order, the lot—isn't mere makeup, covering and coloring the narrative. Rather, it is a decisive element in that narrative, governing or reflecting what can be told and how, the rate of revelation, the attitude of the novelist toward his world, the relationship of writer to reader. Sentences can welcome us or rebuff us, but they always make a statement.

Now, that Faulknerian monstrosity. It comes from *Go Down, Moses*, and runs for a zillion pages in my edition. Arising in the middle of the story "The Bear," it attempts to capture, if not the world, the whole sordid history of the slave-owning South. The section begins simply enough, with an uncapitalized initial letter in what would be a sentence, and then launches into another sentence that runs approximately forever.

then he was twenty-one. He could say it, himself and his cousin
juxtaposed not against the wilderness but against the tamed land
that was to have been his heritage, the land which old Carothers
McCaslin his grandfather had bought with white man's money
from the wild men whose grandfathers without guns hunted it,
and tamed and ordered or believed he had tamed and ordered it
for the reason that the human beings he held in bondage and in
the power of life and death had removed the forest from it and
in their sweat scratched the surface of it to a depth of perhaps
fourteen inches in order to grow something out of it which had
not been there before and which could be translated back into the
money he who believed he had bought it had had to pay to get it
and hold it and a reasonable profit too . . .

Whew! And that's just the start. It goes on for pages and pages
and pages. It even has paragraph breaks, and dialogue, and the occasional full-stop, although those periods are part of a character's
statement rather than of the narrative. For me, this is one of the
great performances in all of fiction. The only problem is, I don't
know where it ends. Or begins, really. The section begins and ends
without a capital or period, so we might see the entire thing as a
single utterance, a kind of freak sentence, an interior monologue
going on forever but taking the form of one statement. Or do those
periods within the passage actually constitute some sort of sentence
changeover? I just can't tell.

Of course, first-time readers generally have a different question.
Why?

Isaac McCaslin has been reading his grandfather's farm ledgers
regarding all aspects of plantation business—including the buying,
selling, and misusing of human beings. He's from Mississippi, so

the concept of slavery itself isn't shocking to him. What is shocking is that he finds that his grandfather, old Carothers McCaslin, has fathered a child with one of his slaves, Eunice, and then later fathered another child—with that first child, Tomasina. Eunice, the mother/grandmother, has subsequently drowned herself six months before the child, Terrel or Tomey's Turl, is born, to which Ike's father's (Theophilus) only comment is to record the death as another loss of property. His more "humane" brother, Amodeus (Uncle Buddy) circles over the fact of that death, ultimately wondering whoever heard of a slave "drownding him self?" All of this is what Ike finds shocking: the compounded horrors of not only using slave women against their will for sexual pleasure but of practicing incest into the bargain, the callousness of the grandfather's response, the depths of despair that led to Eunice's suicide, the death in childbed of Tomasina, the routine, unthinking inhumanity of his father and uncle, both of whom were sufficiently progressive to have freed their own slaves before the Civil War, the inevitable intertwining of races into a single, enormously dysfunctional family. In other words, everything Faulkner wants us to understand as the terrible, logical outcome of owning other human beings. Which is to say, everything about the history of the South. And he wants to do it all at once, to capture Ike's moment of epiphany.

See? You can't even write about the book without having sentences lead into a morass. And for Faulkner to tell it, it's a sixty-page-long sentence fragment. When "The Bear" is published as a stand-alone story, section four is nearly always omitted, and for good reason. We need the context of its novel to make sense of it. The writer may have claimed to want to capture the whole world between a capital letter and a period, but section four has no cap at the beginning and no period at the end. Nor it is entirely clear that any of the periods or question marks—and they are few—in the section actually break the flow of this torrent of words.

So whether it's three words by Hemingway or thirty-five pages by Faulkner, a sentence—or fragment—can tell us a lot more than it says. Which do I prefer? Neither. Both. The one that does the job. But here's the thing. That job is inextricably linked to its pieces. The novel will dictate what sort of sentences it requires; the sentences will determine the sort of novel that can be written. Hemingway's books embody a cultural amnesia, or maybe a desire for short-term memory loss. Who would want to remember the terrible events of this century, this war? Faulkner's articulate a war between nostalgia and revulsion, a wish for a stable past containing horrors that he cannot avoid confronting. His aim is to include, to draw from everywhere, Hemingway's to exclude, to keep at arm's length. No surprise, then, which one would write complicated prose, which one simple. Their sentences are nothing alike, except for one thing: they're perfect.

13

Drowning in the Stream of Consciousness

ONCE UPON A TIME, narrative was simple. You said what characters did, you quoted their dialogue, and, if need be, you told what they thought: "This is easy, Joe thought, as he ambled down the quay." The only tricky thing here is knowing what a quay is. But then, as Virginia Woolf points out, "On or about December 1910, human nature changed." Certainly the novelist's relationship to consciousness did. As a result of huge changes in the scientific and philosophical understanding of the mind—the by-products of work by Freud and Jung and William James and Henri Bergson (who won a Nobel Prize in *literature*)—the depiction of consciousness became much more fluid. And messy. As a movement, stream of consciousness had a short tenure, only three decades or so. Yet it helped to define the modern novel, change how later writers approached character, and bewilder generations of English classes. But we'll be bewildered no more.

Or maybe just a little.

So what is this beast, stream of consciousness? Oh, that's easy:

it doesn't exist. Lot of help, right? Nevertheless, it's true: there is no single thing to which we can point and say, "Stream of consciousness." There are a lot of works that *seem* to fit the notion, but they're hardly all doing the same thing. It's a lot like obscenity: no one can define it, but everyone thinks he knows it when he sees it. Okay, we have something that may not exist, that no one has satisfactorily defined, that existed only briefly, and that tends to confuse readers. Where do I go to sign up? And can it possibly matter?

Oh, yes, it matters greatly. On one level it matters because of all those bigwigs of modernism who attempted new things. They came, they went. But something stayed behind, and that something matters. Prior to the start of all this—let's take Woolf's 1910, plus or minus a few—readers and writers could automatically expect a certain level of authority in the telling of a tale. There was a narrative center that existed outside the characters in the tale. That center is easiest to see in the omniscient narrators of the great Victorian novels, whether *Bleak House* or *Vanity Fair* or *Middlemarch*. There is clearly an intelligence that exists external to the story, one that shapes the story and says, in effect, "We exist outside this story, but through my agency, we can go not only into the story but into the thoughts of the characters at will. That is, at *my* will." That outside center, however, also exists in the first-person narratives. Outside? Of course, outside. The Pip who narrates *Great Expectations* is clearly separate from the child Pip who stumbles into the clutches of Magwitch at the novel's opening. Most of his life to date has taken place in the intervening years. But he's also separate from the Pip who talks to Joe Gargery about being a gentleman late in the novel and who has his final, memorable meeting with Estella. The narrating Pip exists both outside and after those character Pips. How can we be sure? Verb tense. The past tense of the narrative—not simple present or some progressive form—argues for distance from the events and the self within the narrative.

So? How does that make a difference? It means everything we know about the character, and especially everything we know *from* the character is *mediated*. There's a conscious presence imposed between us and young Pip or Esther Summerson filtering their thoughts—selecting, arranging, rewording—so that we *know* them only in this shaped, rather distant form. For all their variety, the one thing common to stream-of-consciousness novels is their desire to do away with that mediation, to get not merely close to but inside the characters' heads.

Swell idea, but where's the road map? As it turns out, the woods in 1900 were just full of cartographers.

As I said before, there is no single technique known as "stream of consciousness." Rather, we use the term, very loosely, to describe the effects produced by a number of techniques, and more generally to describe a certain type of fiction that seeks to reproduce consciousness in all its complexity and with a minimum of narrative mediation. And while they differ considerably from one another, they have this in common: the loss of a narrative center outside character. Instead, narration began to find a home within characters' minds, and not always the minds of which they were aware. Because, as it turns out, "mind" gives way to "consciousness," and consciousness is composed of multiple levels.

Pretty much everybody seems to have had this idea of depth at the same time. The term first arises in William James's work *The Principles of Psychology* (1890), where he prefers it to "train" or "chain" of consciousness. The fluidity and continuum of depths suggested by "stream" make it more nearly ideal as a descriptor of James's notion of consciousness. Some of his brother Henry's late works begin to explore consciousness as operating simultaneously on a variety of levels, although none of them could be properly described as stream-of-consciousness novels. So far so good, right?

But here's the thing: it had already begun to exist in practice. Two years earlier, Édouard Dujardin did something remarkable in his short novel, *Les lauriers sont coupé* (the first English translation: *We'll to the Woods No More*, the second, *The Bays Are Sere*—clearly imprecise renderings). He employed, for the first time I believe, a technique that is recognizable as *interior monologue*. It's a lot like a regular monologue except that it is unspoken, inside the head, and largely unshaped. What Dujardin recognizes at once is that thoughts go where they will, leap in ways that defy logic, and take on a life of their own.

> *A drop of wine. Empty, the seats opposite; between the seat and the mirror, leather upholstery. I must see what happens with a note—anyway. My card-case; my address card, that's more suitable; my pocket-pencil; very well. What shall I put? A rendezvous for tomorrow. I must indicate several. If that solid solicitor knew what I was up to! I write: 'Tomorrow, at two, in the reading room of the Magasin du Louvre . . .' The Magasin du Louvre, not very chic, but still the most convenient; and then, or somewhere else? The Louvre? go on with you! At two o'clock. Need to allow enough time; at least from two till three; that's it; I change 'at' to 'from' and I'm going to add 'until three'. Next 'I . . . I will wait for you . . .' No, 'I will wait'; that's it; let's see.*

Perhaps not surprisingly for an experimental work, Dujardin's novel lapsed into neglect and was largely forgotten in 1902 when Joyce stumbled across a copy in a bookseller's shop in Tours, France.

The impact is undeniable, for despite a twenty-year gap, Joyce copies Dujardin's style exactly for many of Leopold Bloom's monologues in *Ulysses.*

Didn't catch me napping that wheeze. The quick touch. Soft mark. I'd like my job. Valise I have a particular fancy for. Leather. Capped corners, riveted edges, double action lever lock. Bob Cowley lent him his for the Wicklow regatta concert last year and never heard tidings of it from that good day to this.

 Mr Bloom, strolling towards Brunswick street, smiled. My missus has just got an. Reedy freckled soprano. Cheeseparing nose. Nice enough in its way: for a little ballad. No guts in it. You and me, don't you know? In the same boat. Softsoaping. Give you the needle that would. Can't he hear the difference? Think he's that way inclined a bit. Against my grain somehow. Thought that Belfast would fetch him. I hope that smallpox up there doesn't get worse. Suppose she wouldn't let herself be vaccinated again. Your wife and my wife.

Part of being a genius is knowing when you've found a winner. What the interior monologue does for Joyce is allow him—and us—to follow the meanderings of his characters, especially Leopold Bloom, who is a world-class meanderer. Of his wife Molly, more anon.

The intellectual sanction for this new fiction is largely derived from the work of French philosopher Henri Bergson. In works such as *Matter and Memory, Laughter,* and *Time and Free Will,* Bergson lays out a theory of mind, memory, and the subjective experience of time that gives free reign to the novelistic explorers of consciousness.

At the center of experience in the "new" fiction is memory. Bergson distinguishes between *mémoire volontaire*, which is a product of reason and will, the portion of memory we can control, and *mémoire involontaire*, which is the part writers can make use of. This latter is capricious, flowing uncertainly, never quite graspable. We see when we look at writing by Joyce or Woolf, for instance, just how much of memory is involuntary, how little control we have over the images that float to the surface, often to haunt or mock us.

Another key notion is *la durée*, or durational time. As opposed to clock time or metronomic time, humans experience time subjectively, so that moments are almost infinitely elastic, as in the instant before the car crash when one "sees" one's life flash before one's eyes. The notion of durational time, curiously enough, is picked up by the *imagist* poets for their tiny creations and by novelists with ambitions as large as the author of *Ulysses* and *Finnegans Wake*. In the practice of fiction, durational time allows for almost limitless exploration of a single moment, as the mind can be functioning on a host of levels and covering a wide array of subjects all at once as time seems, at least sometimes, to stand still.

The change in the narrative presence is most notable in the stream-of-consciousness novel. This is not to suggest, however, that narrators disappear entirely; rather, the narrator ceases to act as mediator or filter for the characters' thoughts and acts more as presenter or conduit for direct transcription, with little or no authorial commentary. Where Dickens would tell us what someone was thinking and what it might mean or portend, Faulkner or Joyce give us not only the thoughts (the word suggesting an awareness and even a control by the character), but the whole jumble of thought, instinct, pre-thought, reflex, and response to stimulus to which the character is subject. In stream-of-consciousness fiction a character's thoughts are presented directly, without mediation by an intrusive narrator; he speaks, as it were, to himself. Hence the use of contractions and of the second person. The effect of the latter is to give what is said a more general significance, the speaker assuming that his reactions and thoughts do not hold for him alone but for any human being.

If the entire history of stream of consciousness had been a failure, it would have been redeemed by a single section of a single novel. In fact, this section may be why the entire field developed. In the trade the episode, which begins and ends with the word "yes," is called Penelope, but Penelope has nothing to do with its brilliance. It's all about Molly:

> *they might as well try to stop the sun from rising tomorrow the sun shines for you he said the day we were lying among the rhododendrons on Howth head in the grey tweed suit and his straw hat the day I got him to propose to me yes first I gave him the bit of seedcake out of my mouth and it was leapyear like now yes 16 years ago my God after that long kiss I near lost my breath yes he said I was a flower of the mountain yes so we are flowers all a womans body yes that was one true thing he said in his life and the sun shines for you today yes that was why I liked him because I saw he understood or felt what a woman is and I knew I could always get round him and I gave him all the pleasure I could leading him on till he asked me to say yes and I wouldnt answer first only looked out over the sea and the sky I was thinking of so many things he didnt know of Mulvey and Mr Stanhope and Hester and father and old captain Groves and the sailors playing all birds fly and I say stoop and washing up dishes they called it on the pier and the sentry in front of the governors house with the thing round his white helmet poor devil half roasted and the Spanish girls*

laughing in their shawls and their tall combs and the auctions in
the morning the Greeks and the jews and the Arabs and the devil
knows who else from all the ends of Europe and Duke street and
the fowl market all clucking outside Larby Sharons and the poor
donkeys slipping half asleep and the vague fellows in the cloaks
asleep in the shade on the steps and the big wheels of the carts of
the bulls and the old castle thousands of years old yes and those
handsome Moors all in white and turbans like kings asking you to
sit down in their little bit of a shop

For forty-five tightly packed pages. Molly's soliloquy is the
most amazing literary achievement I know of. Her whole life is in
there—past, present, and future; attitudes, considerations of career,
and love life; her menstrual cycle; everything. What's more amazing
is that people often think at first glance they can't read it: it's too
dense, too allusive, to scary, too something. In reality, though, it's
really pretty simple. These are the nocturnal, sleepy-but-not-asleep
musings of a passionate, not terribly well educated, proud, loving,
talented woman. She's at the end of a very long, taxing day. We've
been following her husband through funeral and newspaper office
and music room and pub and brothel, but she's been busy in her own
right. Her current lover, Blazes Boylan, has made love with her in
the afternoon. She's been preparing for a series of singing engage-
ments. She has begun her period. And she's had her sleep interrupted
when Bloom arrives home with a very drunken Stephen Dedalus
in tow. Given these conditions, her monologue makes perfect sense
and is actually not difficult to follow. On some levels, it may be the
simplest thing in the book, since it's pure interior monologue, so we
don't move between narration or description, dialogue, and thought.
Instead, we're in there and we're staying.

Virginia Woolf practices her own form of consciousness narration, and in each book it differs somewhat from what she's done elsewhere. James Naremore in *The World Without a Self: Virginia Woolf and the Novel* (1973) points out that "stream of consciousness" is not entirely adequate to describe what Woolf attempts in *Mrs. Dalloway*, preferring instead "indirect interior monologue," a variant of "free indirect discourse." This jawbreaker of a term refers to a special mode of third-person viewpoint in which the narration takes its cues from the consciousness of the character so it's quite close to but not quite first person. You can think of it as the language the character might use if she could get outside her own consciousness to articulate it. Needless to say, the ironic possibilites are legion. This distinction would be equally true for *To the Lighthouse* or indeed most of her mature work. There's really nothing in the way of direct interior monologue as it appears in Joyce or Dujardin. Rather, it is filtered through a narrative presence whose chief job is to change the first-person "I" to a third-person "he" or "she." Hence the "indirect" part of Naremore's characterization.

One of Woolf's abiding concerns is the degree to which characters are connected psychologically and linguistically. This is in part an outgrowth of the philosophy of G. E. Moore, under whom the Bloomsbury males studied at Cambridge. Woolf was excluded from that experience because of her gender, of course, but she absorbed much of what she learned from her brother Thoby; her husband, Leonard; and her other friends. The part of Moore's thought she's particularly interested in here are his ideas on friendship, so much so that by the time she writes *The Waves* in the 1930s, characters' monologues are impossible to separate entirely one from another. A professor of mine once said that he thought any monologue belonged only about 80 percent to the character who voiced it and the remaining 20 percent to the other friends. She's only beginning to explore that possibility in *Mrs. Dalloway*, although we see some of it in Clarissa's time together with Peter Walsh, for instance.

Consider this passage from *To the Lighthouse*.

> *While he walked up the drive and Lily Briscoe said yes and no and capped his comments (for she was in love with them all, in love with this world) he weighed Ramsay's case, commiserated him, envied him, as if he had seen him divest himself of all those glories of isolation and austerity which crowned him in youth to cumber himself definitely with fluttering wings and clucking domesticities. They gave him something—William Bankes acknowledged that; it would have been pleasant if Cam had stuck a flower in his coat or clambered over his shoulder, as over her father's, to look at a picture of Vesuvius in eruption; but they had also, his old friends could not but feel, destroyed something. What would a stranger think now? What did this Lily Briscoe think? Could one help noticing that habits grew on him? eccentricities, weaknesses perhaps? It was astonishing that a man of his intellect could stoop so low as he did—but that was too harsh a phrase—could depend so much as he did upon people's praise.*

This passage has numerous telling features of the Woolf style: a wide range of topics that barely hang together, parenthetical insertions, sometimes using dashes instead of parentheses, question marks in mid-sentence positions, a sliding narrative center (is a specific thought coming from William Bankes or Lily Briscoe?), and as a source of that sliding quality an indirect way of revealing thought. The thought flows from character, but we're never sure how directly or what degree of mediation has been practiced in conveying that thought.

It's a mystery, always, and a good one. So here's the Law of Streaming Narrative: All representations of consciousness are arbitrary and artificial. It's impossible to see into another mind, so writers therefore employ devices that create the illusion of consciousness. It's the same as any other sort of narration. Omniscience doesn't exist among humans, yet we accept the illusion of it in fiction. The "limited" or "sympathetic" viewpoint is an imaginative construct, not a journalistic reality. With all these approaches, we suspend what we know, namely, that they are untrue to our experience of the world, in favor of the possibility that they will help us arrive at something we desire, whether that is insight into the human condition or pleasurable reading. We're neither dupes nor dopes. Rather, we want something the writer has to offer, and we agree to play along with her game in order to acquire that something. It's not about what's "easy" or "hard" but about what achieves the mutual ends of both participants in this transaction. We're even willing to meet new and challenging demands, sometimes, if the rewards are great enough. The demands of stream-of-consciousness fiction were steep, so not all that many readers were willing, at least initially, to meet the challenge. Time, however, has shown that those writers were onto something. Responding to the new psychology and the new philosophy, they created in their turn new fiction that gave insights into the workings of the mind that no earlier techniques had ever provided. Not a bad day's work.

Woolf and Joyce, Faulkner and Dorothy Richardson, Djuna Barnes and maybe John Dos Passos. There are a few others, but the club that could be stream-of-consciousness writers was never large. So why all the fuss? Not because of how many imitators they inspired, but because of how their techniques influenced other writers. Novelists found new ways of presenting consciousness because of the daring experiments of a few pioneers. If no one after them writes stream of consciousness, it's because everyone after them does. Writers as various as Lawrence Durrell, Margaret Atwood, Graham Swift, Anthony Burgess, Henry Green, Edna O'Brien, and John Updike can pick and choose among the techniques developed by Woolf and Co., employing the devices within otherwise comparatively stable and even conventional narrative frameworks. We don't have to be Einstein, thank heaven, to have access to relativity; he did the heavy lifting for us.

Oh, right, a quay? Just a dock that knows somebody. Which leads me to . . .

14

The Light on Daisy's Dock

HERE'S ONE THING I learned teaching introductory creative writing: would-be fictionists don't understand character. When I would give the first characterization assignment, I always got back the same thing—height, weight, hair color and length or lack, size of nose, shape of mouth, number of freckles. The full package. You could take the details and paint a life-size portrait. You could, I couldn't, but that's a function of artistic ability, not lack of student description. What I could do, however, was hand the character sketches back with this question: what does Huck Finn look like? Or Jake Barnes? Or even Emma Bovary?

The answer is, we don't know. Sometimes, as with Huck, we haven't been told; he lacks sufficient self-awareness to bother describing himself. We know about Jake's signature war wound, since it matters so much to the story, but not much else about his appearance. And Flaubert, for all his exact rendering of detail, can't even settle on Emma's eye color, which leads to the riff on Enid Starkey in Julian Barnes's *Flaubert's Parrot*. Sometimes Emma's eyes are black, or sort of blue in certain light, or maybe brown if looked at just so. Starkey, a real Flaubert scholar, took him to task on the shifting iris coloration, and Barnes's protagonist, Geoffrey Braithwaite, in turn takes her to task for her shortcomings. But looks ultimately don't matter all that much. In order to understand Braithwaite—or Huck, Jake, or Emma—we don't need to know what they look like.

We need to know what they want.

Take Emma's eyes. Maybe a bit vague or inconsistent. Still, we have a pretty good idea about her eyes, really, but it's not the eyes that matter. We're not her lovers; we're her readers. We're looking to understand her, not fall in love. What matters for Jim is not how he drives forward but what drives him forward. Again, I say, we need to know what they want. Really, really *want*.

And usually, we know what they want by what they obsess on. If I were to ask ten people to name one object from *The Great Gatsby*, nine of them would come up with the same item—even if they hadn't read the title of this chapter. There it is, that green light on the end of Daisy Buchanan's dock, commanding Jay Gatsby's rapt attention and presiding over Nick Carraway's final paragraph. This thing, the object that drives him forward to calamity, stands for everything that's wrong with him, and also what's right—his capacity for self-delusion, his ability to hope, his belief that some things, some people, no matter how flawed, are worthy figures of the Dream. It's quite literally the last *thing* we see in the novel, before those phantom boats driving against the current. Fitzgerald was taking no chances that we might miss his point.

That point is central for writers, and hence for readers, the Law of Character Clarity: To understand characters, you have to know their deepest desires. More often than not, that desire finds an emblem—an object or action—to give it tangible expression.

Since we're out on the water's edge, consider another longing gaze, this one directed out to sea from the Cobb, a long, snaking pier at Lyme Regis, toward a man the gazer knows is never coming back. The Cobb is actual and historical, the woman fictitious, the man perhaps a figment of *her* imagination. She is Sarah Woodruff, the elusive if titular female in John Fowles's *The French Lieutenant's Woman* (1969). Why would a woman spend her off hours scanning the waters for a French officer who, if he ever existed, is certain not to return? Why would a woman in 1867, the year in which the novel is set, subject herself to the community disapproval resulting from this unseemly (and therefore obviously sexual) display of romantic grief? Ah, there's the question that drives the novel and to which Fowles never provides a clear answer. Is it deliberate debasement, a desire to incur social opprobrium, a suicidal impulse, inconsolable romantic mourning, pure existential misery, self-dramatized posturing, out-and-out madness? Whichever view one ultimately takes— and there are adherents to each of those possibilities within the narrative—will decide how one feels about Sarah and about the novel. The options are nearly endless, but the gesture itself is abundantly clear. What *your* experience of the novel is like will depend greatly on what you believe Sarah is looking at, or looking for, or looking out for, out on the Cobb. Of course, she's not the only or even the main character, even if she does own the title. Charles Smithson holds that distinction, and he has wants of his own. One of those desires turns out to be Sarah Woodruff. Charles doesn't even know this, or if he does, he spends great energy on denying it, for much of the novel. We have to figure this out for ourselves as we watch him clamber over the cliff faces in search of his fossils, his "tests," referring, in this case, to fossilized shells of sea creatures. Do you think that's all that Fowles means? Charles is a hunter, of fossils first of all and of the mysterious Sarah later, but most of all of meaning. His life fills him with ennui and a vague but inescapable sense of pointlessness. Although as a Victorian man he lacks the vocabulary to express it, he is living out the existentialist crisis, confronting absurdity and nothingness in cravat and dundrearies.

Okay, I promise this principle holds true on dry land as well, but just one more example from the waterfront. In theory, the purpose of a vacation is to get away from our troubles and concerns, but it rarely works out that way, as Virginia Woolf shows us in *To the Lighthouse*. While appearing to tranquilly summer in the Hebrides, nearly every character is driven forward by desires, usually by the desire to *achieve*, although that can take many forms. The most famous example of wanting in the novel is, of course, the lighthouse itself. James, the youngest of the Ramsay children, is consumed by a wish to see the lighthouse across the bay. He has been promised a trip the following day by his parents, and Mrs. Ramsay clings to that promise even as Mr. Ramsay correctly if thoughtlessly insists that the weather will force postponement. James accordingly hates his father but loves his mother all the more. My students generally read this conflict as being about some dichotomy—men and women, Mr. and Mrs. Ramsay, nurturers and takers—and there's some truth in that. But it's also a good deal more complex. This little scene of the six-year-old James wanting his trip to fantasyland, his mother supporting him despite concerns about the morrow's weather, his father almost absentmindedly stomping on his dream, reveals an entire family dynamic.

What we really find here is a conflict of desires. They complement at times but enter into battle at others. And yet they seem so simple. What are they, these deepest heart's wishes? Mrs. Ramsay is driven by a dinner entrée, Mr. Ramsay by a letter of the alphabet. Yes, you heard me right. Throughout the course of this day that comprises the first long section of the novel, Mrs. Ramsay obsesses over her *boeuf en daube*—will it be a success, will the family and guests like it, will it have enough of this or that, will it, in short, be a credit to her? The beauty of this obsession is that she does not cook it; Mildred, her maid, spends three days preparing the dish, which is declared a "triumph," so much so that Mrs. Ramsay cannot help taking credit, saying that it is "a French recipe of her grandmother's." Silly, you say? Perhaps, but show me the person who has never worried over the outcome of a party or dinner and I'll show you someone who has never hosted one. Her concerns, moreover, are entirely domestic and allow her to concentrate her attention on her children, and especially on her youngest. Besides fretting over the meal, she also knits a brown stocking—probably the most famous sock in literature—for the lighthouse keeper's son, who has a tubercular hip. Neither of those activities distracts her greatly from her maternal duties. Nor, it should be added, are they presented as inconsequential or trivial. Both show her as committed to the comfort and well-being of others, and that is not negligible. And her husband? Mr. Ramsay spends his day barging around the grounds, largely lost in thought and reciting Tennyson's poem "The Charge of the Light Brigade," and obsessing on "getting to Z." I'm sure you've often wanted to go there yourself. Like his wife, his thinking, although presented humorously at times, is not trivial. He is fuming over his intellectual limitations, which are few and, by our standards, tiny: he's not the greatest thinker of his generation. One man (and it would be a man in his mind) in a generation, maybe one, can get all the way from A to Z; he reckons he's made it to perhaps Q and can squeeze through to R or S, but that's about it. Hard to sympathize, isn't it? Most of us weren't the greatest thinker in our dorm room. Thought of differently, though, it's not so petty. He wants to be more than he is. Now *that* we can relate to. And I've been a little unfair to him. His concern is less about competition than it is about achievement; he wants to reach as far as he can, which he realizes is not as far as he had hoped. Call it a midlife crisis, if you will; it certainly has elements of that. For our purposes, however, the drive itself is the point of interest. He's so caught up in his own desire that he can't recognize the needs of others, even those of his own children. Mrs. Ramsay, on the other hand, is very sensitive to and even protective of everyone who comes into her sphere of interest—smoothing ruffled feathers, playing matchmaker, offering advice, and generally being solicitous. When someone like Augustus Carmichael, an old family friend, seems not to need her aid, she receives this attitude as personal hostility.

And Lily Briscoe? Lily has her painting. In the first part, she is stymied in her attempt to capture the scene in front of her, to grasp the domesticity punctuated by error and aggression that is the Ramsay household. Part of what she wants is approval or acceptance; that is why the comments of Charles Tansley, Mr. Ramsay's latest protégé, that "Women can't write; women can't paint" frustrate her efforts almost completely. She seeks that approval from Mrs. Ramsay, from Mr. Ramsay, and even, unwittingly and very much against her will, from the "odious" Tansley. Only in the third section, "The Lighthouse," does she understand that it must come from the inside, from herself. It is then that she can make the bold line down the center of the canvas and finish her painting. She gets the last words of the novel, and they are about neither Mrs. Ramsay nor anyone's approval: "I have had my vision." That's what it has all been about for her, the ability to have a vision, the space to pursue it, the maturity to express it in her own way, free of outside influence. Is that desire? I believe it is.

It's always about desire, which may or may not involve sex but is just as powerful nonetheless. Characters are driven, and the thing that drives them is desire.

Is this why saints so rarely feature prominently in novels? Perhaps. Mostly, though, they're just not really very interesting, narratively. Consider the *Confessions* of St. Augustine—is this the focus on his many years as priest and bishop? Not at all. He wrote them around age forty and had only converted to Catholicism at age thirty-three; moreover, the narrative of his life more or less stops at his conversion, with the last several chapters taken up by meditations on such religious matters as Genesis and the Trinity. Or Herman Hesse's *Siddhartha*. He may reach something like enlightenment, but the bulk of the novel is taken up with the searching, error, and struggle prior to attaining insight. Why? Because saints lack desire. They don't want anything and as such aren't going anywhere we'll be interested in watching. Admire? Sure. Emulate? We'd do well to. Read about with fascination? Not happening.

Faulkner knew this. He doesn't have much truck with saintly types, and when he does give us a Dilsey, in *The Sound and the Fury* (1929), he keeps her firmly in the background. Out front, the Compsons are frantically clawing and scratching at their desires, whether Benjy's to return to a happier childhood when his beloved sister Caddy was still around, Quentin's to assuage guilt and shame at his own conduct and that of his family, or Jason's to acquire material gain. Faulknerian characters are the neediest, most obsessive creatures ever invented. His novels teem with brooding, scheming monomaniacs pursuing their idiocentric mythologies. Even his saints, or the would-be versions, display wild fixations. Isaac McCaslin, who in *Go Down, Moses* (1942) truly wants to atone to his heretofore unacknowledged black kinsmen for the treatment of their forebears by his white ancestors, particularly his grandfather Carothers McCaslin, gives away the estate in ways that destroy his marriage and make him suspect in the eyes of his neighbors. His refusal to own the plantation drops it into the hands of his cousin McCaslin Edmonds, who is a less understanding and moral person than Isaac himself. He does make sure that money entailed for the descendants of McCaslin slaves gets into the right hands, even traveling to Arkansas to hunt down one heir. Isaac is ethical but also excessively scrupulous. From the Snopes family avarice to Sartoris honor, Faulkner's characters create mayhem and calamity for themselves through their obsessions, and those obsessions come to readers through emblems. Pick up one of his books and you'll soon find driven people and their signs. Any book will do.

And then there's *As I Lay Dying*. We have many reasons to teach this gem of a novel, but one of the most compelling is that character motivation is so darned available. Everyone in the dysfunctional Bundren family (a tautology when reading Faulkner, but these people are special even for him) has a secret, a burning desire, an obsession—and a thing to represent it, what T. S. Eliot calls an "objective correlative." Jewel, the angry son, has his spotted horse. Forty years later and it would have been a muscle car, a Mustang or GTO that he had worked and scrimped to be able to almost afford and that he would lose, as he does the horse, through the agency of his improvident, self-involved father. The joke, of course, is that Anse is not his father, that Jewel is illegitimate, and that his obsession is escaping the leaden, earthbound condition of his family. Jewel couldn't tell you what his desire is, and if he tried, he would probably say it's the horse, but it's not the horse. It's so much bigger than that. Anse himself wants a new set of teeth, or seems to. His "determination" to get Addie to Jefferson for burial masks his wish for new chompers. Yet they're not the real desire. That has to do with going on with life, maybe even with finding, as he announces in the novel's last line that he has, a new wife. Now, you can't very well say, before your wife is even in her coffin, that you're aimin' to go to town and get yourself a new one. Even someone as low as Anse Bundren probably can't admit *that* to himself. But you can say you need new dentures and, as long as you're headed that way anyhow, well . . . why not? Vardaman, who is still a child, needs to understand things beyond him, matters of life and death and what dying really means. He's so concerned that his mother is in that box and still alive that he drills holes into the coffin lid—and into her—to provide air for her. His objective correlative is easy, since he tells you all about it: "My mother is a fish," he says in the shortest and most memorable chapter in all of literature. Vardaman catches an enormous fish, nearly as big as he is, and when Anse makes him clean it himself, he confuses the fish and the mother and living and dying and about every other thing in his world, so that, when he comes out with his famous pronouncement, it shocks not because it's outrageous but because it's so perfectly understandable. What else would he say? Even Cash, who seems to be concerned only with making the coffin for his mother, is driven by desire. His is to feel nothing, to push feeling, with which he is profoundly uncomfortable, as far away as he can. He does this by obsessing on the box's construction, one of his narrative chapters consisting entirely of a list of his thirteen reasons for cutting the corners on the bevel. Focus is good. Attention to detail is good. But when a person focuses that intently on a fairly straightforward bit of logic, he is seriously trying to avoid something else. Dewey Dell, the teenaged sister in this tragicomedy troupe, wants as badly as her father to get to Jefferson, where she's heard the druggist might have a cure for her complaint. She's pregnant. Only Darl, the eldest son, seems immune from his family's penchant for obsessive thinking. What a relief, we think—one semi-normal person in the bunch. He winds up in the insane asylum. The Bundrens are, by turns, appalling, hilarious, touching, frustrating, and shocking. But mostly, they are—and this makes them a teacher's dream—readily accessible.

It is ever thus. Novelists want us to understand their creations, or at least their creatures. So they post road signs along the way, suggesting what we should look for. Sarah Woodruff has her French lieutenant, the unlucky Mr. Micawber his faith that something will turn up, and Jay Gatsby, of course, the green light on Daisy's dock. What is it, we ask, that Joe Christmas really wants? How does what Pip wants differ from what he needs? Can he figure out the difference? What does Jake Barnes not see when he looks at the mirror, and how does it matter to the novel? Every character has his *telos*—Aristotle's term for the necessary endpoint in a goal-oriented, even compulsive, process—not the place he actually winds up but the thing toward which he's driven, his ultimate goal. Our job is to find it. Are they always so obvious? Sadly, no. Will it explain everything about him? Again, no. But it will explain a lot, and we need to find out what drives the character if we want to know what drives the novel.

15

Fiction About Fiction

So who's the first postmodern genius? You're thinking Beckett, maybe, or Alain Robbe-Grillet? Think what you want, but I'm going with Chuck Jones. Yup. That one. Animator extraordinaire for the Brothers Warner. In one famous episode, "Duck Amuck," Daffy Duck undergoes a series of baffling and ridiculous transformations, acquiring a tutu, a head like a flower, the body of a lion, and so on. At the end, we're amused but hardly surprised to learn that the impish wielder of the cartoonist's pencil is, indeed, Bugs Bunny. Warner Bros. took this self-reflexivity even further in the television series *Animaniacs*, which plays like an extended dialogue with the history of cartooning. In fact, cartoons seem uniquely well suited to this whole self-referential thing, whether made for television (*The Simpsons*, *Family Guy*, *South Park*) or feature films (*Who Framed Roger Rabbit?*). But even live-action shows get in on the game. The television series *Moonlighting* (admittedly not representative of anything in Hollywood) ended one season in midchase to collect the costumes and props because the season had ended before the episode had. Somehow, though, when serious writers do it, some readers may suspect they've been cheated. Yet cheated is the last thing we are; rather than closing down possibilities, the strategies we've come to know and love as *metafiction* opens them up.

It's just that readers, and student readers especially, get a little impatient with funny business in their reading.

How impatient? Read on.

Sometimes we speak of a novel soaring, of narrative flights. Sounds nice, doesn't it? Impressive. One envisions the passion of Morrison, the wit of Wodehouse, the scope and scale of Tolkien, the invention of García Márquez. No question about it, there are some wonderful novels in the world. Some of them seem to have wings. But that's not what I mean. I'll give you a soaring book: *The French Lieutenant's Woman.*

The most thrown book in American colleges.

I know when, and when will get you why. What, you want the exact paragraph? We have two options, so take your pick. Sometimes it flies in Chapter 13, when the narrator, having just asked at the end of Chapter 12 who Sarah is and "Out of what shadows does she come," answers with this little gem: "I do not know." Not the answer we typically expect. Here's the rule: when a narrator asks a question, he is obliged to answer. Fowles's narrator does answer, only not to our satisfaction. But wait, it gets worse. Not satisfied confessing ignorance, he actively breaks the illusion he has maintained for a dozen chapters:

> *This story I am telling is all imagination. These characters I cre-*
> *ate never existed outside my own mind. If I have pretended until*
> *now to know my characters' minds and innermost thoughts, it is*
> *because I am writing in (just as I have assumed some of the vo-*

cabulary and "voice" of) a convention universally accepted at the time of my story: that the novelist stands next to God. He may not know all, yet he tries to pretend that he does. But I live in the age of Alain Robbe-Grillet and Roland Barthes; if this is a novel, it cannot be a novel in the modern sense of the word.

At which point, wham! Against the wall, shaking the *Sports Illustrated* swimsuit calendar and rattling the South Padre Island souvenir beer mug nearly off the shelf.

The second place is perhaps less definite, but here's where it begins: "No. It is as I say. You have not only planted the dagger in my breast, you have delighted in twisting it." Nothing in there, in itself, to create flying paperbacks. Except that we've read it before. Exactly. And quite recently. This particular passage comes early in a final chapter, which had, a moment before, seemed superfluous. Chapter 60 ends with the finality of a novel's ending, complete with a small child, a forever-after embrace, and (I'm not making this up) a thousand violins. So who needs another chapter? Well, Fowles does, for one. Chapter 61 offers us a different ending—no evermore, no string section. He uses the device of an author-surrogate setting his watch back fifteen minutes as the pretext for creating an alternative ending, one considerably less happy, if perhaps more in tune with modern sensibilities. And when some students find out that THE conclusion is merely A conclusion, and there is also a B, then Air Fowles flies again. To be sure, some readers see the extra chapter—and the extra alternative—as a gift.

There's something maddening, at least for those reading under a deadline, about the revelation that novels are illusions. At some level we know, don't we? Novels are made-up things? But they're more than that. Novels are in a sense *learned* activities—learned by cultures and learned by individual readers and writers. A novel is, as Fowles suggests, a compilation of conventions, a series of if-then propositions: if the main character is a child at the beginning, then the goal of the novel is to deposit him at some state of adulthood by the end; if the narrator is limited to only knowing one character's mind in Chapters 1 through 5, she can't suddenly pretend to know everyone's mind when the crunch comes in Chapter 23. Or this: if a narrator pretends to omniscience throughout the first twelve chapters and *then* poses a major question about a character, he damned well better have an answer when we turn the page. None of this suddenly becoming helpless as a babe; there is no off position on the omniscient switch.

Unless it's a game. Unless you're merely employing conventions to strip them of their illusion, in which case you had better be prepared for the backlash. This is what drives student-readers crazy: What if he's just playing around? What if he's not serious? It seems unfair somehow to the apprentice reader who is working very hard (usually to find things the professor has promised are in there—magical things, mysterious things) that the novelist might have regarded this not work but play. Not only that, but it seems to cause doubt about the whole fictional enterprise: if we can't trust Fowles, and he's using the devices and practices of the conventional novel, how can we trust any of them?

Well, we can't. But is that a problem, really? You know a novel is made up when you open it. Does the illusion have to be "real"? Does that question even make sense? It does and it doesn't. We've just entered the literary equivalent of quantum physics, where propositions can be simultaneously true and false, where waves and particles overlap and matter and energy may be the same thing.

Welcome to metafiction.

Metafiction: fiction (that part is a no-brainer, right?) that is *about* (meta, meaning "going beyond" or "involving"), well, fiction. It's a relatively new term for a very old practice. If you own the first edition of *The American Heritage Dictionary* from the early 1970s, you'll find it missing. The novelist and philosopher William H. Gass came up with the term in his book of criticism and theory, *Fiction and the Figures of Life* (1970). He means by the term those works of fiction that self-referentially take as at least part of their concern the making of fiction; words like "self-referential," "reflexive," and "self-conscious" routinely pop up in discussions of metafiction. In the first instance, Gass was trying to describe a phenomenon of his own time: the many stories and novels that were then appearing by writers like John Barth, Robert Coover, B. S. Johnson, Christine Brooke-Rose, Italo Calvino, Fowles, and of course Gass himself. But the sort of story he means goes way back. How far back is "way back"? Maybe all the way. It goes something like this: on night one, Caveman Alley told a story, and on night two Caveman Oop told one that, at some point included the phrase, "Now here's what stories typically do, so I will (a) do it or (b) not do it with my story." Or he would have done that had parentheses been invented. In fact, Caveman Alley may even have started off with, "So you know how stories go . . ." After all, why wait for night two? In any case, metafiction was born.

You doubt? Tom Stoppard's *Rosencrantz and Guildenstern Are Dead* (1966) is a play that toys with a couple of hapless minor figures from *Hamlet*. So that's metatheater, a near cousin to metafiction. But so is its source. Hamlet has that whole business of a play within a play and instructions to the players on how to present his little drama, and that's 1600. Shakespeare does that sort of thing all the time, play after play, where either there's an actual play, as in *A Midsummer Night's*

Dream, or there's an act being put on for someone else's benefit, as in *Much Ado About Nothing*. And we know he's not the first. Geoffrey Chaucer's *Canterbury Tales* (1384) involves a set of pilgrims going to the great cathedral town for Easter, during which trip they tell stories. Sometimes the stories conflict with other stories, or animosities from real life spill over into the stories (or vice versa), or, as in the case of the Pardoner and his tale, the teller gets so carried away that he forgets where he is and does something inappropriate, for which the other pilgrims give him a tongue-lashing. There's a lot of material in the *Tales* for the savvy critic of metafiction.

But wait, as the infomercials say, *there's more*. It turns out the idea isn't original to Chaucer. The recently deceased Giovanni Boccaccio got there first, with his *Decameron*. His group of ten young people fleeing Florence during an outbreak of the Black Death each tell ten stories over the course of two weeks. This tidy phalanx of narratives covers a pretty full range of possibility, and the framing device necessarily calls attention to the artificiality of the setup: these are stories made to order for a special situation. The work constantly reminds us that it is a work of fiction, that in fact there's nothing natural about this enterprise. Is that as far back as we go? Hardly. Homer and Virgil both invoke muses, but with a difference. Homer, to the extent that such a personage existed, was an oral poet-singer; he needed all the breath and wit he could muster, so routinely at moments of great stress he calls on the muses to help him out. Virgil, by contrast, is a *writer* and not a singer, so no such need of breath or immediate recall; when he calls on the muses, he does so in virtual quotation marks, because that's what composers of epics do. We could go further back if need be, but you get the point.

So this meta-whatever has been going on for a good little while. What's that you say? *Chaucer and Boccaccio, to say nothing of Virgil, aren't novelists.* Ah, I see. Consider the constituent elements of the novel: book-length, fictive, multicharacter, main plot plus subplots, narrative, prose. What's missing? Only the last one. And I'll admit, it's a big one. But in the time of Chaucer and before, virtually no respectable literature was written in prose. Ergo, verse. Given the interests of all three writers, the complexity and shapeliness of their narratives, they clearly provide models for early novelists. Besides, the word is not "metanovel" but "metafiction." And never forget this other fact: novelists will steal from anywhere. Anyone. Any time. The magpies of the literary world, novelists.

Small wonder, then, that when we come to the "first" novels, they're already highly self-aware, reflexive. One might almost say postmodern. If one wanted to get hit. One doesn't. The point is, we tend to think of self-referential writing as something that comes along late in the day, but in the case of the novel, that would be an error. The first metafictional novel? *Don Quixote* (1605). Also, as it happens, pretty much the first novel. In English, metafiction makes an appearance at least as early as *Tristram Shandy* (1759–1769). Both works are shot through with jokey, irreverent textual play—puns, reversals of expectation, print-based gambits like full blank pages, anything that Cervantes or Sterne could think of to do with this new form that they obviously weren't taking too seriously. And the ink was barely dry on Samuel Richardson's *Pamela* before Henry Fielding—he of *Tom Jones*—offered up his parody, *Shamela*. In some ways, the early days of the novel were like the Wild West: very few rules and a lot of outrageous activity. Part of that was not having any model of how the novelist must behave toward his novel. There's no reverence toward tradition before there is a tradition. Those early novelists could do anything, and they did.

Only later did novelistic conduct get codified. I've talked elsewhere about the specifics of Victorian publishing practices. What we're interested in here is the way those practices—serial publication, mass audiences, linear narratives, sprawling canvases—tell us about the narratives themselves. Chiefly, they suggest a regularization of the novel: more and more, novels resembled each other in structure, and for reasons philosophical as well as commercial, tended to be less experimental than in other eras. The later Victorians pursued realism, by which we mean not merely accuracy in portraying the world but a systematic effort to create the illusion of reality, with a zeal that was near-religious. Or maybe not merely "near." The idea was for readers to snuggle right into a novel as if into the story of their friends' lives (and readers often did think of these characters, with whom they lived for many months, as bosom friends or mortal enemies). In any case, if your worldview, economic principles, and publishing practices conspire to make the realistic novel the highest form imaginable, you're probably not going to spend a lot of time calling attention to the artifice of the form. This is not a failing. As a reader, would *you* want to be reminded, with Tess D'Urberville lying on a slab at Stonehenge waiting to be taken by the police, that we're just playing with form here? I think not.

Does that mean that Hardy doesn't notice that he's sitting for months, building up five hundred or so manuscript pages, that he's *making* an artistic creation? Of course not. But it does mean that he chooses not to emphasize the made-ness of the book. That emphasis is called "foregrounding" in the criticism trade, meaning that an aspect of the work is moved to the front in order to call special attention to it. Literary realists, for the most part, tend to foreground story and relegate the messy business of artistic self-awareness to the background. Very deep background.

There's a tendency to see all this metafiction business as "postmodernism" (a term so amorphous as to be almost entirely bankrupt), as merely a function of a certain historical moment when, presumably, writers had run out of ideas. And in truth, there did seem to be some danger of that. Right around the time of Gass's book there was a lot of death-of-the-novel talk going round. In 1967, John Barth published his celebrated *Atlantic Monthly* essay, "The Literature of Exhaustion," in which he argued that the novel had exhausted its possibilities, that perhaps everything that could be done with the form had been done. Yet a mere fourteen years later, he published a companion essay, "The Literature of Replenishment," announcing a miraculous recovery by the patient, whose narrative pneumonia had turned out to be a mere case of the sniffles. What a relief!

Yet that tendency of fiction to examine its own bases and practices, to doubt its veracity even as it insists on it, has been there from the first and sometimes shows up in very realistic novels. You remember the soaring Fowles? Chapter 13, right? Well, he wasn't the first. There's another novel, also Victorian in form, where right in the middle of the narrative the author pauses, in a chapter called "In Which the Story Pauses a Little," to lay out her theory of novel writing and to talk about the limitations on what she, as novelist, can know. Hers is Chapter 17, not Fowles's "unlucky" 13. So who is this innovator? Angela Carter? Jane Smiley? Nope. She's that great postmodernist, George Eliot, in *Adam Bede* (1859). Now if Eliot, the realist of realists, displays this self-referential element, even a little, it has to be a strong impulse. Well, of course it is. And why?

Because novels don't grow in gardens. They are made things, and their makers get their know-how by reading lots and lots of other novels. And you can't read all of those novels, pick up the old quill, and suddenly forget that you've ever read a novel. So here it is (you knew it was coming), the Law of Crowded Desks: When a novelist sits down to begin a novel, there are a thousand other writers in the room. Minimum. There are even writers present whom she's never read. But that way madness lies, or at least a serious headache.

So what does that mean? Yeah, yeah, one room, lots of buddies. But in practical terms, what does it mean for the writer? It means that nobody's innocent. You simply can't sit down to write a novel as if the world isn't already full of novels. It is already full of novels, and so is your head. That's just how it is. One response I hear in class to any self-conscious novel is that it's a stunt, an artificial posturing. My students are right. It is a stunt. Well, guess what? So is the novel that ignores all those other writers in the room. To pretend innocence or lack of self-awareness is exactly that: pretense.

And there's nothing wrong with pretense. The writer assumes a pose. Always. The narrator who is not strictly the author? A pose. Omniscient, godlike narrator? Definitely a pose. We read novels to follow writers pretending to be things and know things that aren't exactly true. Self-awareness—or its lack—is just one of those things that gets pretended.

But another pair of practical considerations: you can't do anything that hasn't already been done; everything is possible. If you know that everything that can be done has already been done, you have a couple of options. One is to shut down completely, or at least never try anything in that vein. We could see this as the path pursued by Alain Robbe-Grillet and the French anti-novelists of the so-called *nouveau roman*. They attempted to break down the illusions of the novel, to dismantle the customary operations of fiction—you know, get rid of extraneous things like plot, character, narrative continuity, theme—and reduce narrative to a fragmented series of subjective apprehensions of things. There's a reason Robbe-

Grillet never really caught on in the Anglophone reading world. The other option? Get on with it. Write your novel. Of course you know there have been other novels like yours before now. Of course you can't be first to the quarter pole. It's okay. Fiction isn't a race; you don't have to come in first to win. In fact, no one's entirely sure what winning is.

Here, too, you have a couple of options. You can pretend that all those other novels don't already exist and attempt to write a novel that's like a window on its world. Jerome Klinkowitz calls this pretense "transparency," the writer's attempt to make the apparatus of his novel invisible so that readers see straight through to the contents. Or you can call attention to the artifice of the novel in a strategy he calls "opacity." A work of fiction is opaque to the degree it requires readers to notice it even as they may be trying to focus on the story. Most fiction ever written has strived for transparency. But not all, and not even all of it we might think would. You can think of in terms of the theater. Does the playwright pretend that the audience isn't there, that the actors and props are "real," that the proscenium arch is merely a window? Or does she "break the fourth wall," address or engage the audience directly, remind us that this is only a play? Or do both? Shakespeare chiefly tells his stories and engages us directly, but periodically he throws in the aforementioned plays within plays and discussions of stagecraft. So, too, with fiction writers. Every once in a while, they'll surprise you.

Is one way better than the other? Yes. The one that works for a particular author in a particular work is the better one. Do I prefer one to the other? That's like asking if I prefer pie or cake. Why would they be mutually exclusive? I want Dickens or Hardy or Lawrence to insist on verisimilitude. It would be deeply upsetting if my favorite mystery writers suddenly went all metafictional. But I want

Fowles to be a metafictionist, and with him Calvino, Barth, B. S. Johnson, Julian Barnes, Angela Carter.

Then there are the O'Briens. Three of the best novelists of the past, or indeed any, century are named O'Brien. Edna, the girl from a repressive Irish village who grew up to smash all the conventions of propriety surrounding Irish women's fiction, absolutely insists on transparency. Her mode of storytelling requires that readers be drawn in and not let go until *finis*. From the trilogy *The Country Girls* in the 1960s through more experimental works like *Night* (1972) to the sociopolitical later novels *House of Splendid Isolation* (1994) and *In the Forest* (2002), her novels either repel readers due to subject matter or hook them and reel them in from the first pages. In part, Edna O'Brien is working unclaimed land; when she began, there were few, if any, models to follow for the sort of novels she wanted to write. But such self-conscious narrating isn't really her style in any case. Even when, as in *Night*, she is wrestling with the ghost of James Joyce—the novel is a reworking of the concept of the Penelope episode of *Ulysses*, a long, rambling, nocturnal, female meditation by a character looking back over her life so far—there's only the slightest nod to the prior work. The American novelist Tim O'Brien balances narrative immediacy with a certain degree of reflexivity. That may be the more true in his Vietnam novels, *Going After Cacciato* (1978) and *The Things They Carried* (1990). It's hard to write about war without Hemingway looking over your shoulder, stupid to pretend he's not. But Tim O'Brien mixes sources from fantastic fiction like *Alice in Wonderland* in with his Hemingway, even as he immerses us in the experience of war. His novels are a heady brew. And then there's Flann O'Brien, who as I've said before is not even an O'Brien. Born Brian O'Nolan, he took his pen name for his first novel, *At Swim-Two-*

Birds, a hilarious if sometimes confusing pastiche of Irish student novel, American western, Irish epic (much of it is drawn from the legends of Finn MacCool and Mad King Sweeney). A novel within a novel within a novel, *At Swim* has three openings and three endings, a novelist-character whose characters rebel and take him captive (drugging him so he can't write them into more difficulty), and a *pookah,* or demon, who takes control of the offspring of the inner novelist and one of his own characters. Now *there's* a form of incest we rarely encounter. Mercifully. His other novels, particularly *The Third Policeman* (1967) and *An Béal Bocht* (1941, translated as *The Poor Mouth*, 1973), do similar damage to the novel form; the genre has never fully recovered.

Does that cover the full range of possibilities for metafiction-or-not? Probably not. Someone's always figuring out something a bit different, and every writer has different strategies. But these three O'Briens give a sense of what can be done. Besides, in their very different ways, they're all terrific. One could do worse than to adopt a policy of only reading novels by writers named O'Brien.

So maybe we don't want a name-controlled reading list. What do metafictional novels look like? Well, like a lot of things.

Some are rewrites of classic stories:

- John Barth's *The Sot-Weed Factor* (1960, eighteenth-century poem of same name)
- Valerie Martin's *Mary Reilly* (1990, *Dr. Jekyll and Mr. Hyde*)
- John Gardner's *Grendel* (1971, *Beowulf*)
- Julian Barnes's *Flaubert's Parrot* (1984, "A Simple Heart" and *Madame Bovary*)
- Jean Rhys's *Wide Sargasso Sea* (1966, *Jane Eyre*)

- Jane Smiley's *A Thousand Acres* (1991, *King Lear*) and *Ten Days in the Hills* (2007, Boccaccio's *Decameron*)

Others are recycling earlier or other forms:

- John Fowles's *The French Lieutenant's Woman* (1969, Victorian novel), *A Maggot* (1985, eighteenth-century primary document assembly, in this case, from a private legal prosecution)
- Barth's *Letters* (1979, eighteenth-century epistolary novel), *The Last Voyage of Somebody the Sailor* (1991, *A Thousand and One Nights*)
- Iris Murdoch's *The Unicorn* (1963, gothic novel)
- Tim O'Brien's *Going After Cacciato* (1978, Hemingway and *Alice in Wonderland*—go ponder that for a while)
- T. Coraghessan Boyle's *Water Music* (1982, mixture of eighteenth-century adventurer's tale and picaresque)
- Vladimir Nabokov's *Pale Fire* (1962, narrative poem and poetic exegesis)

Some are intricate forms of play, as with *Tristram Shandy*:

- Fowles's *The Magus* or *The Collector*, in which dueling narratives call into question the very notion of narrative reliability or veracity
- Italo Calvino's *If on a Winter's Night a Traveler*, which explores the world of popular novels by using opening chapters from a host of genres, or *Invisible Cities*, in which Marco Polo seems to have gone to the court of the Great Khan expressly to describe fabulous and even impossible cities he has passed through en route, or, for that matter, any Calvino

✏ Murdoch's *The Black Prince*, which, like Fowles's *The Collector*, exploits subjective perception by offering contrary versions and interpretations of events through a primary narrative by the protagonist and commentaries by other characters

They're interesting, baffling, fascinating, sometimes maddening, but always fresh and new. And that's one purpose of metafiction, to make it new, because . . .

You can do anything. If a writer can imagine it, she can do it. There are no rules that say, you can only go this high, can only stretch the truth this far, can only be this outrageous.

We readers are sometimes too serious. I think we have to grant our writers a bit of latitude. Let them horse around, joke, trick us and trip us up. What is the novel, after all, but play? Unlike all those nonfiction genres—exposé, pamphlet, sermon, harangue, lab report, news article, biography, history, and, yes, literary essay—fiction cuts itself loose from the moorings of reality so that it can give pleasure, so that the imagination can run free of any constraints but its own. Best of all, it invites us in to play as well. We forget that at our peril.

We are less put off, perhaps, when these sorts of authorial hijinks occur in our popular culture, but we should have the same delight with Angela Carter that we have with Bugs and Daffy. When writers play these metafictional games, they're merely inviting us to play in their world. Writers since at least Sir Philip Sidney have been telling us that the purpose of literature is to instruct and delight. Fiction about fiction can teach us a lot about our own psychology, about what we expect from stories, and about the nature of, well, fiction. Besides, it's a whole lot of fun.

16

Source Codes and Recycle Bins

YOU'VE SEEN IT HAPPEN. It's the public-reading train wreck, right up there with "Do you write with pen or pencil (or the keyboard equivalent)?" If you go to even a very few readings, you take your seat with a certain dread clinging to your slumping shoulders: when will it come, when will the awful thing be asked, will it be the first or the second question? It meanders around the hall throughout the reading, until the tension is almost too much for mere mortals to bear. Then, the author's thanks to the audience, the general approbation, and the call for interrogation. Here it comes, to be followed by an almost inaudible groan: "Where do you get your ideas?"

Um, from my head? To the credit of the writing community, I've never actually heard that response, but you can see the thought form, push forward, be squelched by the higher being, and slink sulkily back to the dungeon of wisecrackery. It sounds so naïve, so shallow, so dumb. It sounds like, "How did you get to be creative, when the rest of us aren't?" Sometimes it even sounds like, "What is wrong with you?" I think, however, it's more than that, although those questions may be part of the package. It seems to me the question also has to do with some larger issue of creativity: Why this idea and not that? What makes one idea more suitable for a novel than some other? What brings you to borrow from this source rather than some other? Or even, how do you decide from whom to steal? Sounds better, doesn't it? But let's face it: it's just the same. Those of us who don't write novels are always going to wonder at those who do. Where *do* they get their ideas? In general, despite the multitude of sources, there's one common answer.

Look around.

In a course I regularly teach, there is a novel based on the Old English epic *Beowulf*, another based on the author's time as a soldier in Vietnam, one that grows out of the writer's family life on an Indian reservation, yet another that comes from an early-morning vision combined with a vast knowledge of Victorian novels, one that is the product of the novelist's encounter with African American history, and one that can best be said to spring from, among other things, drug-induced paranoia coupled with prodigious, and quite useless, erudition. So where *do* they get their ideas? Everywhere. And from one place in particular. Novels come from a host of sources, the most important of which is always personal experience.

So they're autobiographical?

No. I mean, yes. I mean, what do you mean? "Autobiographical" is one of those highly charged and, therefore, highly suspect terms. Like that other degraded (and related) form, the *roman à clef* (literally, "novel with a key," meaning something close to a one-to-one correspondence with real-life persons and events). "Autobiographical" generally means that "about me"-ness lurks in the novel or poem or whatever. Often in the worst way, or at least the way of least imagination and most lawsuits. Think *The Devil Wears Prada* or one of those thinly veiled Hollywood tell-alls. That's not exactly what I had in mind by personal experience, although it's certainly one side of it.

Let's go back to that course I mentioned a minute ago. What kind of person writes a novel based on *Beowulf*? How about a scholar of medieval literature? That was John Gardner—writer, critic, medievalist, creative-writing teacher extraordinaire, student of the novel, philosophy, mythology, and Batavia, New York. His novels engage pretty much all of his interests. *Grendel* (1971), obviously, is taken from that first English literary work, Grendel being the monster who can only be subdued by a hero from outside the warrior community. *Freddy's Book* (1980) made further use of his interest in the Middle Ages: the novel is a frame tale; the inner narrative is a saga of sixteenth-century Sweden written by the reclusive giant of the title. He turned to even older source material in *The Wreckage of Agathon* (1970), a novel consisting chiefly of a dialogue between an ancient philosopher and his pupil, and *Jason and Medeia* (1973), a verse retelling of the story of the Argonauts and of a wronged wife's revenge on her faithless mate. Rust Belt western New York comes into several of his novels and many of his short stories, most famously in *The Sunlight Dialogues* (1972), an encounter between the morose police chief of a mythical Batavia and a magician/madman/genius/natural-philosopher known as The Sunlight Man. Their sometimes madcap conversations range across the fields of ethics, religion, contemporary society, freedom, justice, government, and about anything else eight hundred pages can hold. *The Something Dialogues* could be the title of almost every Gardner novel. His characters are contentious, thoughtful, and unusually well informed. Each of *Grendel*'s chapters, for instance, makes use of a form of philosophy unavailable to the characters of the source text; Unferth is a "whiny existentialist" (Gardner's phrase) about twelve hundred years too early. In *October Light* (1976), his National Book Award winner, an elderly farmer and his even older sister have an ongoing dialogue, or argument or maybe border war, through the door where either he has imprisoned her or she has locked herself (agency, or at least motive, is a little murky). And in his final novel, *Mickelson's Ghosts* (1982), the main character is a philosopher and many of his dialogues are with persons who are not, cannot, be there. The novel may or may not pass muster with professional philosophers, but it wrestles with the big issues of life and death through the medium of fiction. And it certainly demonstrates one of Gardner's abiding preoccupations in full flower.

So where does it all come from? Personal experience. That experience can take lots of forms: reading, social observation, history, myth, obsession and preoccupation, family events, personal failings and successes, the lot.

It comes as a deep shock, no doubt, to find out that literary works grow out of literary sources. Wow! Writers read other writers—what a concept! This phenomenon is sometimes less happy than it might seem. The world is currently awash in novels drawing on, extending, reinventing, and generally maiming poor Jane Austen. I wasn't aware that we needed a novel on Mr. Darcy's cousin's housekeeper's romance, but I'm pretty sure I saw one in the bookstore the other day. Someone, often a corporate someone, will always want a sequel to a proven moneymaker, to *The Wizard of Oz* or *Gone with the Wind* or, yes, *Pride and Prejudice*. And there will no doubt be a certain audience for such works. But I'm really thinking more here about imaginative reinvestigations of a work than in commercial exploitation.

Nor are those sources inevitably novels. Jane Smiley has made use of *King Lear* in *A Thousand Acres* and the *Decameron* in *Ten Days in the Hills*. Of course, one needn't know either Shakespeare or Boccaccio to appreciate the novels. The kingdom being divided in the former is not England but an Iowa farm, the concerns not Elizabethan but contemporary; the rivalries and desolation wrought by that decision are no less for that. She maintains many of the themes and issues of *Lear*—those of gender roles, sibling rivalry, generation and inheritance, and love true and false, but brings them into her own time, adding others to them. In the latter novel, she follows the pattern indicated in the title of Boccaccio's great work: ten persons, ten days, something like ten stories per day. Her ten-person party is divided evenly between men and women, rather than into his seven women to three men, and the event they're escaping isn't the plague but the beginning of the Iraq War, but conceptually, this book is very much the child of that famous progenitor. There are stories of every type, through which characters reveal themselves, sometimes more fully than they intend. It's bawdy and sexual, if perhaps more explicit than the original. These are, like their predecessors, privileged individuals, the hills being not Florentine but Hollywood, and most of the participants being attached to the film industry in one way or another. Lacking a true aristocracy, Smiley makes do, like her society, with celebrity. The *Decameron* has been inspiring other works from the moment it appeared, most famously *The Canterbury Tales*, which Geoffrey Chaucer published within nine years of Boccaccio's death. What does Smiley gain by this connection? For one thing, a certain resonance, a sense that others have used the device of character-generated stories to plumb the mysteries and miseries of human existence. And there's a sanction for following a group of well-off, self-involved, and, dare we say, shallow people for the length of the novel. Whenever readers might object that her characters are insipid or trivial, well, are those of Boccaccio or Chaucer any less so? Chiefly, though, I think she gains a ready-made structure. There's a template for tossing together a bunch of chatty folks and seeing what comes out, and that template has been around since 1371. That's a long enough pedigree for anyone.

Some writers have made careers out of cribbing from older sources, even when the sources aren't all that old. J. M. Coetzee springs to mind. Occasionally the connection is little more than a title, as in *Waiting for the Barbarians* (1980), which is drawn from the title of a poem by the Alexandrian poet C. P. Cavafy, the signature line of which is, "Because it is night, and the barbarians have not come." In true Coetzee fashion, the barbarians are not the wild people on the outside, but the forces of empire and "civilization" within. It is they who commit the atrocities, killing, maiming, blinding their victims, suppressing all dissent or humane action, and actively engaging in a campaign of extermination. He upends Cavafy: not only have the barbarians arrived, they've been here all along. In *Elizabeth Costello*, the protagonist has in her youth written a novel, *The House on Eccles Street*, that reimagines Joyce's *Ulysses* from Molly Bloom's viewpoint.

Later chapters also make free use of Franz Kafka's work, returning to a source he used extensively in *Life and Times of Michael K.* (1983). Anyone even mildly aware of Kafka will be familiar with his penchant for the letter *K* in connection with his besieged heroes, and particularly with Joseph K. of *The Trial*. Clearly, Coetzee revels in postmodern, intertextual games, yet he does not undertake them lightly or randomly; there is method and seriousness to his play. Perhaps nowhere on earth could more appropriately be called Kafkaesque than apartheid South Africa, with its arbitrary rules and punishments, its thoroughgoing oppression, its brutality.

Coetzee makes it more so by rendering a dystopian version where civil war and concentration camps replace race as the dominant mode of inhumanity. Michael K. is a victim of biology, intellectually challenged, and marked by a harelip. His journey to return his mother's ashes to her birthplace is filled with peril and hostility, including robbery by a soldier. The place he finds seems a refuge, but eventually he is found and arrested for suspicion of abetting insurrectionists he's never met—a thoroughly Kafkaesque moment. The narrative is shot through with references to Kafka, including a phone call to "the Castle," but the narrative and ethical force are all Coetzee, as is Michael's eventual escape and resolution. Rarely in Kafka—I can think of no instances—are characters afforded a revelation that leads to contentment. This use of prior texts to highlight social commentary or moral investigations is typical of Coetzee's work. He is no slave to the intentions of others.

So what else can he do? How about introducing a female viewpoint into the most famous buddy narrative in English literature, *Robinson Crusoe*? His *Foe* plunks a female character, Susan Barton, down on Crusoe's island, where she finds things not entirely as reported by Daniel Defoe (the "Foe" of the title). Friday is clearly African, as against the nearly European original, and he has been rendered speechless by the mutilation of his tongue, although agency in this horrific act is never established. Cruso (as it is spelled throughout) dies on the return voyage, and it is only through Susan's importuning of the titular author that his story is told, however distorted in the process. Needless to say, the novel turns an adventure yarn into a meditation on race, gender, and the consequences of colonialism, topics of which Defoe was blithely unaware. It also reminds us of his sources. Defoe typically drew from real-life counterparts for his narratives, from the lives of various female criminals, probably including the notorious Mary Carleton, who had published an autobiography during her own crime spree. Unlike Carleton, who died on the gallows, his Moll repents and is transported, although her protestations of reform and remorse are never as convincing or as engaging as her tales of bad behavior. For Crusoe, he drew upon the most famous castaway of his time, Alexander Selkirk, who spent four years on a desert island before being rescued and whose tale was told in various fictional "autobiographical" accounts as well as in an interview with the famous journalist Richard Steele. What better figure, then, to draw from than someone who made a practice of reworking sources himself?

Okay, so novelists borrow from other narrative. We've got that. Novels, memoirs, letters, stories of all sorts. Check. Sometimes those narratives are really old. Older than writing. Older than anything. The American novelist John Barth has shown that he'll borrow from anywhere, but he prefers *A Thousand and One Nights*. And why not? There's a story there for every occasion. Plus, the really interesting story, for Barth, is the talking-for-your-life tale of Scheherazade herself, whom he sees as a sort of Ur-novelist, a figure compelled by circumstance or fate to spin tales endlessly. A good model for the novelist. In *Chimera* (1972), he weaves together the tales of his bedtime story genius-heroine and her sister Dunyazade, Perseus, and Bellerophon, along with a figure purporting to represent the novelist himself as genie (or "Djean"). In *The Last Voyage of Somebody the Sailor* (1991), we're pretty sure who will make an appearance. Sure enough, when the contemporary man Simon Behler falls overboard off the coast of Sri Lanka, he somehow awakens to find himself trapped in ancient Baghdad and locked in a contest of storytelling prowess with Sindbad the Sailor, no slouch at yarn-spinning. Barth is always enthralled with other storytellers and with earlier literature, and that fascination takes him back toward the great stories, and thence to the great myths. Here's what matters, though: this is personal experience for him. As much as being a twin, as living in Maryland, as being a sailor, as teaching English, as dealing with publishers and editors all help define him, so does his reading, so do his obsessions and preoccupations.

When Barth encounters these tales, of course, he's playing his postmodern games with them, but that's not the inevitable path. Joyce makes use of Odysseus and the Greek gods in *Ulysses*, Finn McCool and other—many, many other—myths in *Finnegans Wake*. D. H. Lawrence borrows myth everywhere he travels, perhaps most notably the myth of the Mexican god Quetzalcoatl in *The Plumed Serpent*. The modernists frequently turn back to ancient myth as organizing principle for their stories of modern struggle. Lawrence and Joyce, though, have a contemporary who made myth seriously fun. A Greek. *The* Greek. How can you not love somebody named Zorba? You remember Zorba, right? Anthony Quinn playing very far over the top? Well, before it was a Quinn movie (actually, a Michael Cacoyannis movie, but who remembers him?), it was a Nikos Kazantzakis novel. Kazantzakis worked for decades on a long verse epic, *The Odyssey: A Modern Sequel*. He became notorious in his own lifetime and then much later, when Martin Scorsese filmed *The Last Temptation of Christ*, although the novel is simply *The Last Temptation*. He wrote novels about St. Francis of Assisi and Alexander the Great, and he wrote *The Greek Passion*, about a passion play that gets out of hand, where, essentially, Christ is recrucified. So he's pretty familiar with recycling myth. But what made him very famous and much loved, naturally, is *Zorba the Greek*. Wait a minute, you're saying—that's the least mythic of them all. True, if you mean the immediate story. But Alexis Zorba's no ordinary man. He's all passions and desires, drink and sex, music and dancing, dark energy and deep digging. He is, in other words, Dionysus. The unnamed narrator, with his emphasis on the mind, his instinctive recoil from sexual urges and the body generally, and his bookishness, is almost pure Apollonian, according to the dichotomy that first comes to us—and to Kazantzakis—from Friedrich Nietzsche. Zorba represents the other, livelier half, of that opposition. Zorba is connected to wine, of course, to harvest bounty more generally, as well as to music and dance, but also to deep drives and urges, particularly those like lust and anger that are most difficult to tame. He has a way with women, reminding us that Dionysus had a cult of wild women, the Maenads, who held orgiastic rituals in the wooded darkness where among other activities they drank, danced, slaughtered animals and consumed them raw. Dark urges, indeed.

Dionysus was the most alarming of the Olympian gods, in part because his specialty, fruitfulness and the vine, was both mysterious and terrifying in its negative consequences. If grapes or olives failed, a community was in great danger of annihilation. What we often regard as the high-water mark of classical Greece, the drama, grew out of primitive dithyrambic rites (dancing and sung narratives) meant to appease and celebrate him. In the theaters there was always a seat in the front row reserved for him, and performances were generally preceded by an animal sacrifice in his honor. He alone of the major deities was not pictured directly in his own person, but as a figure or face reflected in the clouds. Well, one can't very well write a novel about the god himself, can one? So Kazantzakis gives us Zorba, both the representation of the god and a recognizable figure in himself: the unschooled workman in touch with the earth and its pleasures, the man whose genius is for living.

If a farm kid from Ohio writes such a story, it may come off as a bit contrived. I can speak with some authority on this point. But Kazantzakis grew up in a world infused with knowledge of the ancient world and its deities. He was a scholar and translator of philosophy and classical works, a student of various religious traditions. His Dionysian figure owes as much to Nietzsche as to the ancient tradition. Not for nothing is the narrator writing a book on the Buddha, whose teachings lead invariably away from the body and from desire generally. Does this mean he "believes" in the ancient myths? Not literally, but he does place them in the context of a broader wisdom tradition, reminding readers that salvation (one of Zorba's favorite topics) relies not only on the spirit and the mind but also on the stomach, the sexual organs, and the body. Those are the lessons of Zorba/Dionysus, and they are available to Kazantzakis through his direct, personal experience of the world.

Okay, that's one sort of personal experience, but maybe not the most obvious. Much more commonly writers draw on observations of the current social scene, on history, and on their own lives. We'll speak of history in another chapter, since it warrants a separate discussion. And the rest? For one, there's the ripped-from-the-headlines school. Okay, maybe that's a largely degraded subset because of lousy books and movies that thinly veil current events for sensational effects. Maybe we're better off thinking of ripped-from-the-back-pages as a type of fiction. That's what much of Fitzgerald could be called. While the Scott-and-Zelda marriage often reads like a novel—by a novelist sadly unfamiliar with limits and decorum—and while the real novelist did use personal events and situations, what really makes his fiction go is the ability to observe the social situation of his time. *Gatsby* is not autobiographical, yet it draws on persons he met and well-established 1920s types. *Tender Is the Night* (1934) has a generous helping of Gerald and Sara Murphy, who in some significant ways provide the models for Dick and Nicole Diver; some of Scott and Zelda, chiefly in the disastrous outcome of the grand times; and a great deal of the era. That Fitzgerald could observe his world so carefully, even when drunk, and could work his own flaws and failures into his narrative design, is a powerful testament to his artistic abilities. That he wrote so few novels is a testament to how deeply he fell into the world he so accurately critiqued.

Most of our great writers have been keen observers of the social scene. Mark Twain may have said that any library with no Jane Austen in it is a good library, even if it contained no other books, yet he and Austen share some—okay, maybe just a few—important abilities. The most important is the ability to see what's flawed in society. And what's funny. I'm pretty sure Twain had only limited experience with conjoined twins, but he had abundant experience of slavery and racism. When he started out to write what he later categorized as an "extravagant tale," *Those Extraordinary Twins*, he had little plan except to tell an extended tall tale that came to him as a result of seeing Italian conjoined twins when he toured Europe. That plan, however, later melted away, as new characters hijacked the narrative. Why? Because Twain, for all his fanciful leanings, is a realist. He's at his best when scrutinizing the actual world, ruthlessly dissecting its shortcomings. That's what he does in this tale of switched babies and disastrous outcomes. The slave infant passes for white in the world, but money and privilege teach him to become cruel and selfish, ultimately leading him to commit robbery and murder. The white infant whose place he takes becomes moral and hardworking through his upbringing and circumstances, but he's also illiterate and saddled with the dialect of Southern slaves; when finally restored to his rightful place, he can never fit in. In novel after novel, Twain skewers the pretensions and hypocrisies of nineteenth-century America.

And Austen? Twain once said in a letter to Joseph Twichell, "Everytime I read 'Pride and Prejudice' I want to dig her up and beat her over the skull with her own shin-bone," but he should have had more fellow feeling. She, too, skewers the pretensions and hypocrisies of her era, as different as it was from Twain's. She, too, finds great hilarity in human folly, whether the ill-advised manipulations of Emma Woodhouse or the romantic mayhem of the Bennett females and the snobbery and class consciousness of the surrounding characters. One would think Twain would have some sympathy for *Pride and Prejudice* simply for the portrait of the puffed-up, social-climbing clergyman-cousin Mr. Collins. He may not be the Duke and the Dauphin, but he's not far off.

Both writers are brilliant observers of their times and unsparing in their criticism of pomposity, bombast, and societal duplicity. Most great novelists, in fact, specialize in capturing the telling details of the social scene. But be forewarned: results may vary. In *A Changed Man* (2005), Francine Prose writes about the white supremacist who came in from the cold. A young skinhead suddenly shows up in the offices of a human rights organization run by a Holocaust survivor, leading to much consternation and intrigue from all parties. John Updike has specialized in capturing the historical moment, whether in the Rabbit novels, where Rabbit Angstrom lives through the various changes in the second half of the twentieth century, or in novels such as *Couples* (1968) and *A Month of Sundays* (1975) that meticulously anatomize the foibles of the historical moment. In a much more sober vein, John Steinbeck specialized in capturing the physical and spiritual rootlessness of the first half of twentieth-century America in works like *Of Mice and Men* (1937), *Cannery Row* (1945), *East of Eden* (1952), and, most famously, *The Grapes of Wrath* (1939). In much of his work, there's a journalistic quality of capturing the historical moment, and indeed, *The Grapes of Wrath* grew out of a series of newspaper articles that he wrote on migrants escaping dust-bowl Oklahoma in an often futile search for a better life in California. Autobiographical? No. Experience-based? Absolutely. He poured a tremendous amount of himself into the book: observations, outrage over treatment of Okies, leftist political beliefs, hostility to the property-owning class, toughness and tenderness, optimism and something like despair. Nearly every action in the novel proves futile, yet the book ends on a hopeful note through Rose of Sharon, having lost her stillborn baby, nursing a starving man and Tom Joad, on the run from a murder charge, issuing his famous promise to his mother about always fighting for the downtrodden and oppressed. *East of Eden* is even more personal, addressed as it is to his young sons, even though the story is not "his" story, not his autobiography. The competing sons, the biblical parallels, the war between good and evil—all that is in a sense the purest Steinbeck. Part of what makes this work, like so much of his fiction, personal and gripping is his absolute fidelity to place, to the Salinas Valley and Monterey, that part of central California that inhabited him as much as he inhabited it.

So, who else? Pretty much everybody. D. H. Lawrence's novels follow him around from Nottinghamshire to London to the Tyrol to Italy to Australia to Mexico new and old. His characters undergo many of his experiences; his wife Frieda once coldcocked him with a stoneware dinner plate, and that incident becomes Hermione Roddice's conking of Rupert Birkin with a piece of lapis lazuli in *Women in Love* (1920). And Lawrence's early personal and romantic tribulations form the basis for *Sons and Lovers* (1913), his breakthrough novel. Joyce draws heavily on his own childhood and adolescence for *A Portrait of the Artist as a Young Man* (1915). Hemingway? Bullfights, fishing, war, personal turmoil, toughness and tenderness in an uneasy mix. Other than that, not much. Dickens? At least half of his novels are, in one way or another, about debtor's prison, where his father was sent when Charles was twelve years old, and his own work in a bootblack factory at the same age, two experiences from which he never really recovered. Did Franz Kafka live through the events of the posthumously published *The Trial* (1925) and *The Castle* (1926)? No, but he certainly understood on an extremely personal level the alienation and the rejection they depict, as well as the absurdity of existence. And what of Kerouac and the Beat writers? Much of his work is seemingly direct transcription of experience. We know that much of this self-created myth—the single long roll of paper containing the typescript of *On the Road*; the almost untutored, offhand narrative stance; the sense of unfiltered reportage— is studied nonsense, that in fact the effects he achieves are the result of considerable labor, or at least they are until he begins to believe the myth, but we like him that way. And you can't deny that the narratives grow out of personal experience, that he and Neal Cassady dashed cross-country in cars seeking out as much of life as they could drink in (*On the Road*, 1957), that he and Gary Snyder went hiking in the mountains (*The Dharma Bums*, 1958), that he used his adventures with his friends for all of his subject matter, sometimes changing characters very little from the originals, aside from some minor name deformation.

Okay, okay. You get the idea. So what does this mean for the reader? What do we do with this information?

Writing grows out of experience. That part's unassailable. Well, guess what? So does reading. They're not the same experiences. Happily, you don't have to have lived in the Salinas Valley or 1920s Paris, don't need to have bombed across Kansas in the late 1940s or have read the same ancient epics, don't need any special experience to connect to the novels. This is a place we can meet, reader and writer. Whatever the sources of the narrative, what matters ultimately for readers is the sense that this *thing* is genuine, that it has the solidity of the real deal. It's ephemeral, yet we feel we can reach out and touch it. Which leads us to . . .

The Law of Novel Paradox: Novels grow out of intensely private obsessions, which writers then must make public and accessible to readers. They have to move from autobiography, or even diary, to public discourse. They have to make us care about something that we may never even have thought about, and make it seem like our own idea. Did we care, or even know, about the injustice in the George Edalji case? Not until Julian Barnes made us aware of it in *Arthur and George*, where we find ourselves caught up, amazed, outraged, and ultimately gratified. It's one of many paradoxes in the novel. You can follow your star, but you have to make it ours. You can use old material, but it can't be old hat.

Here's one that's related: we treat fictional narrative as true, even while acknowledging that it is manifestly false. Sure, we know the tale is made up. All the best writers tell us so, if we ask. You didn't even have to ask Mark Twain; he'd tell anyone who'd listen that he was a professional liar. Yet he was also a professional truth-teller. Amidst all the lies, made-up stories, and outrageous jokes, he finds the things that matter. Bigotry. Hypocrisy. Loyalty. Morality. He found a lot of them. We know they matter, moreover, because his writing just feels right—strangely honest. The novel is both counterfeit *and* authentic. Okay, Bub, we say, you can tell us falsehoods, but you better not be faking it.

Interlude

Read with Your Ears

AND LIKE A FOOL, all this time you've been using your eyes. It's not your fault; you were trained that way. In fact, you've been trained that way for hundreds of years. Thousands, even. Ever since print became the privileged form of knowledge exchange, the eyes have it. Back when our old pals Snorgg and Ongk sat around the cave talking about the mastodon hunt, or even when a hundred or so guys who would become Homer were roaming around the Levant telling tales of Odysseus and Achilles to rooms of drunken warriors, building epics up out of fragments and borrowed narratives, stories came in at the ear. Even then, though, the end was nigh. In something like twenty-one thousand lines of poetry that comprise *The Iliad*, there is precisely one mention of writing. But you know what? One's not none. If we accept that this poem achieved the form we know sometime in the eighth century BCE, then the writing, as it were, was on the wall for oral storytelling roughly twenty-eight hundred years ago: the print-oriented bastards are coming. Okay, so maybe it wouldn't refer to Marshall McLuhan directly, but you get the point.

Besides, as Joyce has Stephen Dedalus remind us, we are trapped by the "ineluctable modality of the visual." What that cluster of jawbreakers suggests, aside from the speaker having studied Latin too much, is that there's no escaping visual data, that what the eyes take in dominates our consciousnesses. Hard to argue with him. He is, after all, Joyce.

But let's say you're reading a novel (*insert punchline here*). That novel reminds you of something else you've read, which something may or may not be fiction—news stories, ancient epics, recent movies, biographies of the famous or notorious, and, yes, even other novels. How do you get that reminder? Do you *see* the other text? Or, rather, do you *hear* something that *sounds* familiar?

Most of the time, to be sure, that hearing is a little vague, but it comes in clearer after a bit. Here's a f'rinstance—two books, one of which you might have heard of and the other you should have. Like nearly everyone of my generation, I discovered E. L. Doctorow before John Dos Passos. Specifically, I discovered *Ragtime* (1975), a novel with three interrelated storylines and a historical mosaic. Two of the three plots involve persons without names: Father, Mother, Mother's Younger Brother, Grandfather, and the Little Boy are the white, middle-class family in New Rochelle, New York; Tateh, Mameh, and Little Girl are the Jewish immigrants struggling to survive. Among the main characters, only the black couple, a ragtime pianist named Coalhouse Walker Jr. and his sweetheart, Sarah, have names. Their three narratives weave together to move toward an ending that is both tragic and uplifting, since Doctorow is shrewd enough to recognize that no story of America is all one thing. A place of freedom and opportunity, it is also a haven for racism and unequal treatment, a place where immigrants are simultaneously welcomed and reviled, a place where fortunes can be made and lost almost overnight. This tale of individual destinies is interwoven with a larger tapestry of America at the beginning of the twentieth century, from J. P. Morgan and Henry Ford, to the tragic love triangle of Evelyn Nesbitt, Harry K. Thaw, and the architect Stanford White, to Emma Goldman, to Harry Houdini, to Booker T. Washington. Nor are these historical figures merely wallpaper in front of which the "real" plot plays out. Rather, they interact with the fictional characters, forming friendships and love relationships, offering or needing assistance or obstruction, performing official functions and private blunders.

Now Dos Passos, as I've discussed elsewhere, is the creator of the *U.S.A.* trilogy, comprising *The 42nd Parallel* (1930), *1919* (1932), and *The Big Money* (1936). In it, the central narrative is interwoven with sections of biography of the notable and notorious, Newsreels whose texts are literally ripped from the day's headlines (chiefly from the *Chicago Tribune*), and Camera Eye snapshots of the America in which Dos Passos came to adult consciousness. Sound familiar? Then you're smarter than me. I distinctly remember reading *The 42nd Parallel* for the first time with two responses: this doesn't sound like anything I've read before, and I'm missing something. In fact, I read the whole trilogy without twigging to the connection. There was that persistent sense of an echo of something, but I couldn't bring it clearly into mind while confronted with the tremendous originality of Dos Passos's creation. It wasn't until I reread the first novel some years later (having in the meantime taught *Ragtime* once or twice in book and movie form). Then, about halfway through, I thought to myself, I know what this sounds like. Dos Passos, Doctorow, similarities, check. My only question was why it took so long to arrive at that recognition. Your honor, the defense pleads mitigating circumstances. First, and there's no way around it,

Doctorow is a much better writer, particularly in managing a plotted story with characters, even if they are handicapped by the absence of names. *U.S.A.* is a cubist masterpiece. That's not the same as a narrative gem. Dos Passos is not great with his dialogue, which is often stilted in a kind of working-class king's English. Second, the flow is so much smoother in the later work than in the earlier. Dos Passos employs the herky-jerky qualities of those two signatures of the new medium of cinema, the montage and the newsreel; Doctorow the comparatively smooth flow of the nickelodeon-like flip books created by Tateh. And finally, the historical figures are woven much tighter into the main storyline in *Ragtime* than in *U.S.A.* In fact, part of the charm of each is the distance or nearness to the historical context, which may be a function of proximity. Dos Passos catches the look of the country at the moment of writing his novel but uses it as background to the stories of Mac and Janey and his other fictional characters. Doctorow, on the other hand, is writing many years after the fact, and all the famous figures are safely dead, so he can have Evelyn Nesbitt engage in a sexual relationship with Mother's Younger Brother without fear of lawsuits. Hey, don't laugh; these practical considerations are too onerous to ignore.

Here's an analogous situation. You're sitting in the theater watching *Pirates of the Caribbean: At World's End*, and suddenly you're in a spaghetti Western. Remember the scene? Things are looking distinctly bad for the pirates, who've just discovered they're facing a fleet only slightly larger than the Spanish Armada (in fact, the word "armada" gets employed repeatedly), and Elizabeth Swann, no dummy, calls for "parlay." Suddenly we cut to a shot of boots crossing sand, and while they're definitely pirate boots, they're not in a pirate movie anymore. Against all odds, this sand, on the edge of the ocean, is the most desiccated stuff you ever saw. Sand that's bucking for promotion to dust. And boots in the dust equal showdown. Good guys squaring off with bad. Gary Cooper in *High Noon*, John Wayne at the end of *Stagecoach*. Okay, John Wayne in about anything. But most of all, men with no name. No one in film history showed more boots striding through more dust than Sergio Leone. And he's the one we're supposed to think about here. How do we know? The soundtrack ceases to be Hans Zimmer and becomes, for the duration of the walk, Ennio Morricone. It's all weird instrumentation and over-the-top effects. I'm willing to swear, although I'm sure it's not true, that I heard whistling in there. And as anyone born before 1960 can tell you, Morricone means Leone. Old school chums, they never went anywhere, creatively, without one another. And look what they did together. *Once Upon a Time in the West. A Fistful of Dollars.* And most of all, that other one.

And then it hits you. *That's* what this is. The amoral Leone universe. Is the good guy good or not? Can Charles Bronson really be the hero and Henry Fonda the villain? Whose side is Clint on? The angels or the demons? Can we even tell? One thing's for certain, though, for all that water, this is *The Good, the Bad and the Ugly.* Everybody's playing his own hand (or hers, since Elizabeth becomes a real player here), and nobody, with excellent reasons on all sides, trusts anyone. There are double-crosses on the double-crosses. It may all work out, but somebody's gonna hafta die. All that from boots on the sand. And listening.

Okay, wise guy, how'd you get there?

The inner ear. I thought of calling it the third eye, but that image is too disturbing. Let's just say that readers use a special sort of hearing when they process information, whether said information comes from print or film or whatever. If you simply read the *text* of the pirate movie, you see, what? Boots, sand, a bit of water. You have to bring your own data to the part. That Morricone soundtrack certainly helps, but only if you've heard some of his other work. Gore Verbinski, the director, assumes we have, but there are no guarantees. But even before the melody registers, we can sense where this scene is heading. By step two, the Leone echo is rolling; the musical cues merely reinforce something we're already hearing. Verbinski's reference is arch and fairly obvious, but it would be "audible" even if delivered with greater subtlety. And that subtlety is why we need to open ourselves to nuance. Looking too intently at a text can overwhelm our other senses, can make us miss the echo, the sympathetic chimes in a work.

The Law of Universal Connectedness: Every novel grows out of other novels. So, you ask, does this mean everything's derivative? On one level, yes. Writers can't avoid being influenced by works they've read, stories they've heard, movies they've seen. If you see that influence as derivative, then it is. Yet that's not the whole story. There is also the influence on us. We may hear things that weren't available to the novelist at the time or writing, or that she wasn't aware of—even that hadn't yet existed. The echoes we hear need not run in only one direction. Words change meaning over time. The same's true of novels: they change meaning over time. The words stay the same, naturally, but their meanings can change, although that's not the major force. The world changes around the novels. We change. Are we the same today as Americans in Twain's lifetime or as subjects of the queen in Dickens's? Hardly. Society has gone through great upheavals in the last century or so; Comet Halley has come and gone in its seventy-six-year cycle since its visitation at the time of Twain's death. Both countries have experienced multiple wars, recessions and depressions, alterations in the racial and ethnic landscape, and internationalism undreamt of in the nineteenth century. How can their work possibly remain static?

More importantly, other writers have engaged them in conversation. W. H. Auden said in his elegy for William Butler Yeats that, in dying, the great man "became his admirers." That phrase can have a lot of different meanings, among them, it reflected well on people that they did admire such a poet. One meaning, though, must be that, to the extent Yeats would live on, he would do it through those admirers. True enough, I'm sure, but not one of them was him, and each of them would contain a Yeats colored by the possessor. My Yeats is very personal and, I'm equally sure, very distinct from Auden's. One important distinction: I'm not a poet. When Auden makes use of Yeats's verse in his own, as he does in the elegy (where, among others, "Under Ben Bulben," Yeats's own poem about his death and burial, is engaged in conversation), it forces readers to reconsider not merely the man being memorialized but the poetry as well. So, too, with novels. As I write this, a book called *Finn* has recently been published. In an audacious move for a first (or any) novelist, Jon Clinch purports to tell the story of Pap Finn, Huck's violent, drunken, and doomed father. In doing so he brings in numerous details of the original, and we recall many more. Clinch could have told a story of any violent sod living along the Mississippi in antebellum Missouri, but he decided to tell this one, so there must have been some reason. Just as Twain sought to tell a tale of what he saw as the real America, setting it in opposition to earlier novels and stories by James Fenimore Cooper and Washington Irving, among others, that greatly romanticized frontier or rural life. There are things Twain couldn't have said about life in his time, things he might not have noticed, even things that have become true that maybe once weren't. Clinch can say them. In the process, he alters how we think about the book Hemingway claims fathered all of American writing.

Or take Jane Austen. Please. Sorry, couldn't resist that one—must have been the Twain influence. Surely *Pride and Prejudice* stands as one of the seminal works of English letters. That does not, however, make it untouchable. Perhaps no novel has been more touched. As I mentioned earlier, Elizabeth-and-Darcy spin-offs seem to be a major growth industry. Most of those books, mercifully, will sink with little stain left on the culture, but one or two will likely hang around. More importantly, how many romance novels are *informed* by Austen's great book? And to what extent do they color our understanding of the original? Then there's *Bridget Jones's Diary*, Helen Fielding's melding of *Pride and Prejudice* with *Gentlemen Prefer Blondes*. What's that you say? Fielding is no Austen? And neither is Anita Loos? Perhaps. But they're pretty darned funny; you'll have to give them that. Moreover, Fielding's rather obvious borrowings from Austen and Loos remind us that all three are writing the same novel, a book called *Modern Romance*. All three proved highly successful in their own time, were scorned as each age's version of chick-lit, and made witty, satiric observations on contemporary mating rituals. Her book forces us to reconsider the earlier ones through its reworking of themes and situations in the context of a different age. Do we subscribe to the gender roles and centrality of marriage that inform Austen's novel? How does Bridget's active role in courtship shed light on Elizabeth's societally enforced passivity? Given the change toward career women, how do we feel about the 1925 gold-digger model as represented by the wonderfully named Lorelei Lee, a character who seems to exist in perpetual anticipation of Marilyn Monroe to arrive on the scene and play her? Fielding reminds us that our views of women have changed, and that our readings of her famous forebears may, therefore, also have changed.

The word for the day, class, is *intertextuality*. It comes to us compliments of Mikhail Bakhtin, the great Russian formalist critic, by way of the structuralist thinker Julia Kristeva, who coined the term, and has to do with how texts speak back and forth to each other. Bakhtin, in fact, gave us the term "dialogism," speaking of the "dialogic potential of the novel," by which he means the capacity of novels to carry on an ongoing conversation. The two terms overlap a good deal, differing perhaps in the marginally greater sense of conscious decision making implied by "dialogism." For our purposes, the important notion here is of a conversation among texts across time.

Isn't that discussion a little one-sided? Don't the older texts do all the talking?

You'd think so, wouldn't you? But no, it actually doesn't work that way. The model that instantly comes to mind is something like a lecture hall, with the grizzled old-timer telling the assembled upstarts about how good it was in the days of yore. If that's the model, then the seats are full of hecklers. A more apt image, though, is more along the lines of a graduate seminar. One discussant has some priority, in this case temporal, having arrived at the gathering somewhat earlier than the rest, but everyone is bringing questions, insights, critiques, and information to the seminar table. So it is with novels. Take the case of *Bridget Jones's Diary*: yes, it draws upon those earlier novels about women, love, and independence, but in doing so, it also provides commentary upon and, in a sense, revision of those works. Fielding forces us to *revise* our thoughts about Austen and Loos. Bridget's greater social mobility and self-doubt cause a reconsideration of both the limitations and the accompanying self-confidence that the social order affords Lorelei Lee. To be sure, she's less a free agent in terms of where she can go and what she can do, but those restrictions make her surer of the ground beneath her feet. Bridget's anxieties are in some ways a product of the greater freedom of the contemporary woman. The outcomes Bridget seeks also differ from either Lorelei's or Elizabeth Bennet's. A man, yes. But a man is not the end of the story in the 1990s. Men sometimes prove faithless (as we're reminded by Daniel Cleaver), human life tenuous, and in any case a woman needs a career as well as domestic bliss. Oh, we find ourselves thinking, that's something Austen didn't know. All three writers examine women's roles within the restrictions of their respective societies, and since the societies are quite different from each other, so, too, are the issues and stories that result.

So, dialogism. The idea here is that texts have an ongoing conversation, that echoes, citations, parodies, and reiterations will alter both the newer and older novels—*even when the writer has never read the historically prior text.* You'll notice an emphasis on "texts," which is the term favored by late twentieth-century (and even later) criticism of the schools lumped together as "poststructuralist theory." This gets away from "works" and the inevitable implication that if there is a work, then *someone* must have done said work, what we could call the teleological argument for the existence of the author. The notion of texts and "scriptors," as Roland Barthes calls them, as against some sort of quasi-divine "author," goes back to his essay "The Death of the Author" (1967), in which he argues for a greater importance for the reader in the construction of meaning. Elevating the reader for him necessarily demotes the writer, particularly the writer as a sort of tin-pot despot of meaning, a minor god who packs everything in that readers should be so lucky as to unpack at the other end. Rather, Barthes is suggesting that there are things going on in texts of which even the authors may be unaware but which readers may discern. Can a writer *know* everything that may have influenced her choices? Probably not. Readers may actually be better situated to notice such details. So Barthes impishly kills off the notion of the Writer as the site of meaning and the font of signification, shifting it to the Text and, ultimately, to the Reader. Don't you feel honored?

Does it matter, really, whether we focus on texts or authors? At most levels, probably not. At the level of Barthes and his followers (and detractors), very much. Barthes's program in the essay is to establish the reader, and the act of reading, as the site of meaning. I'm not against that, although I find the writer-reader opposition a false dichotomy for a host of reasons. Here's the one that matters here: writers are readers, too. Texts don't simply spring into life out of thin air; they're the product of a succession of writers encountering earlier works, among other things they encounter. They read and reread and invent from their reading of what others have read and reread and invented. Is that confusing enough for everyone?

Here's what I mean about reading and rereading. Who's the single greatest influence in American popular music during the last half century? You might get some argument here, but most people in the business are likely to tell you it's Bob Dylan. And who are his influences? Woody Guthrie, for sure. Hank Williams, Elvis Presley, Lead Belly, Buddy Holly. And in turn, he has influenced all kinds of people—The Band, Bruce Springsteen, Neil Young, Don McLean (whose "American Pie" anthem identifies "the Jester" Dylan as supplanting "the King," Elvis). In any event, this is a pretty specific tradition of the singer-songwriter, with a twang. So naturally, in 2007, an album of Dylan covers came out from . . . Bryan Ferry. You know, English guy. Roxy Music, proto–New Wave with synthesizers and excellent grooming. That sounds like Dylan, doesn't it? On first glance, this might seem one of those weird high-concept disks where Billy Idol sings Irving Berlin or AC/DC goes Gershwin. Yet this project is not, as one might suspect, the product of some marketing genius at the studio. Ferry means it. He's a Dylan fan who in interviews shows knowledge and great respect for this tradition that isn't quite his. The CD is interesting for the way it brings two different styles, two different approaches really, together. It likely won't convert any nonfans of either Ferry or Dylan, but what it will do is make listeners reconsider the two changes. The questions that arise are not simply of the what-did-we-miss-about-Brian-Ferry sort. The most important ones have to do with what we missed about Dylan. For instance, what did he learn from Tin Pan Alley? Were George and Irving and Yip as important as Hank and Woody and Elvis? Is there a secret crooner under the nasal, atonal song-talker? But the questions spread out in all directions. Is the stage of the Grand Ole Opry all that far away from Broadway? Does the Great American Songbook also contain "Your Cheatin' Heart" and "Lay Lady Lay"? And finally, where do all those threads in the web of song extend to, out there in space and time?

What we ultimately learn from the Ferry-Dylan pairing is that listening, like reading, is expansive. Ordinary fans of a genre or performer hear only one thing at work; often, they listen to only one sort of music. The apotheosis of this tendency would be the outrage when Dylan went electric. In retrospect, that shift seems inevitable if we look at Dylan's influences and predilections, but at the time, many hard-core folkies were appalled. Musicians, on the other hand, listen to all sorts of music. Okay, I don't know that Angus Young does love George Gershwin, but I wouldn't be shocked if he did. They both write great hooks. The point is, musicians can appreciate music even when it comes from very different traditions from their own.

Writers are like that, too. They often have interests and tastes that are much more catholic than the average reader. Robert B. Parker names his detective "Spenser" with a medial "s" after a poet very few mystery readers will have read. That doesn't make *Looking for Rachel Wallace* a modern reworking of *The Faerie Queene* (although he does allude to it in that novel), but it tells us just a little about the range of potential influences on Parker's writing. Moreover, writers are touched by many works they have never read, bits and pieces of which come to them through other works and that they have. And they are touched by, and they are touched by, and so on. This is the real "worldwide web," a network that has been going on forever, a conversation the living have with the dead and the not-yet-born.

How is this possible? I'll have more to say on this later on, but we have need of a concept right about here: there is only One Story. It's always been there, is still there, is always the same, is always changing. Every story, poem, play, movie, television commercial, and political speech—the whole shootin' match—that has ever been told, written, remembered (no matter how vaguely) is part of that story. What that means is that literature, in its broadest sense, is all part of one system. You can be influenced by and can know a good bit about novels you've never read, stories you've never heard. Why? Because things you have read mention and make use of them. And sometimes the writers of those works haven't read the original tales. But they've been touched by them. Literature, in other words, is a system, a worldwide shared experience across millennia. There are connections everywhere because everything is connected.

Which is where the ears come in. You don't so much *see* these connections as hear them. Our language about noticing these sorts of connections is auditory. We speak of an echo of Homer in Virgil, or of Austen in Helen Fielding. Can you see echoes? Or hints, allegations, rumors, or soupçons (but then, I'm not sure you can hear that last one, either). What I'm advocating here is an inner-auditory process of reading, that you keep your inner ear attuned to the text for what it's saying, for the sounds that lie just behind the main melody. "There's just a hint of Raymond Chandler in this new mystery writer." "He's heavily influenced by Thomas Hardy with a soupçon of P. G. Wodehouse." Now, *that*, I'd like to see.

17

Improbabilities:
Foundlings and Magi, Colonels and Boy Wizards

FOR THE RECORD: I have never been a South American colonel, a Victorian coquette, a knight errant, a slave on a raft, an eighteenth-century foundling, a Chippewa reservation dweller, a soldier in Vietnam, or an English teacher in a Greek boys school. Had the opportunity presented itself, I might possibly have become a South American coquette-errant on a raft, but things didn't work out that way. On the other hand, I *have* been all those things at one time or another through the agency of novels. Yes, he said with an evil chuckle, and what's more, I'll do it again. And again. That's one of the beauties of reading.

For those of you of a certain age, I ask you to consider three years: 1966, 1969, and 1970, and while you do, recall that these were the years in which the death of the novel was not merely predicted with excessive confidence but announced as a fait accompli. Dead, dead, dead. No future. People are moving on and leaving the "print-oriented bastards" behind. Remember? For those of you who weren't out and about between Monterey and Kent State, you'll have to trust us geezers on this one. A few years ago a friend said to me that she distinctly remembers not being able to walk across campus in 1966 without seeing a copy of *The Magus*. The same was largely true three years later with *The French Lieutenant's Woman*, which was the number one fiction bestseller of that year. It was a very good decade to be John Fowles. Then, in 1970, a very big wave crested and broke on our shores with a loud sound: *Boom*. The Boom, that is—the name for the young lions in the more southerly portions of this hemisphere who were suddenly everywhere and making the novel new and miraculous. Magic realism had arrived in an English translation (God bless Gregory Rabassa) and was called, in its new language, *One Hundred Years of Solitude*. You couldn't avoid it, and I don't know why you would have tried. That wave had built and built through the 1960s, with Carlos Fuentes's *Where the Air Is Clear* (1959) and *The Death of Artemio Cruz* (1962) and Julio Cortázar's peculiar *Hopscotch* (1966). The Brazilian Jorge Amado had been at it even longer, publishing novels as early as the 1930s; his *Gabriela, Clove and Cinnamon* appeared in English in 1962, *Dona Flor and Her Two Husbands* in 1969. Sometimes, though, it takes a single event to crystallize a trend or movement, and the Boom crystallized around Gabriel García Márquez's brilliant novel.

But back to our three years and three books. What is the common denominator among them? I'm sure there are many, including astonishing events, prose mastery that we glimpse only rarely, and great historical insights, but the one that stands out to me is exoticism. We will never have a chance to be Nicholas Urfe, teaching English to schoolboys on a Greek island and having amazing encounters with a mystery man who stage-manages a living psychodrama for our benefit, or Charles Smithson, a Victorian gentleman of leisure with modern existential issues, or any of the fabulous

Buendía family living in the coastal Colombian town of Macondo, that microcosm of South American postcolonial experience. It's not all beer and skittles. When Nicholas is befuddled, we're right there with him, just as confused. We cringe at his misdeeds, his mistreatment of women (I've always wondered how women see him and never been entirely satisfied with their answers).

Films and television let us experience other lives vicariously, or perhaps voyeuristically, as we watch those lives play out. But in a novel, we can become those characters, we can identify from the inside with someone whose life is radically different from our own. Best of all, when it's over, when Huck lights out for the territories or Elizabeth marries her Mr. Darcy, we get to be ourselves again, changed slightly or profoundly by the experience, possessed of new insights perhaps, but recognizably us once more. Part of the allure of the novel lies in its ability to draw us into unfamiliar spaces and improbable lives, to let us become people we aren't, if only for a little while.

Here's something else I've never been: a boy wizard. Not only that, I'm going to go out on a limb here and say that, of the millions of fans and casual readers of Harry Potter, no one else has been, either. So what? The most amazing publishing phenomenon in history and not one person on earth has ever had the experiences of the main character. Suppose there's a lesson in that? Quite a lot of novels for young people have heroes who are quite like their readers in both their makeup and their life stories. In fact, we find that many novels for middle-schoolers feature middle-school characters confronting events and issues that happen to, you guessed it, middle-schoolers. And many of these novels are quite good and quite popular. Kathe Koja, for instance, in *Buddha Boy* (2003) gives us a quite ordinary main character, Justin, who discovers bigotry and small-mindedness in his high school when someone quite out of the mainstream, the Buddha Boy of the title, moves into the district. This setup is an old friend: Tom Sawyer is an ordinary boy in an ordinary town whose wildest adventures are only mildly extraordinary, and certainly in the realm of the familiar. We know that most readers of the first edition did not live in Hannibal, Missouri, or even any town very similar, but they could easily imagine themselves there. Writers can push that envelope a bit by setting the story in the familiar past, as Christopher Paul Curtis does in his Newbery Award–winning *Bud, Not Buddy*, set in the Depression, or *The Watsons Go to Birmingham— 1963*, whose title pretty well telegraphs for grown-ups what they will find at their destination. Most readers, certainly most of Curtis's target audience, did not live through either the Depression (nor were they orphans) nor the turmoil surrounding the civil rights movement and the racist backlash, including the Ku Klux Klan bombing of a Birmingham church, which features prominently in the plot.

Then there is that class of tales to which Harry belongs, which I would characterize as looking-glass novels. A perfectly ordinary young person goes through the looking glass or into the wardrobe or down the rabbit hole, and suddenly they're in a world they, like us, have never inhabited. It works for grown-up tales, also, and has since at least Jonathan Swift's *Gulliver's Travels* (1726). Lewis Carroll took us along with Alice into an incomprehensible world in *Alice's Adventures in Wonderland* (1865) and *Through the Looking-Glass* (1872), where cats disappear but their smiles linger, where there are White Rabbits and Red Queens and Mad Hatters giving tea parties. When the Pevensie children stumble through the back of the old wardrobe in *The Lion, the Witch and the Wardrobe*, the first book of *The Chronicles of Narnia* (1950–1956), they encounter an enchanted world in which a lion can be king and an evil White Witch can freeze the world into perpetual winter. Like Alice, the Pevensies are perfectly ordinary children, no more remarkable than any other. They simply happen upon a world not of their making and in which they can barely understand the events, the rules, or the logic. Sounds rather like a description of childhood, doesn't it?

This, then, is Harry Potter. Yes, he turns out to have remarkable powers, but he knows nothing about them. Unlike all of his Hogwarts schoolmates, he has no experience of witchcraft when he goes and knows nothing of that world. When he unwittingly causes bad things to happen to his richly deserving cousin Dudley Dursley or when he can talk to a serpent, he is as surprised as anyone and has no explanation he can offer to others or himself. What Harry has known in his first eleven years are cruelty, loneliness, failure, isolation, and bad treatment at the hands of others. Aside from being an orphan forced to sleep in a cupboard under the stairs, he is in every way perfectly normal. His normality is the thing that most drives Professor Snape crazy about him. Snape complains that he is not tremendously bright, that he doesn't work hard, cuts corners, breaks rules, and that in general, it's just not fair for someone so *average* to be the chosen one. Snape's right. The world isn't fair, even the magical world, and Harry is normal. It's the world he encounters that is not. Naturally enough, he brings a good deal of mistrust, anger, and confusion with him, and what is of major interest is how he deals with his personal issues. I wouldn't say the magical elements are window dressing, since they are the major focus, and readers may not have picked up the novels without them. But the real problems Harry encounters—aside from, you know, nearly getting killed and having his soul sucked out and such—are ordinary school problems: rivalries, bullies, girls and what to do about them, friendships, envy, loneliness, home-work, and exams. If you went to school, as I assume everyone read-ing these words did, and you didn't deal with these, you just weren't paying attention. That mix—a normal person put into extraordinary circumstances—has captured readers since before there were readers, since the crowd in the palace was listening to the poet sing *The Odyssey*. Odysseus is the least remarkable of the Greek heroes below Troy, no astounding size or abilities, only a clever mind and a determination not to die. And a bit of luck, which in ancient Greece is portrayed as the favor of the goddess Athena. It's the adventures on the way home, Calypso and Circe and the Cyclops and the trip to the Underworld, that are remarkable. Right there, I believe, is the key to Harry's success: luck, pluck, a quick mind, and a sense of when to strike and what to do. It seems to have worked.

Works for hobbits, too. What is Frodo Baggins if not a repre-sentative of the little guy? Literally. Think about it. Here is a book, three books actually, with no shortage of heroes, and none of them is the focal character. Why not Gandalf the Grey, the wizard with wisdom? Why not Gimli the Dwarf or Legolas the Elf? Why, es-pecially, not Aragorn, the once and future king? He seems custom-made for the part. He even has a love interest, unlike Frodo. In an older age this would be an epic poem and Aragorn would be the hero, no ifs, ands, or buts. Achilles gets his own epic, Odysseus his, Aeneas his, so why not Aragorn? Well, that's just it, isn't it? This is not an epic poem; it's a novel. Novels aren't about *heroes*. They're about *us*. The novel is a literary form that arose at the same time as the middle class in Europe, those people of small busi-ness and property who were neither peasant nor aristocrat, and it has always treated of the middle class. Both lyric and epic poetry grew out of a time that was elitist, a time that believed in the innate right of royalty to rule and the rest of us to amount to not very much. Hardly surprising, then, that both forms lean toward the aristocratic in subject matter and treatment. The novel, on the other hand, isn't about them; it's about us, and Frodo is us, despite the hairy feet. He's the small person caught up in the war of huge powers. He's not heroic, preferring his own hearth to the big world with its hazards. He's not even a volunteer. Essentially, he's a conscript, selected not by the draft board but by circumstance in the form of a ring that has been handed to him to deal with. Talk about your raw deals. And yet, the big heroes can't be heroes without him, evil can't be defeated, the ring can't be destroyed. Over and over, he says the task is beyond him, yet he keeps going even as body and mind seem to fail. How many soldiers, I wonder, would recognize their situation in his? How many civilians in Britain, which is where Tolkien is really talking about, found themselves performing useful and surprising service in the fight against Nazism and the drive for world domination? Whatever our nationality, we can recognize that struggle against evil, can see our possible selves in the little guy pushed to heroic extremes.

It isn't always a matter, we should note, of identifying with the protagonist. No one I know, regardless of how much they love his novel, wants to be Humbert Humbert or Victor Frankenstein, although perhaps for different reasons. Or Heathcliff. Ever want to be Heathcliff? I didn't think so. They are not the stuff of our fantasy lives, yet we may revel in their worlds, even while reviling their persons. Consider Humbert. The narrative strategy Nabokov employs is very daring, since it demands that we identify with someone who is breaking what nearly everyone will consider the most absolute taboo. Sexual violation of children is a horrible offense against the natural order, and he goes out of his way to commit that offense. Sympathy is out of the question. What the novel requires, however, is that we continue reading, something it audaciously gives us reasons to do. The word games and intellectual brilliance helps, certainly; he's detestable but charming and brilliant. The other element is that we watch him with a sort of appalled fascination: can he really intend that; does he really do this; would he really attempt even that; has he lost all sense of proportion? The answers are, in order, yes, yes, yes, and yes. Pretty clearly, then, there are pleasures in the text that are not inherent in the personality of the main character. Nabokov's central figures in general do not inspire warm and fuzzy feelings. We tend to find them interesting rather than lovable, tend to want to watch them rather than be them or feel with them.

This is a largely although not exclusively modern trait. For the most part, nineteenth-century novels relied first of all on an emotional response. We may not want to be Tess Durbeyfield, given all the misfortune that life throws at her, but we stick with her, follow her fortunes, suffer with her, feel for her. And Hardy puts us through the affective mill: disappointment, alarm, elation, pity, hope, pity, fear, discouragement, rage, pity, pity, pity. This is, after all, Thomas Hardy. He gives us a higher HMQ—human misery quotient—than any other three Victorian novelists combined. But his fellow scribblers are very much like him in terms of reader response. They want an emotional investment of their readers. Partly, of course, this has to do with the serial publication of so many Victorian works; readers have to be locked in on the characters if they are going to hang around reading magazine installments for two years. We could think of a hierarchy of desired reader responses for the nineteenth and twentieth centuries that would look something like this.

Nineteenth	Twentieth
1) Emotional response	1) Aesthetic response
2) Intellectual response	2) Intellectual response
3) Aesthetic response	3) Emotional response

Obviously, there are mavericks and wild cards out there, but this comparison works on average. Until the very late nineteenth century, novelists did not think of their work as *art*. Literary art consisted of lyric or narrative poetry and drama. Fiction in prose was more or less a branch of commerce, which was not an entirely unfair characterization. Hard to feel like Michelangelo when the printer's boy is standing impatiently in your doorway waiting for the ink to dry on your latest chapter. It's not until fairly late in the century, in 1884, when Henry James begins writing about the novel as a serious art form in *The Art of Fiction*. (Defense Counsel stipulates that this shift occurred somewhat earlier in France, just after midcentury, owing to one Gustave Flaubert.) One would hardly demand an aesthetic response above all else for a form one regarded as second-tier art, if even that. Aesthetic considerations are distinctly modern, much more the province of Virginia Woolf or Ernest Hemingway. Nor were the intellectual demands terribly high on the Victorian reader; not for their novels the word games and puzzles of Nabokov, Fowles, or Italo Calvino. No, the peg on which the Victorian hat hung was emotional.

Their goal: make us love (or hate) the characters. There aren't a lot of terribly subtle shadings of character in Dickens or Thackeray. We cheer and hiss with enthusiasm. Readers responded to these

characters as if they were family members (or threats to them). Character is absolutely central to the ongoing serial. Think of J.R. and
Bobby Ewing. Why has Susan Lucci been able to keep the same role
for three hundred years? Because viewers respond viscerally to her
character. In Victorian times, readers wrote to novelists with their
thoughts on the current book, and writers listened. Thackeray was
told that readers wanted "less of Amelia," the sugary-sweet, somewhat boring girl in *Vanity Fair*, that they wanted to see Laura marry
Warrington in *Pendennis* (which title has always struck me as more
than vaguely obscene, but no matter). Novels were changed based
on fan reaction, sometimes even to projected reaction, as in Bulwer-
Lytton's famous advice to Dickens not to attempt the more logical,
unhappy ending of *Great Expectations*. Again, I give you *Dallas*: why
did they miraculously revive the dead Bobby Ewing? Fan unrest.

In all these cases, the central reality is that readers wish to be
involved in their novels. Wish? Nay, need. The earnestness with
which nineteenth-century readers engaged with characters and their
stories is touching in its naïveté. At the same time we know that,
in our own day, characters on series television sometimes receive
fan or hate mail (more often the latter) and stars of soap operas are
often greeted with either the love or venom their characters, and
not they, merit. Whence comes that need for involvement? I believe
it grows out of the desire to be swept away to somewhere else, and
that's what novels do, even when the place they sweep us to looks
a great deal like our own. A reader in Dorset or Wiltshire might
recognize the landscapes and notable buildings of Hardy's Wessex,
might see exterior Dorchester in his Casterbridge, but the place in
which Tess or Jude live and struggle bears scant resemblance to any
place current or historical. Joyce's Dublin has real place-names in it,
and one can map out every story and novel (and indeed, someone

has, in many cases more than once). And those of us who have been to academic conferences learn, to either our consternation or, more likely, relief, that they are neither as hilarious nor as disastrous as those in the novels of David Lodge or Malcolm Bradbury. They are just close enough to the originals to give a *frisson* of recognition, just far enough away to be entertaining. The American poet Marianne Moore characterized her poetry as the making of "imaginary gardens with real toads in them." In the case of novels, the real—or potentially real—toads are characters, persons we can react to, relate to, accept or reject, identify with, suffer over.

Sometimes those persons and their environments are quite familiar, as in the case of Iris Murdoch's fiction. She was successful most of her twenty-seven times out of the gate with a fairly simple formula: take perfectly ordinary members of the privileged class—academics (like the author and her husband, John Bayley), television executives, publishers, stage people—place them in ordinary circumstances—summer home, retirement villa, suburban terrace house—and introduce one odd event—a surprise appearance of former friend or complete stranger, an accidental death, a crime witnessed—and watch what happens. And we did. Readers flocked to her work from *Under the Net* (1954) to *Jackson's Dilemma* (1995), putting up with sometimes windy philosophical observations from the truly observant and the harebrained alike, just to see what happened next. It was a familiar world, as many of her readers did indeed belong to the class she portrayed, did in fact live in Murdochland, as it was often called, or its overseas equivalents. Why? Because she made us believe in her characters and want to see what they might get up to.

Do we have to love them? Want to be them? No. That's part of the beauty of the novel, that it follows the Law of Us and Them: Readers choose the degree to which they identify with characters.

We can try on experiences and identities for a few hours that we would never want as our permanent condition, or we can stand aloof from the proceedings and take only a clinical interest. We don't have to be Heathcliff or Aureliano Buendía or Tess, but we can be if we want. Every teacher knows this, having had students in the same class divide between those who identify fully with Atticus Finch or Jane Eyre and those who wouldn't touch them with a barge pole. The novel goes on either way, and so does the reading.

If one tweaks that formula slightly, making the event weird rather than merely odd, one arrives at Fay Weldon. Her world is quite similar to Murdoch's (and indeed, she was a one-time worker in the vineyards of British television), but the events that befall them are distinctly peculiar. A woman wakes up one morning to find that her unfaithful husband has cloned her. Repeatedly. That, not surprisingly, is the premise of *The Cloning of Joanna May* (1989). In *The Hearts and Lives of Men* (1987), a child in a bitter divorce is kidnapped at the behest of one parent, but the crime goes awry when the plane she's on blows up in midair and she, sitting far back in the tail section, floats gently to earth, launching her on a bizarre fairy-tale journey that is equal parts hilarity and heartbreak. The novel is a delightful satire of many worthy targets in contemporary society, most of them involving people with more money than brains or scruples. Her most famous creation, of course, is Ruth, a wronged woman who lets her dark side come to the fore in the service of revenge in *The Life and Loves of a She-Devil* (1983). As far as I know, to date no one has ever been a she-devil or been cloned, and the record of tail sections of planes gliding gracefully to earth is discouragingly slim, yet that has not kept readers from identifying with Weldon's characters or becoming absorbed in their adventures and mishaps. Perhaps that is the most miraculous thing about reading, the way in which we can become captivated by both the familiar and the alien alike.

18

What's the Big Idea—or Even the Small One?

QUICK: *FRANKENSTEIN*. GOOFY MOVIE about a guy with elevator shoes and bolts in his neck, right? Well, there is a monster in there. But Mary Shelley's novel is really an expression of romantic philosophy and a treatise about the limits of science. Had she lived at the point in history where we had nuclear power or genetically modified foods or embryonic stem cell research or any of those other things that have been identified over the years as "our Frankenstein's monster," she might have written about them. She, however, had the great good fortune to come along at a time when medical schools were examining the bodies of the recently dead and entrepreneurs were gleefully digging up specimens for the doctors' uses.

There's a popular myth that English professors are all frustrated novelists, but a more interesting question is, are novelists all frustrated philosophers? Okay, maybe not Harold Robbins. But the others. The *Alexandria Quartet* isn't, as my students think, merely about kinky sex. Lawrence Durrell calls his four-decker book a "novel of relativity," although I think it owes as much to Heisenberg as to Einstein. Kinky sex probably doesn't hurt. And then there are Nietzsche and Bergson, who are everywhere in modern fiction.

Or maybe the adjective is incorrect. Maybe the novelist as philosopher isn't all that frustrated. The novels of Saul Bellow, John Fowles, and Iris Murdoch are more accessible, certainly more entertaining, primers and critiques of existentialism than, say, *Being and Nothingness*. And way more fun to read. There's a great passage in *The French Lieutenant's Woman* where Fowles has his narrator say of Charles, as he is forced to make a difficult choice, "He had not the benefit of existentialist terminology; but what he felt was really a very clear case of the anxiety of freedom—that is, the realization that one *is* free and the realization that being free is a situation of terror." The passage is typical of the novel, the idea of all of his novels. Fowles has great fun in his "Victorian" novel with counterpoising the mores and crisis of the era with those of his own, finding not, as we might expect, that the Victorians were particularly quaint or hypocritical but rather that their predicaments very much mirror our own, circa 1967, the year of the novel's composition. Their anxiety over the new threat to religious certainty posed by Darwin nicely anticipates, for Fowles, the anxiety over existence as articulated by Jean-Paul Sartre and Albert Camus. Their "piety" becomes our "authenticity," their "hell" our "nothingness." The questions with which Charles Smithson, gentleman of 1867, must wrestle—duty, honor, dignity, purpose, honesty—still resonate with the modern person, even if the outward trappings have changed.

Fowles wasn't just guessing that they would resonate, of course. He had already taken them for a test drive three years earlier in *The Magus*, where they were a smashing success. The two books are full of surface differences, but at heart they ask the same questions. Nicholas Urfe's dilemmas are very much those of Charles Smithson, updated: How do I conduct my life? Is it meaningful? Am I being honest? What gives it meaning? Those big, existentialist terms like anxiety, absurdity, nothingness, and authenticity are in many ways the age-old issues. What gives a human life value? If the person experiences a separation from God, where, then, does meaning reside? Of what, if anything, can we be certain, and how do we live with uncertainty? How can we keep death from negating the worth of our lives? The difference between the two Fowlesian protagonists is that unlike Charles, Nicholas knows the terminology and even hides behind it. Yet his protective coloration cannot save him from the genuine issues. That he discovers the need to confront them through an elaborate fiction—the godgame, as it is called in the novel—merely announces the parallel for readers, who engage ethical problems and questions through their encounters with fictional texts. We may sit down to read story, but we stand up from the novel having wrestled with issues of personal conduct and moral behavior.

And therein lies a key to ideas in fiction. If the books are to be any good, the story and its telling must work in the first instance. Who's the kingpin of idea-oriented fiction? There are probably numerous candidates, but my vote goes to George Orwell. His big two, *1984* (1949) and *Animal Farm* (1945), are in their separate ways Big Idea novels, the former a futurist cautionary tale and the latter a barnyard fable Aesop never thought of. The thrust of both is the encroachment of the state against individual autonomy—revolutions gone wrong, principles turned inside out in the slide toward totalitarianism, obsession with enemies turning all citizens into enemies. Nothing wrong there. Ample instances in the twentieth century, and Orwell didn't even know about Mao's Cultural Revolution, the Khmer Rouge, or genocide in Rwanda or Bosnia.

But here's the thing: none of that makes a good novel. Absolutely none. What makes a good novel, and these two are more than good, is plot, character, language, narrative: in a word, story. Immanuel Kant had wonderful, amazing ideas, but that didn't make him a novelist. Jonathan Swift, on the other hand, had some pretty fair ideas, and in *Gulliver's Travels* he set them in a sufficiently compelling story to keep people reading.

The Law of Fictional Ideation: It doesn't make any difference how good the philosophy is if the fiction is lousy. That master of malaprop Samuel Goldwyn said of message movies: "You got a message? Call Western Union." That may not be quite the match of "A verbal contract isn't worth the paper it's written on," but it's pretty good. But I'd go old Sam one better. If you want to write a novel of ideas, first write a novel. And make it work. Any creative-writing teacher can tell you that student fiction (bad) comes in two basic styles, the all-action-all-the-time shoot-em-up-blow-em-up and the deadly earnest message piece that is deadly dull. The first, what creative-writing guru Stephen Minot calls "mock Faulkner" (but you can substitute Stephen King or Bruce Willis movies just as easily) will have three murders, one suicide, a barn burning, a rape, and a car chase in twenty-five hundred words. The other will have absolutely nothing happening in the same space—two morose teenagers tossing around Ingmar Bergman dialogue about their boredom. At least the former provides some unintentional levity. One suspects this is why products of creative-writing classes and first novels in general wind up chiefly in desk drawers and not on bookstore shelves.

The novels that last, and have something to say, capture us with narrative, then hit us with ideas. Generally. There are no absolutes. John Bunyan's *The Pilgrim's Progress* has hung around since 1678, but not on the strength of narrative dazzle. It's earnest, devout, and an absolute grind. So anything's possible. For the most part, however, novels need to be novels. They need to engage their readers and not rely on religious or ideological fellow feeling. That *The French Lieutenant's Woman* was the bestselling novel in the United States in 1969 is a testament to Fowles's narrative prowess, not to his ideas, interesting as they are. That the novel continues to resonate, avoiding the fate of most bestsellers, does have something to do with those ideas.

The postwar years gave us dozens of writers on both sides of the Atlantic for whom ideas form a large part of the fictional enterprise. Sometimes, as with Nabokov or Alain Robbe-Grillet, those ideas are aesthetic or formal, having to do more with the shape of the novel than its thematic content; indeed, in *Pour un nouveau roman* (1963) Robbe-Grillet proposes eliminating theme from the New Novel as one of the outdated elements, along with character and plot, that fiction no longer requires. Writers as diverse as Italo Calvino, John Barth, Claude Simon, B. S. Johnson, and Edna O'Brien attack the problem of form in a variety of ways and in novel after novel. Fowles says that a change of narration is a change in theology, and we can extend that to say much the same about a change of literary form. But many of the postwar writers confront issues we recognize as such, questions of existence and conduct, the roles dictated to the individual by society, the presence or absence of gods in the world.

Often the greatest pressure on ideation in the novel has come from writers from "emergent" groups—minorities, women, citizens of former colonies—who understandably have a lot to say after being spoken for and spoken about for so long. Take women novelists. When I went through school—including graduate school—one had the impression that there was one woman writer per era. Nineteenth-century America? Emily Dickinson. Britain? Okay, there were two,

George Eliot and one Brontë (but not two and never three). Modernist Britain? Woolf, but uneasily. And so on. And now? Two things happened. One was that pioneering feminist scholars and critics such as Bonnie Kime Scott, Sandra Gilbert and Susan Gubar, and Elaine Showalter among many others, changed the landscape of literary studies, so that modernism included not just the men and the token Woolf or Djuna Barnes, but also Willa Cather, Edith Wharton, Nella Larsen, Dorothy Richardson, H.D., Mina Loy, Vita Sackville-West, Zora Neale Hurston, and a host of others. In other words, writers who had been there all along and who had actually had quite a lot to say for themselves.

The other element was the emergence of powerful, sometimes shocking female voices. By now it's pretty clear that I hold Edna O'Brien in high regard. So do a great many readers, and for precisely those qualities in her fiction that got her work banned in Ireland, novel after novel. O'Brien refuses to write about "good" Irish girls, or to be one. Her *Country Girls Trilogy* violated a lot of taboos, one of which was that Irish women ought not be pictured as openly sexual. Showing Irish men as withdrawn, emotionally stunted, or violent probably didn't help, but it was the sexuality that did in the saga of Kate and Baba. Yet whatever the censors may have thought in the early 1960s, the sex wasn't there for prurient interest. It was an idea, and a very basic one at that: until women are accorded their full humanity, bodies and sexuality included, they can never be accorded their full rights as human beings. Male writing had tended to present Irish women as variants of some combination of nun, mother, the Countess Cathleen, and the Shan Van Vocht, or Poor Old Woman, who is symbolic of Mother Ireland herself. These are not people but emblems, and it's really hard, insists O'Brien, to live one's life as an emblem. She even has a crow to pluck with Joyce's

Molly Bloom, who is perhaps more like a real person, and certainly more sexual, than any of Yeats's women, for instance. In the short novel *Night* (1972), she offers her version of a woman's night meditation. Her protagonist, Mary Hooligan, is as engaging, full-blooded, sexual, and profane as Molly, but she also comes across as a more completely realized human being and less of an artistic conception. That's an idea at work.

Nor is O'Brien alone. At roughly the same historical moment, Doris Lessing, the Margarets Drabble and Atwood, Muriel Spark, Erica Jong, and a host of slightly younger writers such as Barbara Kingsolver have been writing about what were once called "women's issues," but which are really human issues. Dignity, the right to live freely and express oneself, equal treatment by one's fellow creatures, self-determination, the right to make one's own mistakes—those all sound pretty basic to me. What matters, of course, is that these are novelists rather than essayists or polemicists (at least, when they are writing novels), so their fiction must succeed *as fiction*. Which it has, splendidly. Lessing packs ideas and issues—about social justice, women's rights and men's wrongs, sanity and madness—into *The Golden Notebook* (1962) and her *Children of Violence* novels (1952–1969). The first work in particular is one of the great achievements of twentieth-century writing, at once complex and direct, encompassing the personal and the political, the emotional and historical. One of the most interesting features of the novel, which is structured as four differently colored notebooks recording various aspects of a writer's life, along with a framing gold-colored notebook, is the way that a series of compartments, the notebooks, ultimately defeat the effort to compartmentalize, arguing for unity in existence. Since the novel is concerned with the life of a fictional novelist, Anna Wulf, it ultimately reflects on the process of its own creation and the way that everything in a writer's life comes together and exerts pressure or influence on the written work.

Both Atwood and Kingsolver have achieved great popular success while addressing important issues as well. What they ultimately reveal is that "women's" issues simply form one thread of the broader issues that make up fiction. Atwood's Booker-winning *The Blind Assassin* (2000), for example, plays with multiple narrative frames, with novels within novels and truth within fiction, even as it explores issues of female identity and personal history. From *Surfacing* (1966) forward, Atwood has been a major feminist voice in the world of fiction, but she is perhaps never as simultaneously subtle and pointed as in *The Blind Assassin*. The play among truth, falsehood, guilt, redemption, authorship, unknowability, fiction, and identity is fascinating, perhaps the more so when the novel is paired with Ian McEwan's idea-laden *Atonement*, which appeared the very next year. That two such remarkable, similar, and yet very distinct novels would appear so close together probably says something very profound about our age, although we're likely too close to it to know what that statement might be. At the very least, we can note that metafiction in these two writers has long ceased to be a mere sleight-of-pen and become a major constituent of fiction's larger program. Kingsolver's *The Poisonwood Bible* (1998) is on one level clearly concerned with the wrongs committed by United States and European powers during and after African colonialism, but those concerns blend with the damage suffered by girls and women at the hands of colonizing male power. That the colonizer is at both the imperial and familial levels at least slightly mad goes perhaps without saying, that the damage leaves permanent scars is both expected and shocking. From her first novel, *The Bean Trees* (1988), Kingsolver has married the personal to the political and shown ethical behavior toward the world to be indistinguishable from responsibility for the self. Just as Taylor Greer, in finding her own way, must do right by the native child who is thrust into her care in that novel, so the Price girls must carve out a relationship with the world, and particularly with Africa, as they strive to sculpt their own lives.

The big, often very uncomfortable, ideas run rampant in those disquieting categories, "minority" and "postcolonial" fiction. That's nearly inevitable. How can a novel by an African American or African Caribbean writer *not* take stock of the legacy of slavery and racist mistreatment? How can an African or Indian novel, or any other from a former outpost of empire, not speak to, among other things, the experience of oppression or the chaos that so often follows when the oppressor withdraws? Chinua Achebe has a famous essay of complaint against Joseph Conrad's *Heart of Darkness*, itself a pretty dense little novella of ideas, but his better rejoinders are his fiction from *Things Fall Apart* forward. The essay states his ideas; the novels embody them. History, as I suggest elsewhere, is the one inescapable fact. Stephen Dedalus's "History is the nightmare from which I'm trying to awake," is merely a sign of his callowness. Writers as outwardly different as Salman Rushdie, R. K. Narayan, Kiran Desai, Caryl Phillips, Toni Morrison, Alice Walker, Louise Erdrich, and Edward P. Jones have in common the making of fiction filled with ideas in response to what history has handed them. Jones shocked readers of all races with his novel of black slave-owners, *The Known World* (2003), but that material ironically freed him to talk about issues of race, privilege, class, and right and wrong in ways that a conventional white-black slavery tale might not have. So, too, with Phillips, whose *Cambridge* (1991) is an astonishing experiment in voice, bringing together a nineteenth-century English woman sent to the West Indies to look over her father's sugar plantation and the slave, freed and eventually resold into bondage, whose name gives the novel its title.

What matters most, perhaps, in all these novels, and what makes the novel matter as a place for ideas, is the ability to bring broad ranges of experience down to the individual level. Groups don't lead lives; persons do. Rushdie's *Midnight's Children* isn't the story of "India" gaining independence; it's the story of Saleem Sinai, one person, the family into which he is born, his experiences as an individual in an emerging nation. It is through him that the collective can be expressed.

Right there is the genius of the novel form. It is the perfect medium for capturing individual existence, and in turn to be a near-perfect medium for capturing the experience of the group. The life of the ordinary person—right there is a big idea, the first one the novel ever had. The earlier literary forms were highly elitist. Tragedy and epic are both about the ruling class, although for rather different reasons. Comedy often had lesser nobility for characters; I can't speak for you, but my ancestors would show up in Shakespeare, if at all, as the grave diggers and comic servants, the entirely expendable class whose stage time is counted in seconds. Even the lyric was intended for the leisured classes capable of reading—it had shepherds in it but wasn't for (or even about) real shepherds. No, if your surname indicated the work you did or where you did it—Miller, Cooper, Smith, Farrier, Forester or Forster or Foster—you were excluded from the old literature. Then this new form comes along, catering to an emerging middle class and often about its members, and it's capacious enough that there might be room in there for someone who actually works for a living. It's still better to own things than do things, but it's a start. No accident about it, though: the rise of the novel coincides with the rise of a middle class, and of liberty, and of democracy.

This is a form in which ordinary people just might matter. But it's not about a class, only about individual members thereof. In fact, it's the first form in the history of Western civilization to suggest that a single person might actually matter in the grand scheme even if that person doesn't wear a crown. What a concept!

You doubt? What do these people have in common: Tom Jones, Clarissa, Huck Finn, Jay Gatsby, George Babbitt, Augie March, Bridget Jones, Emma, Silas Lapham, Don Quixote? Eponymous characters all; that is, they give their names to the titles of novels in which they play starring roles. When did that happen before? Oedipus? Hamlet? *King* Lear, for crying out loud? If you wanted a title on the stage, you needed royal blood. The novel, on the other hand, goes for red blood rather than blue. This constitutes a huge change not only in literature but in the history of ideas. This chapter seems to suggest that the twentieth century has a lock on idea-centered fiction, which is too bad. Ideas, and important ones, have been invigorating fiction since its beginning, and one idea above all others. Sure, Thomas Hardy's cosmic doubt or Dostoevsky's investigations of man and God or of crime and punishment are indubitably philosophical, but so is Henry Fielding's comic narrative of the foundling Tom Jones and his attempt to find his place in the world. And so is Dashiell Hammett's mystery with a detective named Spade, digging, maybe reluctantly, for the truth.

For novelists, there is one big idea, always present and always demanding of attention. It goes something like this: what does it mean to be human? How can we conduct our lives to best effect? For many readers, the novel is as close as we ever come to philosophy. And it may be quite close enough. Ideas, big and little, should never be discounted in the novel because "it's only fiction." It's fiction, all right, but not only.

19

Who Broke My Novel?

REMEMBER WHEN NOVELS USED to run front to back, straight through, in order, from A to Zed? When narrative was a seamless continuum of story that connected the dots and didn't leave you dangling, except at the ends of chapters? When only Burma-Shave signs had gaps in between? Man, are you old. My advice? Get over it. Mr. Dickens has left the building.

Oh, you can still find novels that read like novels, very linear and all present and accounted for. Lots of them, actually. It's just that so many novels are told upside down and backwards in a mirror that we almost don't notice.

Ever picked up a "novel" only to find it's a collection of short stories? What's up with that? Stories are stories and not chapters, right? We're being cheated somehow by a bunch of semirelated, autonomous, short narratives getting hooked together by a "novelist" too lazy to do the job properly! That about the size of it? I've heard this complaint many times in class, often in quite heated tones. Here's my advice: put a cool compress on your forehead and relax. This trend has been going on for a while now and probably won't be going anywhere soon.

One of my favorite writers of these composite novels (I wish I could claim the term, but it's Joanne P. Creighton's) is Louise Erdrich. Beginning with *Love Medicine*, she has written a series of hilarious and heartbreaking novels of life in and around a Chippewa reservation in the upper Midwest. Her own tribal affiliation is with the Turtle Mountain Chippewa of northernmost North Dakota, right up by the Canadian border. The novels's various stories, and indeed the publication order of the books themselves, often violate chronological order. *Love Medicine*, for instance, should be the penultimate novel in the cycle, but it was the first to appear. In it, the narrative begins with a story in the "now" of the novel, the early 1980s, when the death of June Morrisey Kashpaw sets the plot in motion, then jumps back to 1934, when the old people of the tale were young and relationships were being forged. There are similar jumps in chronology, point of view, and voice, with the principal storytellers being Nector and Marie Kashpaw, Lulu Lamartine, and their great-nephew/grandson (it's a maddeningly tangled family tree), Lipsha Morrisey. But some stories are told in the third person, and a few shift midway. Clearly, the traditional three unities of the theater—time, place, and action—have taken a powder.

So why tell a story this way? Well, why not? I mean that literally. *Why not?* There's nothing magical or sacred about any organizing principle, and that most certainly includes chronology. We may be accustomed to it more than to any other method, but it's only a convention, and those exist chiefly to be ignored. The thing that should never be ignored is narrative logic, and that leads us to . . . the Law of Narrative Unity: The best way to organize a novel is the way that makes the most sense for that particular book. No universals here. The only unity a novel has is whatever the writer imposes upon it and the reader discovers in it.

So why is this form of unity right for *Love Medicine*? You'd have to ask Erdrich, and I'm pretty sure she wouldn't tell you. Writers are funny that way. I can't say for sure, but here's what I think. First of all, it's a group novel. That is, the story and the outcome matter both singly (Lipsha, for instance, very much wants answers to his questions) and collectively (these people are related by blood, personal and group history, geography, and shared suffering). There is also the matter of collective knowledge—and ignorance. In any real human society, some people hold certain information, some hold other information, but no one holds all of it. And all of them together? You'd think that you would merely have knowledge by accretion, that collective knowledge would be the sum of all individual knowledge, but while that may be true, there's also collective ignorance, that the sum of what individuals don't know, or choose not to reveal, adds into the group's information database. And to a great extent this novel, and each novel in the cycle, relies on what people do not know as much as what they do. A third-person narrator, particularly one approaching omniscience, would know and reveal far too much. The two people who in some ways matter most, moreover, the deceased June and the notorious Indian activist Gerry Nanapush, are never given their own chance to narrate their stories. Why? Because what counts most in those stories is what other characters make of them. To see the various uses to which those two life stories are put, we need to hear from other characters but not from June and Gerry. This is a trick Erdrich seems to have learned from Faulkner, who knew, for instance, that Caddy Compson remains a much more vital and intriguing figure if she never explains herself but is instead interpreted by brothers Benjy, Quentin, and Jason. Erdrich, in fact, appears to have learned quite a lot from the great Mississippian, while avoiding some of his more overwrought linguistic tics. Those are some reasons we can extrapolate from observable effects in the novel, but there may be one more. I once heard Seamus Heaney say that he didn't have a long poem in him, that he was not made for epic or extended narrative verse. This is not, I believe, a fault; if one can write lyric poetry as he can, one needs no other arrows in the quiver. It may be the same for Erdrich, that she is most attuned to short bursts of narrative, most comfortable assembling those pieces into coherent, if discontinuous, wholes.

If that's the case, it applies to quite a lot of her contemporaries. Tim O'Brien has made a career out of cobbling stories together into novels, most famously in his two Vietnam novels, *Going After Cacciato* and *The Things They Carried*. He has said that writing in shorter, self-contained units has several advantages. For one thing, stories (unlike chapters in some novels) have beginnings, middles, and ends and thereby give emotional satisfaction to readers. Writing story-chapters also allows him to publish pieces ahead of the novel's appearance, allowing him to gauge readers' response and offering the chance to make money on the stories themselves. A warning here to budding writers: there are so few paying venues for short fiction these days (even compared to when O'Brien made those comments in the 1980s) that this angle is not a strong rationale for this mode of writing. I don't want to set up any false expectations. We see it in that other O'Brien, Edna, in her alarming *In the Forest*. The main character, or perhaps main focus or inquiry, is a seriously unhinged young man who commits multiple murders. For good and sound reasons, we'd rather not spend any more time inside his head than we must, so it falls to others to report his conduct and that of the village that creates him.

These novels are many things, but cookie-cutter is not one of them. You'll never think, "This was built from a kit." Precisely because each one needs to justify itself, to establish its unity in its own way, each one is unique. And that goes for novels by the same writer. One of my favorite practitioners of the mode is the English Julian Barnes. He made his name in this country with *Flaubert's Parrot* (1984), about a doctor, Geoffrey Braithwaite, whose life story suspiciously resembles that of Emma Bovary's hapless husband, Charles. The novel is filled with Braithwaite's mini-essays, personal reminiscences, pet peeves, jokey lists, and even a parody final examination. It has really only one conventionally narrative chapter, called "Pure Narrative," and it is heartbreaking indeed. One sees in that chapter why the main character must approach his issues indirectly, through the filter of Gustave Flaubert and especially his two signature works, *Madame Bovary* and the short story "A Simple Heart." The novel establishes its unifying rationale through Braithwaite's psychological needs and intellectual defenses. His subsequent work, *A History of the World in 10½ Chapters* (1989), is much less character-driven and indeed proves resistant to classification. Is it a novel, a set of essays and narratives, a collection of short stories, or what? I tend to follow the writer, and since he says it's a novel, that's okay with me. Even when he returns to character-driven fiction, as in *Arthur and George* (2005), a tale of Sir Arthur Conan Doyle's involvement in righting the judicial wrongs done to George Edalji, who was improperly committed in a case of animal mutilation early in the last century, Barnes shies away from the sort of conventional narrative favored in Doyle's Sherlock Holmes stories and novels. The pressure of the tale—from event to accusation to trial to conviction to appeal to eventual vindication—pushes the novel toward linearity, toward, in fact, the detective story, yet Barnes, who also writes detective fiction under the pseudonym Dan Kavanagh, understands how to exploit the genre without sliding into it. The tension between expectation and performance adds to the drama of the narrative: we know what the Holmesian version of this would sound like, and this isn't it. Rather, it's something far richer, far more capable of complexity and nuance, yet still possessed of the same urgency as the best detective stories.

You know by now that I'm a fan of slightly deranged narratives. One of my favorite creators of same is the Belfast poet Ciaran Carson. Poet, Gracie? Yes, very much so—poet, musician, memoirist, essayist, fabulist, novelist. Plus, in poetry he's almost normal. A lyric poem is a lyric poem in his hands, but a prose narrative? Almost unclassifiable. Sometimes more than almost. *The Star Factory* (1997) may be a memoir, but it's a memoir like no other, combining personal experience of growing up in Belfast before the Troubles and of life there during them, industrial history, local legend, etymologies, and meditations on the sign system of his father's glowing cigarette tip in the darkness. When he turns to more purely fictive material, as he does in *Fishing for Amber* (1999), the weave is just as complex, bringing together tales from Ovid's *Metamorphoses*, usually ribald in the retelling, Irish fairy stories of a particularly dark cast that generally focus on abduction and hazard, wild tales of painters and painting from the Dutch golden age. The book is quite beyond genre. Carson subtitles it *A Long Story*, which is undeniable. It is book-length, fictive, and somewhat unified by subject matter, theme, and form. Is that a novel? It sounds like one, sort of. Is it as unified as we would like a novel to be? That depends on who's doing the liking.

And this brings us to the problem of definitions: What is a novel? What do we mean when we call something a novel? Can we find agreement among our various expectations? How important is a story through-line? How much thematic or topical unity is sufficient?

Of all the vexing questions about the novel, and they are legion, the most vexing of all is also the most basic: what is a novel? It's the discussion that every instructor dreads, and it almost always begins in the negative: *Love Medicine* (or *Winesburg, Ohio* or *Flaubert's Parrot* or *Go Down, Moses* or, well, take your pick) isn't really a novel, is it? And so always, you're off to a bad start because there's that disapproval in the discussion; novels are novels, the comment seems to say, and you're pulling a fast one here. The question, moreover, is loaded with assumptions and embedded answers: "*I* know what a novel is, we all know what novels are supposed to have and do and be, and this ain't it, Chester. Now, weasel out of that one. If you can. Which I doubt." Yea, verily, the instructor rarely can, because the person who poses the question has already made up his mind. The work in question will never be a novel. Now here's the interesting part: when you get right down to the discussion, the students won't all agree. Neither will professors, but, happily, they rarely show up in multiples in the classroom. The question, or challenge, however, presumes a single possible answer—this is what a novel is, accept no substitutes. Yet the novel, or rather, The Novel, is almost nothing but substitutes. We can set up a side-by-side taste test to show the problems.

Presumed Ur-novel	Novels We Know and Love
A work of fiction (a made-up story, more or less)	Check.
A work of fiction (a made-up story, more or less)	Check.
Book-length	Check.
Possessing characters	Check, mostly.
Featuring a main character	Um, maybe?
A single story line	Houston, we have a problem.
A single viewpoint, or at least a single type of viewpoint (allowing for multiple first-person narrators, for instance)	Now you're just being silly.
A continuous, if not chronological, narrative	Read much, do you?
Unity as to plot, genre, theme	Unity of some sort is nice.

Maybe the divide isn't that clear-cut, but it does exist in readers' minds, as any teacher of twentieth-century fiction can tell you. And the Ur-novel of column A does exist, with innumerable avatars. All of George Eliot, for instance, or William Dean Howells. Or John Galsworthy or Arnold Bennett or Stephen King or Agatha Christie or Tony Hillerman or J. K. Rowling. Yes, Harry may be a most unconventional boy, but he exists in a highly conventional novel structure. The school-year story arc of each novel makes it ideal for a front-to-back chronological treatment, and it lends a good deal of unity. Chapters have their own pattern of rising and falling action, with plenty of cliff-hangers. Good guys and bad guys are at least as clear-cut as in any Dickens novel (where appropriate cheering and jeering is also invited). This makes sense, of course, in the case of novels for young, inexperienced readers, for seekers of mystery or suspense (where telling tales out of order is really not playing the game), for all those readers of genres that rely on the if-then nature of their universes. And there's a lengthy pedigree back to at least the nineteenth century. The Harry Potter books are, in fact, the most Victorian novels I know of. They even, as the series progresses, have the size to prove it.

Which (form, not length) is my point. What we think of as an immutable truth of the novel—this is what novels have always looked like and what they *should* look like—is actually a historically and economically conditioned form. As I suggested in the extremely abbreviated history of the novel earlier, the nineteenth century, particularly in Great Britain, capitalized on a unique moment in economic and publishing history to try an experiment: serial publication of novels. What we think of as the great fiction of the Victorian era—*Middlemarch, Vanity Fair, Great Expectations*, pretty much the lot, right up through *Tess of the D'Urbervilles*—first saw daylight either in the pages of a weekly or monthly magazine or paper or, wonder of wonders, as a stand-alone series of monthly installments that would be boxed and available at the bookseller's stall. They're not all the same as a result, but they contain some conspicuous similarities. They're long (even the short ones). They're linear. They follow the fortunes of a single hero or heroine, with side trips into subplots on figures of slightly lesser interest. They have emotionally satisfying resolutions that often neatly wrap up every narrative thread (of that, more anon). They tend to employ one of two narrative viewpoints: first person (for the novel about a person growing up) or omniscient (for everything else), both of which work swimmingly for well-padded, three-decker novels. And, on average, they're wonderful, if a little slow for contemporary readers. All these things work well for narratives that stretch out for a couple of years at the rate of two or three new chapters per month.

But here's the thing: they're the new kids, the result of cheap paper and inexpensive book production. And what we think of as this "new" phenomenon of novels told out of order has a fairly impressive lineage. Faulkner and Hemingway, to name only two . . . or even Chaucer and Boccaccio. I know, I know, those last two guys weren't novelists, but you get my point. Discontinuous narrative has been around for a while. And not just in *The Canterbury Tales* and the *Decameron*. Ancient Irish epic, for instance, mixes prose sections with verse sections and shows a pronounced tendency to jump around narratively. We can even go back further, to Homer. *The Iliad* is told in a pretty straightforward manner, from the withdrawal of Achilles in a fit of pique to the death of Hektor. That makes sense: it's a series of causal connections, in which this decision prompts that response leading to the next action and so on. *The Odyssey*, on the other hand, is told in a more roundabout manner. Telemachus goes searching for his father, visiting Nestor, another of the Greek heroes at Troy, and others to gather information. That father, Odysseus, meanwhile is ordered to leave the nymph Calypso, with whom he's been cohabiting for several years (it's a hard life), and when he pitches up at the Phaeacian court, he tells the tale of the last ten years, of all his struggles and adventures. This approach also makes sense: his journey involves far more random wandering and far less causal linkage than the story of Achilles' wrath. It's a narrative instance of horses for courses. One tells the story one has in the way that fits one's material, whether the story is by Homer or Orhan Pamuk. Human beings have always, as nearly as I can discover, had access to both continuous and discontinuous narratives, and the novel is no exception. Today we can find many novels that would read perfectly for a misguided Victorian whose time machine plopped him down in the year 2000-something, but many more of which he could make neither heads nor tails. How did it come to this? Well, you may not have noticed, but it was ever thus. We can go back to Laurence Sterne and *Tristram Shandy* (ever notice how almost anything dodgy about the novel seems to go back there?). In its earliest days, the novel could look just any old way. It could be the journal of a shipwrecked man or a cascade of letters found in a trunk or a confession of a sinner, justified or not, or, indeed, a conventional linear narrative from alpha to omega. The point is, that was just one of several options. And then for the better part of a century, that was *the* option. Well, if you'd come right after that when suddenly the means of production shifted—no more monetary incentive—what would you do? Darned right. Except for those like Galsworthy and Bennett, for whom the conventional novel was a thing of economic beauty, the modernists weren't having a lot to do with the linear novel.

The moderns do just about everything else you can do with or to a novel. I'll not belabor poor old Joyce again, having made hay in that field many times over. But consider John Dos Passos, in both *Manhattan Transfer* (1925) and the novels that comprise the *U.S.A.* trilogy (1930–1936), which are mosaics, assemblages of pieces aimed at portraying not some measly story of puny individuals but the *big* story of the whole thing (New York City in the former, the whole country in the latter), against which we puny individuals play out our measly lives. Dos Passos looks at the country—trains whizzing everywhere, teletypes clattering, speakeasies jumping, leftists agitating and governments cracking down on them—and says, now *there's* a story worth telling. And it is. And he does. The technical problem, however, confronts him: how do you tell a tale this large about a people this fractious? Not the way Howells or Twain could have told it, that's for sure. Maybe the way Picasso would tell it. It presents its subject—contemporary America—from a variety of perspectives, using techniques we don't often associate with fiction. It has a main narrative line with characters, to be sure, but then it also has sections called "Camera Eye," which are snapshots of moments and scenes from around the country, rapid-fire "Newsreels," which attempt to mimic the new cinematic feature in words (employing both the headline style and the telegraphic texts of actual newsreels), and miniature biographies, mostly of admired cultural, often leftist, heroes and villains such as Randolph Bourne and Emma Goldman, Luther Burbank and Big Bill Haywood. To further confuse the issue, many of these pieces aren't exactly in prose. Newsreels, obviously, have their own delivery, scarcely related to the norms of English prose narrative, while the styles he adopts for the biographies, though varied, are largely pointillist and impressionistic. Some, like those of Burbank and William Jennings Bryan, are written in long verse lines more suggestive of Carl Sandburg's poetry or William Carlos Williams's epic *Paterson* than any work of fiction. In fact, in the populist message, the uneasy combination of optimism and disillusionment, the mixing of genres, the wholesale borrowing of real-life materials, and the apparent formal freedom, *U.S.A.* probably resembles *Paterson* more than any other work of literature.

This tendency displays itself all over in modernist literature: in Faulkner and Woolf, to be sure, as well as in Dorothy Richardson's twelve-novel leviathan, *Pilgrimage*, and in Joyce and Sherwood Anderson or Henry Green. Certainly, writers employing conventional linear narrative never went away. One can't imagine E. M. Forster writing like Dos Passos or even his good friend Woolf, or D. H. Lawrence or Fitzgerald emulating Joyce or Faulkner. Then, too, the modernist era was also the age of the great mystery writers— Dorothy L. Sayers, Josephine Tey, Marjory Allingham, Agatha Christie, Dashiell Hammett, Raymond Chandler, Ross Macdonald—none of whom could properly do their job without linear narrative. But in general, modernism takes a sharp turn away from the conventionality of the Victorian novel.

And things were just getting started. The phenomenon really picked up momentum sometime after 1950. The French New Novel, of course, did serious and intentional damage to all aspects of the traditional novel, with Alain Robbe-Grillet leading the way and the Italian Italo Calvino further exploding the form, although the Anglo-American postmodernists—from John Barth, Robert Coover, and John Fowles right down to Erdrich, the several O'Briens, Susan Minot, and Audrey Niffenegger.

This last writer's novel, *The Time-Traveler's Wife*, is particularly interesting in its rationale for a nonsequential narrative. As the title suggests, only one principal character, Henry DeTamble, time-travels, if unwillingly. His chronological dislocations hit him pretty much the way other people are struck by migraines. Clare Abshire, his eventual wife, lives in normal time, and the result is, predictably, difficult. The first time they meet, Henry is twenty-four and Clare five; somewhat later, he is thirty-six and she is twelve. In the normal course of things, such varying age ratios are impossible: I have always been two years older than my next brother and would be greatly disturbed if it were otherwise. The narrative jumps from date to date in a nonsequential order, producing in readers some of the dislocation and confusion to which Henry and Clare are subject, although Niffenegger provides both the dates and ages of each (particularly helpful when Henry's age is wholly unpredictable) at the start of each new encounter. I have frankly never encountered such a strategy before, although I'm sure it exists somewhere. Nevertheless, it's a dazzling exercise in joining discontinuous narrative to increasing-intensity plotting, where the stakes rise appreciably as we near the resolution. To tell such a story in straight chronological sequence would, it seems to me, violate the central concept of the novel, which is, roughly, you never can tell. It would also put a damper on the admittedly dizzying fun.

Why this acceleration of nonlinear narrative in the postwar years? It might have to do with the rise of creative-writing programs, in which the short story is the prized, because manageable and repeatable in the fourteen-week semester, form. It may be due to other environmental factors, such as the exhaustion of (or disgust with) linear narrative through overuse in film and television. Or it may be that writers, like the rest of us, enjoy playing with the new toy, that the exploded novel offers a range of narrative possibilities that have not already been mined out, that there are still new ways of telling stories and new stories, as Niffenegger shows us, to be told. And if there's one thing that a literary form whose name means "new" should never become, it's old hat.

20

Untidy Endings

N.B.: While Management has always done its best to avoid plot spoilers, it finds that there may be no way around them in the present chapter. It regrets any inconvenience and apologizes in advance.

SOMETIMES I WISH I'D been born in the nineteenth century. Sure, there were lots of social strictures one didn't dare violate and those high, starched collars, but on the other hand I could have carried one of those really cool canes with malachite or ivory heads. One could carry one these days, but the look is a trifle affected, don't you think? Also on the plus side: being able to appreciate the endings of Victorian novels. I'm a child of the mid-twentieth century, though, and I find I prefer my endings a little messy. The greatest novel of my century ends with the word "yes," but we're not sure what it's assenting to. My era is one of indeterminacy and equivocation, and I like it that way. When Updike has Rabbit Angstrom run at the end of *Rabbit, Run*, what is he running toward, or from? When Nabokov has Pnin drive out of town at the end of his eponymous novel, where's he going? Faulkner has Quentin Compson cry out in his mind, at the end of *Absalom, Absalom!* in response to the question of why he hates the South, "*I dont. I dont! I dont hate it! I dont hate it!*" What is resolved by that ending? Nothing. What do we learn? By the escalation of end punctuation, going from a period to the succession of exclamation points, something is driving Quentin wild, but we can't say quite what, nor does the text.

I love it. But then, I have lived through the era of *Waiting for Godot* and *Who's Afraid of Virginia Woolf*, of films by Stanley Kubrick and Robert Altman, of novel theory by Roland Barthes and Alain Robbe-Grillet. The novels of my era, *The Magus* and *The Floating Opera* and *Midnight's Children* and *Beloved*, would be incomprehensible to Victorian readers. I live after relativity and quantum theory, after the Battle of the Somme and Nagasaki and Auschwitz, after the Long March and the Khmer Rouge. Certainty is a stretch, particularly in the matter of endings, after all that. Besides, I'd just look silly with a frock coat and an ivory-headed cane. But my Victorian counterparts? They loved order and completion. For them, novels needed to be finished. Resolved. Tidy, even.

Try this on for size. You've been reading a novel for what seems like months (may have been months, in fact). You've got the fat part in your left hand and a very few pages in your right. Now here's what happens. The Hero, who has had some difficulty, is renewed. He finds his old tormentors from childhood still as nasty as ever. Two minor characters who have slid into and out of the story for absolute ages have married, as they should have done four hundred pages earlier (yes, it's that long), and one of them has even died. One villain has been caught and put in prison for life for fraud against the Bank of England (proving, one guesses, the maxim "Go big or go home"); he says the experience has improved him immensely and recommends prison for anyone needing to straighten out his life. But wait, there's more. Another villain is discovered to be in prison as well, this one for a more straightforward robbery that failed. Several good persons are found to be living life as ever, although if they've been especially good, they are rewarded with matrimony. Several characters have died, and although the circumstances are varied, the Hero learns a valuable life lesson from each. The wife who made him wretched has died, and from that he learns not to trust love, or at least the sillier romantic notions of same. One good-hearted soul who was forever in financial difficulty has, unaccountably, been made a judge. The Hero, having learned about love the hard way, discovers that a truer love was right in front of him all the time, back when he was too impetuous and shallow to notice. The owner of this love, unaccountably, doesn't hold the Hero's bad conduct against him, and they marry quicker than you can say Jack Robinson. Or David Copperfield.

You think I'm kidding? Okay, again, with names. Dora, the wife with whom he was so unhappy, dies. In a shipwreck, Steerforth and Ham both die, Ham in a heroic rescue attempt, Steerforth, presumably of drowning but more probably of terminal triviality and cruelty (since he led David down that path, he has to die to show David the error of his ways). Uriah Heep is in prison for life, and really rather happy about it, considering, and Littimer is there, too. In an almost Kafkaesque gesture, Mr. Creakle, the horrible schoolmaster of David's youth, has found just punishment in being effectively jailed himself, although since he is the magistrate in charge of the prison, he cannot see the irony. David overcomes his romantic disillusionment through experiencing real love with Agnes, whom he marries in a lightning-round courtship. Along the way, he realizes the goodness of Mr. Peggotty, Ham, Miss Betsy, Dr. Strong and

Annie, and Peggotty herself. He shows us that transformation to the good is not only possible, it is rewarded, through the fates of Little Em'ly Peggotty, Mrs. Gummidge, and, most especially, himself. The good people get rewarded, the bad punished, the righteous uplifted, and in general, justice prevails in the world.

In the immortal words of that eminent literary critic John McEnroe, you cannot be serious.

Ah, my dears, but I'm afraid he is. And the crowd—for he entertained the masses—went wild. Me? Less wild. You know, Dickens is great. The grotesque characters, the wild improbabilities, the low comedy and high ideals, the full-contact narrative approach, all great. Except the endings. His endings are just so *tidy*. Everybody, no matter how minor, gets his or her story finished. But of course there are still problems, as there are in all novels. Even when things look wrapped up, there are plenty of loose ends.

Don't get me wrong; I love Dickens. He would be my favorite Victorian novelist if there weren't Hardy, but who can resist that much misery and gloom? *Tess of the D'Urbervilles* is the most exquisitely painful reading experience I've ever had. Or painfully exquisite. Whichever is the adjective and which the adverb, I mean them in every possible combination and connotation. *Jude the Obscure* is merely wretched (the emotional ride, not the novel), but *Tess* is the train wreck you can't stop, can't take your eyes off, and can't believe how beautiful the carnage is. Even there, excessive tidiness. Hardy also wraps up his novels with neat bows. The bows drip blood, but they're very neat. The main differences are that, first, Hardy's novels are much less populous, with minor characters falling from view long before the end, and, second, at the end everyone is dead. Okay, not everyone, just villains and heroes. That's perhaps the difference between Hardy as tragedian and Dickens as essentially comedic.

Both cause their characters to battle their share of demons; only one believes they can survive the battle. But what I intended to say before Hardy butted in was that I'm not singling Dickens out for abuse. Allowing for differences in cosmic outlook, Victorian endings are pretty much all the same. Neat. Tidy. They achieve that word that drives me crazy: closure. With a vengeance.

Not only that, I don't think it's Dickens's fault. It's God's. More specifically, it the fault of the God the Victorians fashioned for themselves, one who brooked no nonsense, who meted out punishment and reward absolutely (no half-baked purgatory for them—it was grace or perdition all the way), who was very strict in his requirements, such as insisting on widows wearing black for a half century or so, but who was above all things just and fair, if demanding. Good and evil got what they had coming to them with that God. Apparently, Dickens never noticed the irony of a loving and above all just deity who could consign all of those working people to the most degrading sort of poverty, but we'll let that pass. *David Copperfield* is just early enough that he can believe in that God still. Once his beautiful young sister-in-law dies and his marriage has turned to dust, he begins to have some questions, theologically. He also begins to kill off "young, beautiful, and good" heroines at a serial-murderer rate. Agnes has no idea how lucky she was to be in this book and not the next several. But the endings don't really change much; they still tumble out as so many neatly wrapped packages.

Now I have several objections to the Victorian ending, some literary in nature and some entirely private (and which shall remain so). For starters, and this is no small consideration, life's not like that. Novels, except for the Hardy sort, end as if all the questions of life have been settled even when the protagonists have several decades to go. That's like calling a mile horse race done after six furlongs. A lot of interesting things can happen in that last quarter mile. In fact, that's the part where the crowd rises up and starts paying serious attention. Yet somehow a life's story has been settled at the sixth furlong pole, or the fifth, or even the midpoint. Since many novels not only begin but end in the middle of life's way, laying on a perfect, happy ending seems a bit precious. This tendency is worst in the bildungsroman, the novel of childhood and youth, which ends typically at twenty-four or thereabouts. The best a bildungsroman should say is that the hero is rather less callow (clueless, unconsciously cruel, naïve, take your pick) than before. Yet they are often the worst offenders, as witness *David Copperfield* or *Great Expectations*, giving us the whole nifty bundle in the hero's midtwenties. Good heavens! Most of us at twenty-four have scarcely begun to straighten ourselves out and still have plenty of screwups in front of us. In the real world, in fact, there is only one ending, and it's not particularly tidy. There are always loose ends with a death: estate taxes, probate, disagreements among relatives, varying interpretations of the deceased's life. When Auden says that, dying, Yeats "became his admirers," he doesn't say that the admirers were all in agreement. Auden himself was of at least two minds. At a conservative estimate. Saints preserve us from the untimely definitive ending.

But that's the lesser argument I would make. My chief complaint is aesthetic: too much tidiness kills the book. We find ourselves reading merrily along, following this meandering course where, it seems, anything is possible, and then a couple of chapters from the end, the corps of engineers has shown up, dredged a channel straight as a string, and lined the bottom with concrete. Such a strategy may get you to your destination sooner, but it doesn't make the trip more enjoyable. Rather the opposite. There's more than a little of the deus ex machina at work here. In Greek drama, when the writer had managed to get the plot hopelessly entangled, he would sometimes resort to lowering a god onto the stage by means of a cranelike device (the mechane, or in Latin, whence comes the phrase, *machina*) to apportion reward or punishment and make things work out to the playwright's satisfaction. The problem with such a solution is that it is unearned, that neither the plot nor the characters have taken us to the resolution. In other words, it's a cheat. You needn't take my word for this; ever since Aristotle, critics and theorists have decried such devices as unfair play that cheapens the work. Not only that, but in the case of the novel, there's a multiplier factor. The more plot threads you tie off smartly, the more obviously contrived the narrative becomes. This artificiality is the more jarring in the Victorian novel, since it strives so mightily to hide its artificiality, only in the final chapters to parade that very artifice, and clumsily at that. Were these postmodern works that ceaselessly conk us on the head with reminders that they're all made up, we would be less surprised. Yet those are precisely the works least likely to violate common decency by foisting off an ending with hospital corners.

I've said before, and it bears repeating at this late date, that all novels are inventions. They aren't true, even when they are about real personages. The appearance of reality or fidelity to life is an illusion, achieved through devices every bit as conscious as those of writers pushing the artifice of their creations. Writers, either singly or as a function of their literary milieu, decide the degree to which they will embrace the illusion of verisimilitude. Realism, therefore, is not a necessary condition of narrative but a literary construct. Yet writers of the age that accepted the limitations of literary realism freely rejected those limits when it comes to endings. Why? Commerce. Novels were big business in the nineteenth century. The competition on one level was limited: no films, television, Internet, radio, recordings, or video games. On another, it was fierce. There were dozens of novelists who were quite good and popular (or in danger of becoming so), so you had to woo your readership. And part of that was to leave them, if not laughing, at least satisfied. Provide answers for every question, including a few that weren't asked. Wrap every package. Tie off loose ends. Police the area. This was a big deal, because the ending is the last thing readers see and what they're likeliest to remember. Then, too, as I've already noted, they had lived with the novel for up to two years as it came out every month, and who would deny them this last chance at happiness? Certainly not Dickens or Thackeray.

Which is part of what's going on with endings. It's like chess—opening gambits you can learn from a book, take from a list of possible strategies, but endgames are a combination of necessity and who you are. You make what you can from the pieces left on the board. The possibilities you see will be limited by availability, naturally, but even more so by your tendencies and outlook. Bobby Fischer finished off opponents one way, I'm told, Garry Kasparov another, Anatoly Karpov yet another. All were great, none quite like another. So, too, with novels: Dickens could no more write an open-ended, provisional finale than he could fly. Some of it was who he was and some was how he thought about readers and his relationship to them. Which brings us to the Law of Shutting Doors: The degree of closure in the ending of a novel is in direct proportion to the eagerness of the novelist to please his audience. The nineteenth-century novelists were extremely eager to please, far more so than any "literary" writers since. To find the kind of loyalty in the twentieth century between artist and audience that Thackeray or Dickens enjoyed, you have to look to the popular culture, to romance novelists like Barbara Cartland or to daytime talk television. Think Oprah Winfrey minus the daily visual contact and you'll about have it.

Did I mention that it's a century thing, a tale of different epochs feeling different things about writer and reader? Well, it is. In case you've not heard it before, you should know the secret: literature is a fashion industry. We literature types are often loath to admit this unpleasant truth, yet truth it be. Writerly fortunes come and go with time. From Wordsworth on, for about a century, John Donne and the metaphysical poets of the seventeenth century couldn't get arrested, until the modernists, chiefly T. S. Eliot, came along with an appreciation of irony and intellection to rescue poor old Donne from the trash heap of literary history. And there's a fairly predictable arc of fame and regard when a writer dies. First, there may be an outburst of sympathy and interest, but then there will certainly be a couple of decades at least of neglect when we're *so* over whatever he or she specialized in. Lawrence Durrell? Who needs that anymore? Iris Murdoch? How quaint! Anthony Burgess? Too mannered. Then the wheel will turn another time and the reputation will rise again. Virginia Woolf was buoyed back to the surface and even above it. Henry Green rose slightly, got reprinted, had a few articles written about twenty years after his death, then slid into neglect again. I live for the next revival.

Sometimes we get to see the cycle run through a couple of times. When I first started in the academic racket, D. H. Lawrence was one of the Big Two of modernist British fiction, along with Joyce (with Woolf largely an afterthought). This, I hasten to say, was after his period of enforced oblivion following his death in 1930. By the 1960s and 1970s, he was the hottest thing going. The novellas *The Fox* and *The Virgin and the Gypsy* and the novel *Women in Love* were made into "major motion pictures" in fairly rapid succession between 1967 and 1970. But there were other trends rising, too, and he seems not to have survived the combination of feminism and deconstruction. He's just too sloppy for our contemporary tastes. A world that made Raymond Carver's cool minimalism the toast of the time can never appreciate the overheated looseness of Lawrentian prose. Too much late, dark romanticism there altogether. And while Lawrence would unquestionably have seen himself as demanding that women be strong, his "feminism," if we can even call it that, bears little resemblance to what we know as feminism after Gloria Steinem and Simone de Beauvoir. In fact, Kate Millett was one of the early but by no means solitary feminist critics of Lawrence's sexual politics, which are murky in the best of times. Finally, we can't discount entirely the possibility that Ken Russell's over-the-top cinematic take on *Women in Love* did in Lawrence's reputation. Coming as it did at the end of the decade that began with the 1960 obscenity trial (and acquittal) of *Lady Chatterley's Lover*, it frames the era nicely.

Fair? Not really, neither the rise nor the fall. But whoever said literary fortunes should be fair? Follow a writer long enough, and you'll see the shifting winds of fashion do their work. But I digress. (Now there's news.) The topic under discussion was supposed to be the wheel of history and our previous, "modern" century.

We hit about 1910 (the year Woolf claims human nature changed) and endings just went all to pieces. Modernity, or more particularly modernism, decided it could live without certainty. Oh sure, some of the old guard, folks like Arnold Bennett and John Galsworthy, along with writers of genre fiction from Rafael Sabatini (who had a bestseller nearly every year in the 1920s with books like *Captain Blood* and *Scaramouche*) and Dashiell Hammett were still doing the old thing, more or less. But others were moving on. Consider, if you will, two examples, neither of whom could be described as wildly experimental. E. M. Forster found early success in the first decade of the century with fairly conventional novels like *A Room with a View* (1908), which, as a romantic comedy, ends quite predictably with the appropriate couple honeymooning where they first encountered each other. Fast-forward sixteen years to *A Passage to India*, an altogether more problematic story of intercultural misunderstanding amid the evils of colonialism. At the last, the wronged Dr. Aziz, now exonerated, and the well-meaning but not wholly effectual Cyril Fielding, representing India and England, argue over the possibility of friendship as equals between the two. Even the conversation, which consists largely of exchanging passionate statements of the obvious, cannot be completed; their horses and the landscape conspire against definitive closure. Much the same thing, minus horses, in Lawrence's *Women in Love* (1920), where, after great upheaval and mayhem for the two principal couples, Birkin and Ursula close the novel with an argument whose final words are, "I don't believe that." Critics and readers are sometimes tempted to take Birkin's impassioned speech as the last word, but that honor belongs to Ursula. Not the most definitive resolution you'll ever read.

And what of others? "Isn't it pretty to think so?" After all the bull-running and bull-fighting and bedding and fighting and loving and despising, the ending of *The Sun Also Rises* comes down to an ironic question. Lady Brett Ashley asserts to Jake Barnes, the man she probably loves but can never have a physical relationship with, "Oh, Jake . . . we could have had such a damned good time together," to which Jake responds with "Yes," but then appends his famous query. What does he mean? That he agrees and the idea is pleasant? That he sure wishes they could have tried? That it's easy to say so when the theory can never be tested? That based on current data (Brett's recent amorous record), her claim strikes him as unlikely? That it's killing him that they'll never find out? Take your pick. Or come up with another interpretation. One will work about as well as another. This is pure Hemingway: the statement dripping with ambiguity that forces readers to undertake some soul-searching to reach their conclusions. If Dickens wants to put readers at their ease, buddy to buddy, Hemingway wants to put them to work.

It only gets worse from there. We get novels with two endings, as with John Fowles's *The French Lieutenant's Woman* (1969), novels that leave the protagonist hanging—literally, in the case of Toni Morrison's *Song of Solomon* (1977)—and novels that end with unfinished business, even an unfinished sentence. Joyce's *Finnegans Wake* (1939) ends with "A way a lone a last a loved a long the"—not one you see every day—which seems to tie into the opening, "riverrun, past Eve and Adams, from swerve of shore to bend of bay . . ." You can hardly get more provisional than that. The later twentieth century is full of examples, and we needn't trot them all out to prove a point.

Popular genres typically stick to the tidier ending. Who, after all, wants a mystery novel that doesn't get its man? From Agatha Christie to Sue Grafton, the genre that begins with the smoking gun ends with justice, polite or rough, but justice nonetheless. Romances, Westerns, sci-fi epics, horror novels. And for good reason. Does he get the girl or doesn't he? Who wins the shootout? The aliens and the evil thing are either thwarted or they aren't, no two ways about it. Elmore Leonard, Tony Hillerman, Maeve Binchy, Stephen King, and Robert B. Parker are going to give you pretty decisive endings.

The more "literary" crowd? Not so much. Especially after Beckett, after Heisenberg, after deconstruction, it's hard to embrace certainty with the same enthusiasm that our Victorian forebears displayed. Sometimes the text deconstructs itself. Yann Martel's *Life of Pi* gives us a harrowing tale of a boy, a tiger, and a lifeboat, but then offers a perfectly plausible alternative explanation that undermines the entire narrative. Martel very cannily refrains from giving us a clear reason for choosing one over the other. Some readers will find the strategy frustrating, others exhilarating. What he really provides, of course, is nothing more or less than what many readers would devise for themselves, a rational explanation for a completely irrational tale of survival. Oh no, they'll think to themselves, that couldn't have happened. It must have been *X*. In this case, the author very thoughtfully offers *X* for us. Long before Martel, Henry James offered a beauty of a self-deconstructing finish in *The Turn of the Screw* (1898).

> *I caught him, yes, I held him—it may be imagined with what a passion; but at the end of a minute I began to feel what it truly was that I held. We were alone with the quiet day, and his little heart, dispossessed, had stopped.*

Did young Miles die because of Peter Quint's ghost? Or of being exorcised of it? Or of the smothering adoration of the governess? Or of her repressed anger or her psychosis? James gives no answers and indeed steered clear of any indication that it was other than a ghost story. But then, why the title? Why the emphasis on "another turn of the screw" in the lead-up to the narrative? Readers are forced into making their own determinations as to what really happened and, by extension, what that actual event tells us about the rest of the novella. Now that's canny writing. About the uncanny.

It was ever thus. Even with the most Dickensian of endings, we accept or resist as we will. I never bought the Pip-and-Estella thing, and when I discovered he'd written an earlier, superior (from my perspective) ending, I was all over it. Some endings you can't over-write. Tess is dead and no mistaking it. Jude, too. And Gatsby. Even there, however, we don't necessarily take delivery on the authorized interpretation. My experience from many years of classroom teach-ing is that we read actively, right up to the last word, and as often as not, students don't like the way a writer ends the novel, and say so. In fact, I've had quite a lot of former literature students tell me years later that so thoroughgoing was their rejection of a novel's ending that they misremember their alternative as the actual denouement. Talk about being involved with your reading. And why not? Open-ings tell us where we're going. Endings tell us where we went. We ought to have some say in the trip.

I probably shouldn't tell you this, but I generally read the ending of novels first. Seems like cheating, doesn't it? Well, not first-first, but a long time before I've earned it, usually once I have the novel's premise safely in hand. Chiefly, I'm interested less in the surprise than in how the writer will get there. And it's the ending that is our reward for plugging on, giving us the satisfying wrap-up, but also the hint of what-if, of what-then. Because the worst thing an ending can be is ended.

You want a nineteenth-century novel that has a proper ending? Okay, here.

But I reckon I got to light out for the Territory ahead of the rest, because Aunt Sally she's going to adopt me and sivilize me, and I can't stand it. I been there before.

What will Huck find in the Territory? What will that new life be like? His problems and adventures aren't over but merely beginning in a new realm. Some doors have closed off—the juvenile antics of Tom Sawyer, Aunt Sally and proper behavior, the world of immorality and duplicity that lines the north-south axis of the Mississippi—but others are opening. He'll go west into the uncharted lands, not knowing what they hold, and who blames him? It can't possibly be worse than sivilization.

21

History in the Novel/The Novel in History

I DON'T DO THIS for just anybody, but since you've stayed with me this long, here's some advice. You want to win a Nobel Prize? Literature, now. We're not talking economics or peace or physics or any of those others. Just literature. Here's what you need to do: study history. Think I'm kidding? Try these two lists and see if I'm wrong.

Column A:
- John Updike
- F. Scott Fitzgerald
- W. H. Auden
- Iris Murdoch
- Anthony Burgess
- Geoffrey Hill
- James Joyce
- John Fowles
- Virginia Woolf
- E. M. Forster
- Vladimir Nabokov
- Philip Roth

Column B:
- Toni Morrison
- Orhan Pamuk
- William Butler Yeats
- Nadine Gordimer
- V. S. Naipaul
- Seamus Heaney
- John Steinbeck
- Naguib Mahfouz
- Gabriel García Márquez
- Ernest Hemingway
- Pearl S. Buck
- William Faulkner

Not bad, either group, right? So what separates them? Talent? Technique? Form? Not really. Generalizations are tricky, but we can say that the group on the right is, on the whole, more oriented toward historical and social issues. And the group on the left won zero Nobel Prizes. None. All of the Column B writers are winners. Coincidence? I don't think so. Consider the Booker Prize for British writers. A few years back the judges chose a supreme winner, the Booker of Bookers for the first twenty-five years of the prize's existence. The winner as the most Bookerish of novels? Salman Rushdie's *Midnight's Children*. If you've not read it (and you should), it's about a group of children born at the stroke of midnight on August 15, 1947, the moment of India's birth as an independent nation. How's that for history?

There is perhaps no genre more despised in critical circles than the "historical novel." Okay, maybe the romance. And particularly the historical romance. At the same time, however, we must distinguish between the category novel ("category" or "genre" novels being written to a preset form) we call "historical" and the *genuinely* historical novel. There have always been historical novels, books that look seriously back—or sometimes sideways—at the great contest of historical forces. Leo Tolstoy did well with contemporary novels like *Anna Karenina*, but his BIG novel, the one that makes him TOLSTOY, is *War and Peace*, a little fourteen-hundred-page ditty about the war against Napoleon. It's vast in scope as well as length, and it resembles nothing but itself. It's filled with characters and storylines and digressive essays that simply pop up in the midst of the narrative. Critics at the time had difficulty regarding it as a novel, standing as it did so far beyond the scope of anything they understood a novel to be.

What are these days called "postcolonial" or "multicultural" or "emerging" novels are generally playing fields on which history runs rampant, and sometimes amok. This is hardly surprising. If the history of your people, your island, your country was dominated by some outside power for several hundred years, when that power withdrew or altered its relationship, that shift could hardly be ignored in your writing, could it?

Take an instance from our own country. Native American writers as otherwise different as Leslie Marmon Silko, James Welch, N. Scott Momaday, Gerald Vizenor, and Louise Erdrich have this in common: the stories they tell grow directly out of the tribal and regional histories of their people. Silko's *Ceremony* (1977) deals with the return of a G.I. from World War II to his reservation in the desert Southwest. What Tayo has experienced, and what his Laguna Pueblo tribe has gone through before he was even born, has everything to do with the shape of that narrative. His post-traumatic stress disorder, his biracial identity, his dislocation from the old ways, and his need to become whole and well again all drive the novel forward. Tribal history, national history, and personal history dictate the story Silko composes. Similarly, one could argue that Erdrich's Kashpaw-Nanapush saga grows out of no single feature of Chippewa history as much as the land allotment system forced upon the people by the Bureau of Land Management, that nearly all the resentments and rivalries, the manifold failures and occasional triumphs, ultimately stem from that one cause. The stories in Welch, in Momaday, even in something as screwy and amazing as Vizenor's *Bearheart: The Heirship Chronicles* (1978, 1990), which would take more space to explain than is occupied by the book itself, always have to do at some level with issues of accommodation, assimilation, separation, and the uneasy play of identity for those Americans who also belong to other, long-oppressed nations. The novels may be hilarious or heartbreaking—often both—yet the interaction between fictional creation and the forces of history are undeniable and inescapable.

We see much the same thing in any ethnic American fiction, although most clearly perhaps in African American writing. Perhaps because the history involved is so horrific, not merely the dealing in human beings as commodities, although that in itself is quite bad enough, but also because of the brutalities of slavery and plantation life, the oppression on a grand scale that followed for a century after emancipation, and the ongoing effects of that history, African American novels possess a power that is hard to match. Richard Wright's *Native Son* (1940) can only have come out of a certain pattern of experience, one which no one would wish for himself, yet it implicates all of us in its tragedy. The novels of Zora Neale Hurston, Ralph Ellison, and James Baldwin capture black life seventy and eighty years after slavery, making something both familiar and strange out of the experience. Sometimes black striving with the slave-holding past is comic, as in Charles Johnson's *Middle Passage* (1990), sometimes tragic or strange, as in Caryl Phillips's *Cambridge* (1992—and African Caribbean or African British comes into the picture here, as well), about a freed slave who finds himself re-enslaved, or Edward P. Jones's account of blacks who owned slaves in *The Known World* (2003). Sometimes, it is all those things, which is part of why Toni Morrison may be the greatest novelist of our time. Even her failures (and I have read *Jazz*) are fascinating. And in her best work, in *Song of Solomon* (1977) or *Beloved* (1987) or *Paradise* (1998), the sense that history has come alive and is animating characters in ways they can't quite understand or appreciate permeates the narratives. And the prose simply takes your breath away. Sadly, that history will never leave us but will go on providing material for novelists for a thousand years. And all the novels in the world can't justify or erase the enormity of slavery and racism.

The specific issues differ in postcolonial writing, whether from India, Africa, Latin America, the Middle East, the British Isles, or the Caribbean, and of course they differ from country to country and culture to culture, yet always history announces itself in fiction, frequently in quite overt ways. The original Troubles in Ireland, those spasms of nationalism that eventually led to independence for the twenty-six counties of the Republic of Ireland, from the Easter Rising of 1916 through the Black and Tan War against English soldiers after the Great War, to the Irish civil war, figure down the years from Liam O'Flaherty's *The Informer* (1925) to William Trevor's *Fools of Fortune* (1983) and beyond. At the time the Black and Tans were dispatched to Ireland, Prime Minister David Lloyd George said, "We have murder by the throat." Establishing a pattern, that one didn't go quite as predicted. The later Troubles, the ones in Northern Ireland, show up in such disparate works as Robert McLiam Wilson's *Eureka Street* (1997) and Edna O'Brien's *House of Splendid Isolation* (1994), in which an elderly woman in the Irish Republic is held hostage in her own home by a fugitive IRA terrorist. O'Brien employs the Lloyd George quote as an epigraph to the novel. There are numerous other novels, poems, plays, and memoirs on the Troubles, and there will be many, many more down the years. As I write this chapter, the British Army has just pulled out of Northern Ireland. It went into the province in 1969, the government's idea being that the deployment would last a few months; it lasted, in fact, thirty-eight years and cost over thirty-seven hundred lives, military and civilian. How can such a period not color the writing by residents and onlookers?

Becoming a nation is never simple or easy. Establishing a national identity can be even more arduous and can take many more decades. This process is something Americans know a great deal about, whether they're aware of it or not. Try this experiment. Read several works from any emerging nation. Make sure to read more than one author, and a lot of authors would be useful. Read R. K. Narayan, one of the Malgudi books or even *The Painter of Signs* (1976), and Kiran Desai's *The Inheritance of Loss* (2006), and *Midnight's Children* (1981), or pretty much any Rushdie, and maybe Ruth Prawer Jhabvala's *Heat and Dust* (1975). Feel free to make substitutions. Read Desai's mother, Anita, instead. Pick and choose. The writers and titles don't matter all that much, except that good writers make the best reading. Now here's the experimental part: don't read them as strange visitors from someplace you've never been. Read them as if you're one of them, or they're one of you. Read them as if they're nineteenth-century American novelists. Here's what I think you'll find: minus the surface details, it's the same project as the one undertaken by James Fenimore Cooper, Nathaniel Hawthorne, Herman Melville, and Mark Twain. They're trying to figure out and articulate something that has never existed before, an identity as part of a newly established country separate from that same place and that same people under colonial rule but also (in the case of India, which is vastly older than British rule) from what it had been before, which in any case no one living ever experienced. They're trying to work in a received literary form and adapt it to the sensibility and the reality of their time and place. Kiran Desai isn't Mark Twain—her adaptation must needs be a far cry from his—but she's certainly not Jane Austen or Iris Murdoch, either. Oh, and while you're on the case, read her comic novel *Hullabaloo in the Guava Orchard* (1998), which deserves reading for the title alone.

You can do the same experiment with Nigerian fiction, with Chinua Achebe and Ben Okri and Wole Soyinka and others, or with Naguib Mahfouz and Egyptian fiction or with any place or people. I have for many years been a big fan of Latin American fiction, of García Márquez and Carlos Fuentes and Mario Vargas Llosa and Isabel Allende and Jorge Amado. I have even read Osman Lins, and that takes some effort, even to find him. One of the many things I like, of course, is how they can take me away from the world I know, from suburbs and soybean fields. But I'm always struck more, ultimately, by the "American" than by the "Latin," by how familiar their quests are to someone who grew up with Huck Finn and Tom Sawyer, Natty Bumppo and Ishmael. Once I started reading other literatures, I discovered that "American" didn't even have to enter into it. "It" was about the very human activity of inward voyaging and outward looking, of invention and discovery through the grappling with one's history and culture, however new or old. I think you'll find much the same thing going on, the process of self-discovery and identity creation through fiction. The history connection isn't always as straightforward as *The Scarlet Letter*; sometimes it looks more like *The House of the Seven Gables*. But it's at work, this wrestling with history. The experiment is interesting. Just don't forget to notice how different and wonderful these "similar" novels are.

Remember our two columns up above, and what separates them? Here's the second question about them: how are they alike? Honestly, I should have made a career with the SAT. Famous? Sure. Capable? That, too. How about, shot through with history? Joyce may have had Stephen Dedalus say, "History is a nightmare from which I'm trying to awake," but that doesn't mean the author himself ever awoke, or could. Or even wanted to. Don't forget, Stephen is plenty fatuous. And Joyce wasn't. Among other things, he was among the early generations of Irish Catholics to have the opportunity of attending university. University College Dublin was founded by John Henry Cardinal Newman in 1854 and was necessary because they were, for the most part, excluded from Protestant Trinity College. Joyce came from ardent nationalist stock, from people who had looked to Thomas Stewart Parnell as the Moses who would lead them out of the wilderness of being second-class citizens governed by an imported minority. He lived through, if at a distance, the 1916 Easter Rising, the civil war, and the creation of the Irish Free State. He found himself somewhat closer to World War I and died in Zurich, having fled France after it fell to the Nazis. Does that sound like someone divorced from history? His books are filled with reminiscences and opinions, prejudices and beliefs about history, particularly but not exclusively the Irish variety. The world would be a poorer place without the terrible Christmas dinner row in *Portrait* or the Citizen's fractured history lesson in *Ulysses*.

His literary descendent Roddy Doyle gave us wonderful comic characters and disastrous-hilarious situations in his Barrytown trilogy, starting with *The Commitments*, the first of the three novels, that one ostensibly about soul music but also so much more. The residents of his fictional Barrytown exist because of a particular history that created down-on-their-luck working-class neighborhoods that could give rise to a Jimmy Rabbitte, a young man with the right combination of pluck, vision, and naïveté to found a soul band in Dublin years after the original music died out. Jimmy is every bit as much the product of history as Henry Smart, the young revolutionary tough of Doyle's *A Star Called Henry* and *Oh, Play That Thing*.

It even happens in children's novels, or at least in great children's novels. The Harry Potter novels have already been put through the interpretive mill, so I almost regret what I'm about to do. Still, it can't be helped. I recently saw an article describing them as a literary political Rorschach test where people see what they're already programmed to see. That may always be the case with literature, but we'll leave that question for another day. This article cited such tricks of memory as the link of Azkaban prison to the American Guantánamo and Abu Ghraib detention facilities—nice work, since Rowling had invented her lockup for warlocks several years before these real-world jails had come into being. She can't very well have known about things that had not yet happened, could she? She could know, however, about Nazis and fascists and Communist dictatorships, about totalitarian governments and those who would impose them. And she would know about racism and racial violence, which has been on the rise in Britain during her lifetime, as more and more racial minorities arrived. She would have seen neo-Nazis and Holocaust deniers in action. What did she need with Guantánamo? Lord Voldemort (from the French *vol de mort*, meaning flight of death), with his sense of a mission and his self-loathing (his insistence on racial purity despite being of mixed nonmagical and witch parentage), his charisma and his cruelty, and his desperate need for eternal power, something like a Thousand-Year Reich, recalls Adolph Hitler. Does that mean that Voldemort is Hitler, that the book is an allegory for the rise of the Nazis? No, of course not. She's much too subtle a thinker for something so crude, which would in any case be lost on her target audience. But if you are of the generation born in the twenty years or so after the end of World War II, as Rowling is, much of what you know about evil, about world domination fantasies, and about racial hatred and violence comes from the Nazis. And then there are the events. The fight at the tower that ends Book 6, *Harry Potter and the Half-Blood Prince*, owes not a little to the Battle of Britain, that quintessential desperate fight to save home. There has been, naturally, ample opportunity to understand cruelty by observing the world in the second half of the twentieth century, but much of that is simply a gloss on the Third Reich. The connection may be conscious or unconscious on Rowling's part, but my guess is that she wouldn't even need to think about it. Any English child born when she was would simply know about the years 1933–1945; the knowledge was unavoidable. It would inform the consciousness and therefore the fiction of any writer of her generation.

I know this because her generation is mine, although I'm on the far end of it from her. But there's nothing special about J. K. Rowling, at least in this regard—it's always true. All writers, everywhere, all the time. Here, then, is the Law of Now and Then: Every novel is an act of violence, a wrestling match with the historical and social forces of its own time. Sometimes the novel wins, sometimes history does. Okay, maybe not. But they do not play nicely together. What does happen is that sometimes history is apparent and sometimes it's hidden. In either case, it's always present and the writer has had to carve out the book's place in its historical moment. Until we figure out a way not to live in our own time, we're going to think like people of our own time. Every writer's response to history will be a little different. You can reject it, embrace it, treat it as farce, but you can't escape it.

There's no one who isn't of his or her own time and place. And those are to a large extent governed by history. Updike's Rabbit Angstrom is unimaginable without postwar American society, his Eastwick witches without, somewhere way back there, Salem and its trials. They may not look much like Salem's witches, but they couldn't exist without them. It has ever been thus. Daniel Defoe's *Robinson Crusoe* or Jonathon Swift's *Gulliver's Travels* can tell us more about British attitudes toward colonialism, racism, exploration, imperialism, and what we now call Otherness than any ten textbooks or histories. That's not the point of those novels, mind you; indeed, the writers might be shocked at the statement. It's simply true. Sometimes history bites the writer on the derriere. Anthony Burgess has his four young thugs, Alex and his Droogs, beat up an old man, possibly a writer, and then brutalize a writer and his wife in their home, raping and beating her so badly she dies. This episode may have its origin in the beating and possible rape of Burgess's first wife by four GIs. In *Earthly Powers*, the aging writer, based in large measure on Somerset Maugham, is beaten by street toughs. Burgess himself, in his later years, was mugged by young hoodlums in Rome. You never can tell what history has in mind for you.

The thing about history—like politics and sociology and psychology and bed-wetting—and the novel is that readers have to put in the work themselves. Is it significant when Ursula Brangwen, in D. H. Lawrence's *Women in Love*, calls a robin, disapprovingly, "a little Lloyd-George of the air"? It is if you think it is. Lawrence, whose pacifism and marriage to a German wife (a cousin of the Red Baron, no less) caused him considerable difficulty with authorities, despised Lloyd-George (who keeps cropping up in British fiction), the prime minister during World War I. The novel is otherwise largely oblivious of the mayhem taking place just across the Channel, and the main characters encounter no difficulty when plot exigencies require a trip to the Tyrol, yet current events, along with class warfare and industrial capitalism, do inform the book. How much and in what ways each reader must decide. And that decision will alter what we find in the novel.

This condition obtains almost universally; there are hardly any novels that do not in some way reveal their historical moment. A book may be set eight hundred years in the past or many centuries in the future, may even fly the bonds of Earth to some galaxy far, far away, but it's still a product of *now*, whenever its now may have been. And now is always a product of then. History will come in, whether or no.

There. Don't say I never did anything for you. And remember me in your acceptance speech.

22

Conspiracy Theory

THE FIRST SENTENCE OF every novel says the same thing: *Read me.* The tone may be one of several options, from *Be my guest* to *Ready to ride?* to *I'm gonna get you, sucka,* but the main message is always the same. Novels all have the same need, the same shortcoming—they're nothing without an audience. Not every novel wants to be read by every audience, but each one wants *an* audience, the right audience. The second part of the message may take a bit longer to hit home: "Here's how to read me." But it will appear. Novels do two things consistently and ceaselessly. They ask to be read and tell us how. Think about it. A book of sixty, eighty, maybe a hundred and eighty thousand words is making a big demand on our time. The social contract between writer and reader requires that the writer check back in periodically to make sure we're still turning pages. *Hey, did you see that? Isn't she a stinker? Watch this bit. And do you know what happens next? Hey, wanna buy a watch?* Okay, I don't remember any of them saying that, but almost: *How gullible are you now? What can I get away with this time?* Those are the sorts of tricks writers use to keep us reading and up to speed, right up through the end of the novel. Our part of the bargain is to keep reading or chuck the thing across the room. We get to choose and the choice is important.

Why? Because every novel needs to be read. Without that, it doesn't mean anything. Until it rests in the hand or on the lap, a novel it's just a stack of paper with spots. Meaning in fiction is the result of a conspiracy between two minds and two imaginations. In literature classes we often speak as if the writer is all-powerful, but he needs the reader's imagination to let the deal go down. If you withhold yours, no meaning. Everybody's *Gatsby* is going to be similar; that's Fitzgerald's doing. But nobody's is going to be quite like anybody else's. Is Daisy spoiled, abused, borderline insane, manipulative, truthful, deceitful? In what proportions? Is Gatsby just a crook and a poseur, a lonely dreamer, a guy who doesn't get it? What about Tom Buchanan, Daisy's husband? Nick? We're never going to agree on the fine print. Which, as you know, isn't even printed.

I recently visited a high school English class full of very bright kids. Since it was the penultimate day on which they would ever be high school kids, they were also very happy, but that's another story. We spent an hour together talking about Katherine Mansfield and Shakespeare and the avalanche of Jane Austen films, sequels, prequels, and jonquils, and toward the end Dickens came up. The teacher mentioned that they had read *Great Expectations*, so I asked, less than naively, "Well, what did you think?" And being bright, motivated kids who know the expected answer, they said, more or less convincingly, "It was good." Some used "really" in their sentence, but they all generally agreed. All but one. The class curmudgeon said it wasn't all that great and didn't move him deeply. I liked him better immediately. It takes courage, even on your next-to-last day of high school, to say you're in AP English and aren't wild about one of the established classics. For one thing, there's the weight of more than a century of received opinion going against you. And in this case the wild popularity of those novels in the author's own lifetime. Clearly, this kid was swimming against the literary current. And that's fine. We can't all like the same books, the same films, the same songs, despite what mass-marketing and *American Idol* might have us believe. Or even the same things *about* said books, films, and songs.

Anyway, as I was driving back home past newly planted cornfields and construction zones, his response made me think back on my own encounters with *Great Expectations*. How *did* I feel about it? How do I feel about it now? Let me preface this by saying that it has been nearly forty years, so I may not accurately recall everything about that first reading. I remember clearly, though, two things in particular: a sense of confusion early on, both in Pip's encounter with the escaped Magwitch and in his domestic arrangement with his sister and her husband, and outrage at the ending. The first, I subsequently learned, is fairly typical of the opening gambits in Dickens's novels, and nowhere near the murkiness and fog in the Court of Chancery at the outset of *Bleak House*. That second one, though, that's another story. Ruined the novel for me. No kidding—absolutely ruined it. It was abrupt, suspiciously so. False. Insincere. Hokey. And just plain dumb. So what was it that triggered this venom? Merely this.

I took her hand in mine, and we went out of the ruined place; and, as the morning mists had risen long ago when I first left the forge, so, the evening mists were rising now, and in all the broad expanse of tranquil light they showed to me, I saw no shadow of another parting from her.

Even allowing for some changes in sensibility between 1861, the year of the novel's publication, and 1969, the year of my encounter with it, this was just wrong. Had Pip learned nothing through all his suffering? Could he not see that happiness was never possible with Estella, no matter how much she had been changed by her own experiences? Didn't he have at least a shred of pride? And et cetera.

In case you don't know the story, here's the gist: Pip had once been engaged as a playmate and companion for Estella by an ancient harridan named Miss Havisham, who saw the young girl as her instrument for wreaking vengeance on the male sex for having stood her up at the marriage altar (she lives out her days in her wedding dress amid the wreckage of the aborted reception feast). Pip, although neither knows it, is Estella's practice victim, the boy on whom she can perfect cruelty. She gets rather good at it. Of course they meet later in life, of course she leads him on but marries another, of course he's a fool of the first order to believe that he loves her, much less the reverse; otherwise, there's no need for this famous final scene. Then, after much misery on both sides, they just *happen* (of all Dickens's contrivances, one of the most contrived) to meet at the burnt-out ruins of Miss Havisham's mansion. Some cursory apologies are exchanged, but nothing momentous enough to prepare for the hearts-and-violins ending. So naturally, my future self was appalled. Some of it, I suppose, had to do with being a teenaged male who took rejection by girls about as badly as the next guy. If memory serves, I was also what could generously be called "between girlfriends." In fact, fairly far between. Part of it had to do with having plodded through several hundred pages of hard going, only to have them trivialized by this "easy" ending, as I saw it. Maybe that's what my reading always is, some combination of testosterone, life history, insecurity, male ego, aesthetic judgment, and gut sense (or nonsense). Hard to judge from the inside. In any case, that's what I felt at the time.

But there was one more thing that I felt about that ending but couldn't have defended: *Dickens didn't believe it, either*. It was an idea. A belief. A conviction. With nothing whatsoever to back it up.

Okay, then, a couple of years later, and Tom's reading the novel again. A college class, this time; he would not willingly return to the scene of that particular crime. Same novel, different edition. Now here's the beauty of it: this novel has the standard text *and* the originally intended ending. Much more Hemingway, Jake Barnes, "Isn't it pretty to think so?" Also the story of sage advice from a clearly inferior novelist, Edward Bulwer-Lytton (he gave us "It was a dark and stormy night"—no kidding), to lose the downer ending and please the punters. "Aha!" says Tom. "I knew it. That ending really was contrived." Or words to that effect. So now the novel is merely smudged and not hopelessly blighted.

Which leads to another reading some years on. This time Tom sees something he hasn't noticed before: "I *could see no shadow* of a further parting from her." Not, "There would be no further parting." Well, then, that's different. That's maybe what he sensed but missed the first reading—an out-clause. Dickens seems to be throwing a sop to readers but acknowledging that it is a sop. Pip can't see even a shadow of another parting. So what? When could he ever see a thing before it happened to him? When was he ever attentive to signs and portents? You can believe this, dear reader, if you want, but I'm going to leave a thread of doubt with which the Properly Dubious can unravel this false tapestry.

I heard that. What do you mean, "But did Dickens intend that meaning?" He wrote it, didn't he? Besides, his influence is limited;

Elvis has left the building. It's not his novel anymore. It's ours. His and mine. His and yours. Chiefly, yours and mine. It stopped being his alone when he gave it to us.

Well, what about the writer's intentions? I'm with Huck on that one: I don't put no stock in dead people. And here's the thing: once the writer sends the final edit back to his publisher, he's toast. His impact on the novel is finished. Of course, a lot of the writers we read are dead, and the rest will be (sorry, just my morbid side coming through), but body temperature isn't the issue: in terms of the text, once it's published, he's already past tense. The living presence in the *now* of the text is the reader. The novelist provides the stuff of the novel—facts, events, structure, characters, dialogue, narrative, description, beginning, middle, and end. All the hard data from "Once upon a" to "ever after." Without which, of course, there are no readers. Readers bring interpretation, analysis, sympathy, hostility, cheers, and catcalls. Writers make novels; readers make them live.

So here's something to live by, the Law for All Reading: Own the novels you read. (Poems, too. Also stories, essays, plays—you get the idea.) I don't mean purchase a copy, although for self-evident and self-serving reasons, I'm not against it. I mean take psychological and intellectual possession of those works. Make them yours. You're not a frightened schoolchild asking for extra gruel (there's that Dickens guy again). You're a grown-up person having a conversation with another one. That the two of you have never met and the other one may be dead is immaterial. It's still a conversation, a meeting of minds and imaginations, and yours matters as much as the writer's.

What's interesting about this transaction is how readers both embrace and resist that ownership. Over the years, my work has drifted forward in the twentieth century, from Joyce and Yeats and

Lawrence, which is where I began, toward postmodernism. If you can forgive me for bringing up the metafictionists one more time, one of the things they insist upon is the provisional nature of reality and, therefore, of meaning. We see this most clearly in the dual endings of *The French Lieutenant's Woman*, of course, but it's there in the rest of Fowles, as well, and especially in *The Magus*. When I've taught that novel, the most frequently asked question is, "What happened?" Followed very closely by, "Did it happen?" Is Nicholas the beneficiary, if that's the right word, of a psychodrama staged for his improvement by the mysterious Conchis? How should he interpret it? How should we interpret him interpreting it? And so on. Needless to say, not all members of the class are happy with the lack of certainty Fowles offers in the narrative, but many, probably most, are. Again and again in Fowles and his contemporaries, readers are given opportunities, even required, to construct meaning.

That's certainly true among the metafictional crowd—John Barth, Robert Coover, Angel Carter, Julian Barnes, Salman Rushdie, Italo Calvino—yet it's also the case with those whose writing is somewhat less self-referential. While Iris Murdoch may have seen herself as providing ethical or philosophical instruction through her novels, those books are more puzzles than road maps. Definite events take place. What those events mean, however, and what they tell us about the characters, that's another story. Is there a unicorn in *The Unicorn*? That question always comes up in class, and not because I ask it. Who? Why? What should we think of Hannah Crean-Smith, of Gerald Scottow, of the main character, Marian Taylor? What role are the gothic trappings playing in the novel? Is it imitation gothic, late gothic, anti-gothic? My experience is that intelligent and perceptive readers do not agree on these points. So, too, with *The Black Prince*. In that novel, Murdoch adds to Bradley

Pearson's first-person-central narrative several postscripts by other players in the drama: his former wife; her charlatan psychiatrist brother; the woman, Rachel Baffin, who has framed him for the murder of her husband, Arnold; and his former lover, Julian, the daughter of Arnold and Rachel. Murdoch even supplies a foreword and a postscript by a putative editor, P. Loxias, whose surname is another name for Apollo, especially as related to his connection with the Delphic Oracle. The Pythia, the priestess who reigned over the oracle, you may recall, was notoriously imprecise or ambiguous with information, and Loxias refers to Apollo's obscuring tendencies in matters of prophecy. Murdoch has chosen a name, then, hardly designed to lend credence or solidity to the analysis of events in the novel. Her novels, right up through *The Green Knight*, are full of claims and counterclaims that often cannot be sifted objectively, mysterious pronouncements, true and false advisers and oracles, and uncertainties large and small. Only when readers impose their own imaginations on the novel can a full picture emerge. There are several possible motivations behind any character's actions, and often support is available for more than one. We help shape the narrative by our agency, by keying on certain words, by accepting one explanation as more probable than another based on our understanding of events, by identifying with one character over another.

Of course, sometimes making demands on the reader backfires. If, for instance, one provides an ambiguous text to readers who despise ambiguity, trouble may ensue. Consider, if you will, a novel that is not about the founder of a major world religion but may be taken by certain readers—those, say, with a rigid adherence to writing as scripture and an extremely limited understanding of the concept of parody (or maybe an underdeveloped sense of humor), to be about that founder. You might find yourself living the next decade or so in hiding while under a sentence of death. Did the Ayatollah or his advisers misread *The Satanic Verses*? Of course they did. Did Salman Rushdie collude in his own difficulty? Very probably. Not so much in his subject matter, which on one level is pretty clearly not about the Prophet, but in his assumptions about his audience. The novel uses certain situations that parallel the life of Muhammad— the brothel in which the prostitutes bear the names of his wives, for instance—not to indicate that his wives were prostitutes but to underscore a sort of corruption or hypocrisy at large in the world that makes use of religion for commercial and degraded purposes. Rushdie's intended audience would get that. He probably never anticipated acquiring a readership among the mullahs. On the other hand, mullahs can also be active and creative readers, if not always discerning ones, as he discovered to his pain. This is a special and, we could hope, singular case, although the sad truth is that there are other instances. Egyptian Nobel Prize winner Naguib Mahfouz was stabbed by an extremist while sitting at his favorite café. The more recent Nobel laureate Orhan Pamuk was threatened with imprisonment for "insulting Turkishness." (There was even an assassination plot for which the only appropriate word is "byzantine": According to *The Guardian*, Pamuk "was targeted as part of a campaign to sow chaos in preparation for a military coup, scheduled for 2009.") In recent times a number of writers have been assaulted or assassinated because fanatics of one stripe or another have taken issue with perceived meaning. Rarely is the perception anywhere close to the writers' intended meaning. Yet intentions do not rule out alternative or contrary readings. All a writer can do, ultimately, is write what *she* means and hope for the best.

This can seem, amid the fatwas and general hubbub, a particular problem of this moment. Yet if we go back further in literary history, we see that writers have always demanded that we bring something of ourselves to the act of reading. We can go way back and have the Hamlet-and-his-problems or even Achilles-and-his-problems chat, but we'll limit ourselves to novels and novelists. Who is Heathcliff? What does he want? What drives him? What are his limitations? How about Catherine? Do we believe or trust Nelly Dean? Why, or why not? Well, then, how about Victor Frankenstein? What do we understand about his motivations? How about his monster? Are we all in agreement here? Even fairly controlling writers, Jane Austen, say, and Dickens, since he's already implicated here, leave a lot of room for interpretation. Dickens often gives us the opportunity to sympathize with his dark characters, if not his real villains. Bill Sikes is beyond the pale, clearly. But Fagin? How much, and on what basis? And Austen's amatory novels, those plots aimed at the goal of marriage, may seem to have only one outcome, but the nuances are many. Do we find Mr. Darcy as interesting as we're supposed to? How harshly do we judge Emma Woodhouse's judgmental blunders? The third person, free-indirect style viewpoint—the point of view we can think of as generated out of the character's thoughts but not directly said by her, that is almost-but-not-quite first person—brings us close to Emma's own voice yet keeps us at just enough distance that we never quite settle into identification with her. How much sympathy we extend to her, then, is our call. And don't even get me started on Henry James.

You see the problem? Except that it's not a problem, or not in the usual sense. A conundrum, maybe. A puzzle. Ambiguity is the way of the novel, even when it is not the goal of the writer. There is simply no way to close out all possibilities except the one primarily intended while creating characters who are even remotely human. The essay can successfully restrict meaning; the novel, not so much. Why? In part, we can blame language, that rich vein of multiple meanings. As public figures often discover to their pain, it's very difficult to make statements that are completely accurate, straightforward, and without embarrassing subtext. What are you going to do with a language that contains self-antonyms, those words that are their own opposites, where the verb "to dust" can mean "to remove particles, as from furniture" and "to distribute particles, as with powdered sugar"? And this isn't an isolated instance; there are scores, perhaps hundreds of them. English is always shifting meanings, borrowing from other languages, getting all slanged up, verbing nouns and nouning verbs. It's the most flexible and malleable of languages, but also the most maddeningly imprecise. Novelists can't control that, and mostly they run with it, using that ambiguity to their advantage. In part, too, it's the nature of the novel, which describes action rather than explaining it. Texts that attempt to explicate themselves tend to lack drama and immediacy. Besides, we would regard that as a lack of faith in the enterprise: if you have to explain it for your readers, you must have failed in the initial narration. But I think the real cause is that human beings are fundamentally ambiguous. We say one thing but mean another, fumble to explain ourselves, contradict our beliefs with our behavior, perform actions even we don't understand, hide much of our true being from the world and perhaps from ourselves. If the novel is to be faithful to human existence, characters are going to share in that ambiguous nature.

Think it's just me? Here's what Erica Wagner says on the subject, "Good novels go on beyond their final pages. They leave their authors and enter the minds of readers, who will ask questions, make demands and sometimes find themselves dissatisfied, just as they do with the flesh and blood creatures who inhabit the world outside the pages of a book." Wagner is a novelist as well as the literary editor of *The Times* of London, so she knows a thing or two about reading—and writing—novels. She's right, of course: good novels do go on beyond the text. But I would shift the dynamic just a hair: good readers invest themselves in novels in ways that stretch the texts. Our readings are dialogic: we interrogate the narrative, asking the questions and making the demands Wagner suggests, pursuing some possibilities while giving others a pass and, yes, sometimes finding ourselves dissatisfied.

The novel is *interactive* in the fullest sense. Good reading, and by this I mean not professorial or professional but merely the kind of reading that novelists hope for and deserve, actively enters into conversation with the created narrative, bringing out nuances, developing or resisting sympathies, exploring meanings. We meet the writer on her turf, but it's also our turf. Meaning and significance happen in that place where writer and reader confer. The result isn't merely that we get the most out of the novels, but that we get the most out of ourselves. Great novels, certainly, and maybe all novels, change us, but not merely by giving us something special. They also change us because of what we give to them. That's a winner all the way around.

Conclusion
The Never-Ending Journey

ONE STORY. THAT'S ALL there is, all there ever has been, all there ever will be. And it's more than enough. I've talked about this idea elsewhere, so I won't belabor it here, but it is really pretty simple. Everything we humans tell ourselves and each other is part of a single, gigantic narrative, which is the story of being human. As soon as humans acquired the ability to communicate in language and began gathering around the campfire to relate the events of the day's hunt, that story began. What they did next—I'm guessing here, but evidential record tilts strongly in this direction—is to move from reportage to mythmaking. The first story was almost certainly something on the order of "Ralph Gets Trampled by the Mastodon—Film at Eleven." But I don't think it took very long at all to begin making sense of the world in which Ralph could get trampled by a mastodon, in which Ralph the Flint Knapper was around one moment and gone the next. The prospect of imminent death not only sharpens the mind wonderfully; it begins the flow of questions. Big questions. Thinking on last things almost necessarily prompts thoughts of first things: How did we get here? How did the world look before us? Was there a before-us, is there a higher power than ourselves? What does it look like, act like, think of us? What happens when we die? Where did Ralph go? Little things like that.

What makes you so sure?

I've lived around people long enough to see that the impulse to recount their lives is hardwired into the human brain. And while I'm no anthropologist and so may have missed something, every society I know of has creation myths, which are tied up in a narrative of divinity. Once you have those two elements, reportage and mythologizing, you have the elements for the rest of human communication. I'm just not sure which side of the ledger corporate quarterly reports go on.

Fiction—that body of story about things manifestly not true—came later. Our first fiction grew out of stories of human interaction with the divine. This is what the late, great critic Northrop Frye called the displacement of myth, pure myth (something that only exists in a sort of theoretical realm) being translated into stories involving humans. These are sacred texts and hero tales in which humans have direct contact with gods in ways we ordinary sorts never experience. Is your mother a goddess (well, of course, but I mean literally)? Has she brought you armor forged in a divine smithy lately? Have you experienced any voices emanating from whirlwinds or burning bushes? I'm neither endorsing nor denying the veracity of any stories here, merely pointing out that the earliest human narratives always involve the divine world in a way that the works of, say, Samuel Beckett do not. Epics and sacred texts stand on those two bases, reportage and mythmaking, telling what happened and saying what it all means.

So does the novel. What else is there, really? A detailed account of events and lives, a sense of how those events and lives express the universe in which they, and we, exist. The events may be the Napoleonic Wars or a trip up an escalator to a mezzanine, but that's just detail; the basic function is unchanged whether the writer is Tolstoy or Nicholson Baker. The significance, the mythic level, may be an expression of the divine in the smallest details or an assertion of the emptiness of it all. Neither matters very much from the point of view of this examination. What matters is that they are all, in whatever their particulars, iterations of the One Story. And therefore, they are all related.

So, does it matter? That they're all connected, that is?

Very much. For one thing, we can tease out connections between this work and that, tracing the intertextual play as I suggested when I enjoined you to read with your ears. You listen, you hear the texts talking to one another. You find layers of meaning you would never sense if you kept the walls up between works. Schools of criticism since about 1960, what was called structuralism and then (horrors!) post-structuralist criticicism, including deconstruction, have emphasized "texts" over "writers" in what strikes me as a fatally flawed initial premise. Yet part of their program makes abundant of sense, and it is this: writing is in some ways bigger than the writer. Writers understand their own reading and to some extent that of the writers who have influenced them. If you are influenced by Joyce, you know that he has in turn read Flaubert and Aquinas and Henrik Ibsen and Homer, among many others. But which ones? How many? And whom did they read, listen to, accept, reject? It is impossible to trace out a complete genealogy of any writer because the network has too many strands, which are in turn made up of too many other strands. Besides, where did Joyce get all those jokes?

One possible danger, or so it would seem, is that if all stories are part of one Ur-story, then if you've seen one, you've seen 'em all. Instead, it works the other way. You can have read a hundred novels, experienced all sorts of fascinating and dull characters, noted all sorts of narrative tricks, but you ain't seen nothin' yet. There will always be another novelist, and another, and another, who will do something you haven't quite seen yet. Moreover, those networks lead you from writer to writer, if you're the inquisitive sort, and pretty soon you're reading people you never thought you would. Reading novels is a little like eating popcorn: once you start, there's no stopping. Let's say you remember reading the short story "An Occurrence at Owl Creek Bridge" by Ambrose Bierce when you were in school. You look on Amazon for what else he might have done and discover that a Mexican novelist, Carlos Fuentes, has a small novel, *The Old Gringo*, in which Bierce (or someone very Bierce-like) plays the title role. Then you discover that Fuentes says that all Hispanic fiction comes from *Don Quixote*, and he mentions other novelists. And that's just the start.

Or maybe you've been reading picaresque novels of modern misbehavior. A little *Augie March*, a dollop of Kerouac, perhaps more J. P. Donleavy than is strictly good for you, a touch of Alan Sillitoe. Eventually you're going to find out that postwar America and Britain didn't invent the rascal-hero, and that knowledge can take you places. Okay, maybe Grimmelshausen's *The Adventurous Simplicissimus* won't be your first stop, since the Thirty Years War may not be your idea of a good time. But bad actors doing funny, outrageous things were a staple in the eighteenth century, and England was a center of mischief, so you could try Daniel Defoe's *Moll Flanders*, Henry Fielding's *Tom Jones* or *Joseph Andrews*, or maybe something by Tobias Smollett. Then those writers lead, for a host of reasons, to other writers. Maybe Defoe leads to more Defoe, something like *Robinson Crusoe*, and you find that more than two centuries later a writer in a very different place, J. M. Coetzee in South Africa, wrote a novel called *Foe*, which reimagines a story we all thought we knew. And from there, who can tell?

So be forewarned: this path leads nowhere, and everywhere, and it goes on forever. Books lead to books, ideas to ideas. You can wear out a hundred hammocks and never reach the end. And that's the good news.

Just don't say I didn't warn you.

Reading List
Criticism of the Novel

Since the book you've just finished is a giant reading list, I thought it redundant to plaster the same names in my back pages. There are, however, some names and titles that bear further consideration—the theorists of and guides to this incredibly successful form. This little list barely scratches the surface of all the writing the form has inspired, but it's a place to start. From there, you're on your own. Happy reading.

Mikhail Bakhtin, *The Dialogic Imagination* (1981, written in the 1930s). Bakhtin has done more than any other critic to shape the vocabulary of narrative theory in the late twentieth and early twenty-first century.

John Barth, *The Friday Book* (1984) and *Further Fridays* (1995). Barth doesn't write fiction on Fridays. These essays, on a wide range of topics of interest to the novelist, are the work of that day. They're clever, warm, enthusiastic, and very learned.

Roland Barthes, "The Death of the Author" (1967), *The Pleasure of the Text* (1972), *Writing Degree Zero* (1968). My favorite literary *agent provocateur*, Barthes is outrageous, interesting, impish, and wise, although not always at the same time. He loves to goad readers into responses. *The Pleasure of the Text* offers an "erotics of reading," which is shocking, amusing, and brief. What more can you want in a critical text?

Wayne C. Booth, *The Rhetoric of Fiction* (1963). One of the great standard works on how fiction works, and the source of the notion of the "implied author."

Italo Calvino, *Six Memos for the Next Millenium* (1988). Calvino's provocative and engaging meditations on the stuff of fiction. His categories, with headings like "Lightness," are brilliant and like no one else's.

E. M. Forster, *Aspects of the Novel* (1927). The source of the concept of round and flat characters, these were Forster's Clark Lectures at Cambridge the year previous. Some great insights in audience-friendly language.

John Fowles, *Wormholes* (1998). An assemblage of Fowles's essays, reviews, and occasional writings, this book is full of nuggets about his approach to fiction and about the craft more generally.

John Gardner, *On Moral Fiction* (1978), *The Art of Fiction* (1983), *On Becoming a Novelist* (1983). The combative first book got all the attention for its attacks on his contemporaries, but the second, his creative-writing text, and the third gave a broader understanding of the genre and great insights into the novelist's craft.

William H. Gass, *Fiction and the Figures of Life* (1970), *The World Within the Word* (1978), *Habitations of the Word* (1984). The first of these gives us the word "metafiction." Gass is a philosopher of language and form as well as a fictionist in his own right, and his insights are both profound and closely argued.

Henry James, *The Art of Fiction* (1884). One of the earliest serious considerations of the novel, and definitely the first in English to claim for the genre the status of art.

Jerome Klinkowitz, *The Self-Apparent Word: Fiction as Language/Language as Fiction* (1984), *The Practice of Fiction in America: Writers from Hawthorne to the Present* (1980). Klinkowitz is the only critic I know who also owns a baseball team, and his interests are similarly eclectic, although he's best on postmodern experimentalism.

David Lodge, *The Art of Fiction* (1992), *The Practice of Writing* (1997), *Consciousness and the Novel* (2003). Lodge is a novelist and academic of considerable accomplishment, and possibly our finest writer of academy novels. His *Art of Fiction*, fifty-two weekly installments written for newspaper publication, offers one of the best primers on fiction you'll ever read.

Percy Lubbock, *The Craft of Fiction* (1921). A follower of James, Lubbock wrote an early seminal text on the novel, as much for the opposition it inspired among the modernists as for its direct influence. A better defense of James than offered by the master himself.

Paris Review. Interviews since 1952, with Hemingway as the first writer interviewed by a very young George Plimpton. Tremendous insights on all aspects of the writing craft by poets, novelists, play-wrights, and others. Many were collected over the years in the *Writers at Work* series; more recently, most of the interviews have been made available online.

Francine Prose, *Reading Like a Writer* (2006). This one is good for readers, too. Prose covers a lot of technical ground while also offering a defense of her sort of highly engaged fiction.

Alain Robbe-Grillet, *Pour un nouveau roman (Toward a New Novel)* (1963). The Bible of the anti-novel by its leading practitioner. Traditionalists will find a lot to hate in this call for change.

Robert Scholes, *The Fabulators* (1967), revised and updated as *Fabulation and Metafiction*. He explores the wild invention and narrative shiftiness of novels after World War II, claiming for them that they subvert and expand traditional expectations about the form.

Robert Scholes and Robert Kellogg, *The Nature of Narrative* (1966). One of the touchstones of narrative theory, exploring the constituent elements of fiction with some surprising observations, as for instance that the selectivity of the camera actually makes film more like narrative than drama. Very theoretical, but also highly approachable.

Jane Smiley, *Thirteen Ways of Looking at the Novel* (2005). Smiley has written a wide array of novel types, and her consideration of the novel is similarly wide-ranging, from writing to the ways reading puts two minds in contact with each other.

BOOKS BY THOMAS C. FOSTER

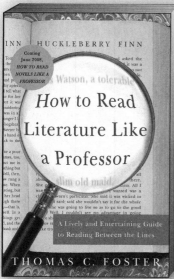

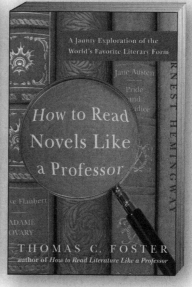

HOW TO READ LITERATURE LIKE A PROFESSOR
A Lively and Entertaining Guide to Reading Between the Lines

ISBN 978-0-06-000942-7 (paperback)

"A smart, accessible, and thoroughly satisfying examination of what it means to read a work of literature. Guess what? It isn't all that hard, not when you have a knowledgeable guide to show the way. Dante had his Virgil; for everyone else, there is Thomas Foster."

—Nicholas A. Basbanes, author of *A Gentle Madness*

HOW TO READ NOVELS LIKE A PROFESSOR
A Jaunty Exploration of the World's Favorite Literary Form

ISBN 978-0-06-134040-6 (paperback)

Out of all literary forms, the novel is arguably the most discussed—and the most fretted over. In *How to Read Novels Like a Professor*, Thomas C. Foster leads readers through the special "literary language" of the novel, helping them get more—more insight, more understanding, more pleasure—from their reading.